INTRODUCTION TO HOSPITALITY INDUSTRY - A TEXT BOOK

INTRODUCTION TO HOSPITALITY INDUSTRY A TEXT BOOK

By:
Prof. S.C BAGRI
&
ASHISH DAHIYA

AMAN PUBLICATIONS
NEW DELHI

In Association with

INDIAN HOSPITALITY CONGRESS

Published by
Rajiv Jain for Aman Publications
LG-4A, Ganpati Bhawan,
4675-B/21, Ansari Road,
Darya Ganj, Delhi - 110002
PH: 23255012, 23282127
E-mail: sshjbs@yahoo.com
in association with
Indian Hospitality Congress

First Published – 2008
Reprinted-2010
ISBN No.: 81-8204-048-9
ISBN No.: 978-81-8204-046-5

SOLE DISTRIBUTOR
JINDAL BOOK SERVICES
LG-4A, Ganpati Bhawan,
4675-B/21, Ansari Road,
Darya Ganj, Delhi - 110002

Jacket Designed by :
S.M. Graphics

Printed by:
Indus Printwell, Delhi, India

FOREWORD

Tourism, Hospitality & Service Industry worldwide is one of the fastest growing economic sector and claims are frequently made that it is about to become or is already the world's largest Industry, employing by some estimates, over ten million people. Clearly, the onus is on the shoulders of trained manpower, which are central resources for the effective operation of this service oriented industry.

The Institutes of Hotel Management sponsored by Ministry of Tourism, Government of India as well as University Departments & Affiliated Institutes are preparing the youth of the country for Hospitality and Tourism. However they, at times do face difficulty due to lack of adequate academic resources as there are very few books, both in terms of text and reference in Indian context available in our country. This ultimately leaves learners yearning for more to acquaint themselves with Indian Hospitality context.

The noble idea of Indian Hospitality Congress conceptualised by the Centre for Mountain Tourism & Hospitality Studies, Prof. S.C Bagri & Sh. Ashish Dahiya to bring the viewpoints of various experts in Hospitality under one roof and giving it a shape of book is a commendable venture. The present book titled "Introduction to Hospitality Industry" as it is laid out, seeks to cover wide range of topics devoted to hospitality as per AICTE syllabus for the facilitation of learners as well as trainers. It is indeed a timely publication.

Scholars wanting to develop an insight into this vital sector of economy in the Indian subcontinent had, so far, to depend on fragmented articles in newspapers, magazines, journals, the internet, etc. The significance of this book lies in, that a multitude of perspectives on the Hospitality Industry, the emerging issues and trends of growth coalesce into a single volume. This book will be an asset to academicians, researchers and professionals from the field of Indian hospitality.

I offer my felicitations to the Editors and the Indian Hospitality Congress for this great academic venture.

R.K. Saxena
Principal
Institute of Hotel Management
Dadar, Mumbai.

PREFACE

The hospitality education in India has witnessed a significant change over the years. Its introduction as a subject goes back to establishment of several Catering Institutes and the National Council of Hotel Management and Catering Technology. From the past few years, universities and colleges in India have also introduced Hotel Management Programmes at degree level. A model curriculum has also been designed by the All India Council for Technical Education (AICTE). However, has been observed that availability of study material in hospitality management is rather limited and does not meet the requirements of the vast curricula. With this book an attempt has been made to assimilate relevant contents on Introduction to Hospitality, keeping the AICTE model curriculum into consideration. The present book is a modest effort to cover the syllabi of Indian Universities and Hotel Management Institutes, and includes the contributors of several faculty members of Hotel Management Institutes across the country.

The book contains *Fifteen* Chapters. In chapter one Mr. Ashish Dahiya and Ms. Sonia Sharma have described the hospitality Industry, its Nature and Status. The chapter familiarizes the learners with hospitality, enabling them to analyse the relationship between hospitality and hotel management along with definition to hospitality in various parameters. In chapter two Ms. Payal Pandey and Ms. Jyoti have discussed the growth and development of hospitality industry in India with an objective to study the history of lodging industry, so as to understand the phenomena in a particular society at a given time phase. Various eras and growth of hotel industry are also summarised in this chapter. Dr. Prashant Kandari in chapter three has focused on hospitality industry and its role in the Indian economy. The linkages, their effects, contribution and working of some economic variables in the context to hospitality industry have been discussed in this chapter. In chapter four Ms. Jyoti and Mr Praveen have given an introduction to hospitality accommodation. The authors have explained different sectors of accommodation facilities, current scenario and the emerging concepts in accommodation. An annexure gives the criteria of star category ranking in India.

In Chapter five *Mr. Yash Pal Negi has discussed the Food Service Industry*. Mr. Abhinav Shandilya has given an overview of ancillary and support services in hospitality industry *in Chapter six*. The author has explained the importance and services of ancillary and support services. In Chapter *seven,* he has given a brief note on hospitality organisations, where the concept of organisation and its organizational structure has been explained. Different types of organisational structures, including few structures of major players in the hospitality sector, have been illustrated for facilitation of learners. Chapter *eight* deals with hospitality distribution channels. Mr Sandeep Malik has focused on Distribution Channels, their importance and role along with different distribution channels used by hospitality organisations. In Chapter *nine* he has covered functions and levels of distribution channels along with their strategy designing, behaviour and organization in a simple and lucid manner.

Chapter *ten* deals with major hospitality distribution channels. Mr Surjeet Kumar has covered in detail reservation systems, global distribution systems and Internet. Mr. Vinay Rana in Chapter *eleven* has talked about the major hospitality players in international scenario. The growth and development of various international hotel chains, the need for expansion and a brief write-up on various chains with their affiliates have been included in this chapter. In Chapter *twelve* Mr. Ashish Dahiya and Mr. Pushkar Negi have covered major hospitality players and associations in India. Different hospitality units at national level and hospitality associations have been discussed here along with their growth and expansion.

Mr. Jatashankar Tewari has explained the concept of marketing, emerging markets and role of support services and infrastructure in developing new markets in Chapter *thirteen*. Mr Surjeet Kumar has further supported this unit by giving an insight into the present status of tourism and hospitality industry in the world in Chapter *fourteen*. Lastly Ms Lata S Patil has explained the role of information technology, CRM, eco-friendly, hospitality and other emerging factors in the promotion of hospitality industry. The future projections of human resources in hospitality industry have also been covered in this chapter.

Overall, the book intends to provide a wider coverage and discussion on hospitality industry in India. The issues dealt with in this, though diverse are unanimous in their forms on hospitality in India.

The editors would like to place on record their gratitude to all the contributors, whose works have been included in this volume for readily agreeing to write on the topics of their respective fields of expertise.

Our thanks are also due to the Indian Hospitality Congress, Aman Publications, New Delhi, and our colleagues and well-wishers without whose sincere efforts and support, the book could not have been possible.

Prof. S.C Bagri
Ashish Dahiya

CONTENTS

1

HOSPITALITY INDUSTRY: NATURE AND STATUS

— *ASHISH DAHIYA[1] AND SONIA SHARMA[2]*

Hospitality is a large and diverse field, providing challenges and exciting career opportunities for people from all walks of life. Various authors have defined hospitality in many ways. However, one thing unanimously accepted in all definitions is that it is concerned with service, confortability and happiness. Often when it comes to the young students or beginners in hospitality profession hospitality is confused with the term hotel management. However as a matter of fact both terms hotel management and hospitality are interrelated. In this unit we have tried to explain these terms from different view points i.e. for a businessman the meaning may be different than that of an employee. Similarly a young learner enrolled in a hospitality programme may perceive a different meaning than that perceived by a guest. Also a housekeeper's view may vary than that of a chef when it comes to defining hospitality.

OBJECTIVES

In this unit we have tried to:

- Familiarise you with hospitality.
- Analyse the relation between hospitality and hotel management.
- Define hospitality and its various parameters.

HOSPITALITY: MEANING AND CONCEPTS

Hospitality embraces nearly all aspects of our life and affects almost everyone in the world, either as guest or host. Consequently, hospitality plays a major role in influencing the quality of life. Apart from its importance to economic benefits, socio-cultural activities, hospitality is related to other knowledge areas as well such

---

1. Reader in Hotel Management at Centre for Mountain Tourism & Hospitality Studies, H.N.B Garhwal University, Srinagar Garhwal, Uttarakhand.

2. Programme Coordinator of Hotel & Tourism Management, Uttranchal Open University – Haldwani, Uttarakhand.

as sociology, history, psychology, marketing, services, business and law. The twin concepts of 'Hotel' and 'Hospitality' have emerged and evolved through a long process and have primarily been an outgrowth of civilization and technological advance. The origin of the practice of hotel or hospitality could indeed be traced back from the origin of man's faculty of walking. However as a regular and professionally meaningful phenomenon, it owes its origin right from the inception of ancient civilization.

Hospitality is a large diverse field providing challenges to people from all walks of life. Hospitality may or may not be a commercial activity, but is associated with all living beings in a way or other, in fact the beginning of hospitality emerged growth and development of civilizations in ancient history. Starting from primary groups to secondary and ahead hospitality is now a well-accepted profession, business and an activity. The dictionary meaning of hospitality is "Friendly Entertainment of Guests". Where one who entertains is called as host and the one is being entertained is called as guest

However for hoteliers and professionals the meaning of hospitality is not confined to the term guest and host. A businessman's viewpoint may state hospitality as a profitable investment with high rate of returns; on the other hand it may be a passion for some one, career for someone who has joined a hospitality programme. A socialist may describe hospitality as treating people like you would want to be treated genuinely. Hospitality can also be termed as a deliberate, planned and sustained effort to establish and maintain mutual understanding between an organization and public i.e. the business making and keeping friends and promoting an atmosphere of better understanding.

Oxford dictionary defines hospitality as "Reception and entertainment of guests, visitors, or strangers, with liberality and good will" Wikipedia encyclopaedia explains hospitality for and in depth understanding of the term from the starting point i.e. etymology of the word itself. The word hospitality derives from the Latin of *hospes*, which is formed from *hostis,* which originally meant 'stranger' and come to take on the meaning of enemy of 'hostile stranger' *(hostilis)* + pets (*polis*, poles, potential) to have power. The Latin word "*Hospitalitias*" means to maintain mutual understanding between the public and an organization, similarly the French word "*hospice*" means to provide care/shelter for travellers." In view of the above hospitality can be defined as "Reception and Entertainment of Guests, visitors or strangers with liberty and goodwill comprised of business which practice act of being hospitable. Those businesses, which are characterized by generosity and friendliness to guests."

Happle, Kipps and Thomson associate hospitality, in modern sense, with four characteristic features/ qualities:

- A host on a guest, away from home, confers it.
- It is interactive, involving the coming together of a provider and receiver.
- It comprises a blend of tangible and intangible factors.

❖ The host provides for the guest's security, psychological and physiologicai comfort.

Also we can say that hospitality is the total of all those activities, which are extended in generosity and courtesy with in limits. However these limits vary from society to society and country to country. However within above parameters the term hospitality can't be concluded. It is a vast term as explained in Fig. 1

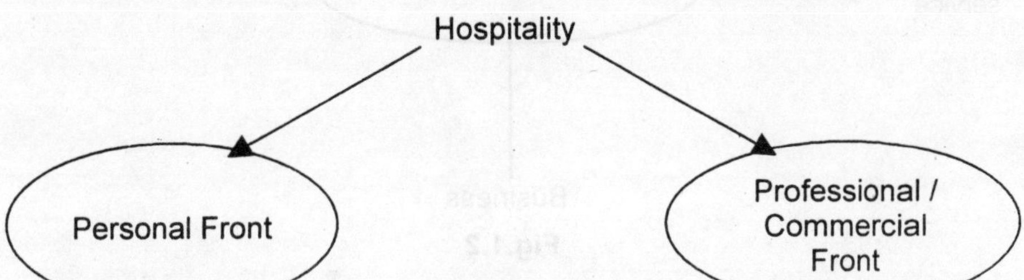

Fig-1

The two fronts can be better understood as:

a) Personal

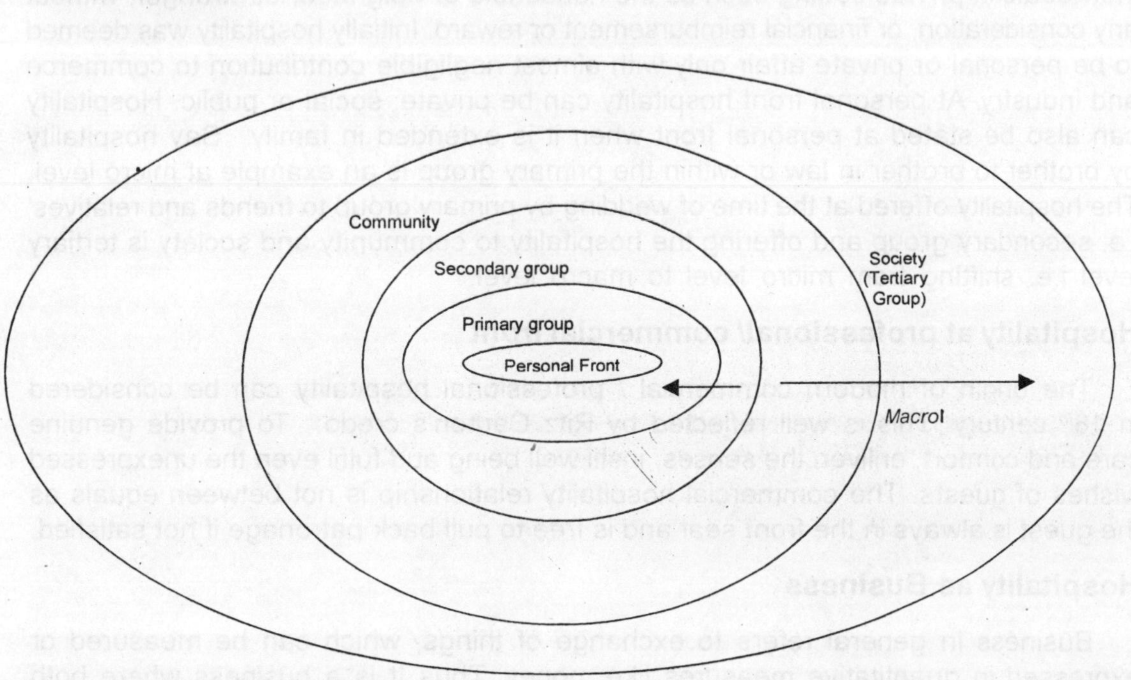

Fig-1.1

b) Professional/ Commercial

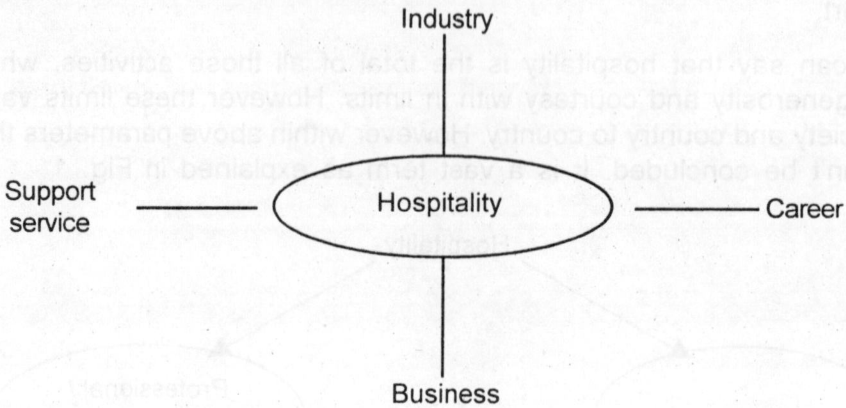

Fig.1.2

Hospitality at professional/ commercial front

A guest coming to your home perhaps needs to be welcomed. The above said aspect involves hospitality at personal front. It involves the acts by individuals towards individuals in private setting such as the household or neighbour or stranger, without any consideration, or financial reimbursement or reward. Initially hospitality was deemed to be personal or private affair only with almost negligible contribution to commerce and industry. At personal front hospitality can be private, social or public. Hospitality can also be stated at personal front when it is extended in family. Say hospitality by brother to brother in law or within the primary group is an example at micro level. The hospitality offered at the time of wedding by primary group to friends and relatives' i.e. secondary group and offering the hospitality to community and society is tertiary level i.e. shifting from micro level to macro level.

Hospitality at professional/ commercial front

The origin of modern commercial / professional hospitality can be considered in 18th century. This is well reflected by Ritz Carlton's credo: To provide genuine care and comfort, enliven the senses, instil well being and fulfil even the unexpressed wishes of guests. The commercial hospitality relationship is not between equals as the guest is always in the front seat and is free to pull back patronage if not satisfied.

Hospitality as Business

Business in general refers to exchange of things, which can be measured or expressed in quantitative measures like money. Thus It is a business where both tangible as well as intangible products are sold i.e. food, accommodation and services are provided to someone, provided the person concerned is in a position to pay for it. This business can be in various forms like hotel, restaurant, cruise lines, Banquets etc. The hospitality as a business can be primary or secondary. For example hospitality is the primary focus of Oberoi's managing "East India Hotels" while it may be a secondary area for JayPee Industries, owing to their prime business is of cement and projects. Hospitality as business in organised sector has gained a significant position. Hospitality providers as business have adopted ISO – Certification, HACCP standards, defined vision and mission. For example: "Amidst a tranquil and romantic ambience, we endeavour to provide a majestic life style, with genuine care and comfort. With our warm friendly and immaculate services, we will create moments of happiness and cherished memories for our guests" is the spirit of Oberoi's team at Udaivilas.

Hospitality as Career

With the emergence of globalisation hospitality has emerged out as an excellent career option for people. It provides wide ranges of job opportunities. As per PATA Total Tourism India Report (2006) India is expected to be the 3rd fastest growing industry in travel and tourism demand over the next 10 years, behind Montenegro and China. Also Conde Nast Traveler (2006) has ranked India as 4th amongst world's must see countries. Thus with the growing demands hospitality services are expected to grow at phenomenal rate and so the demand of manpower. Also the attrition rate in hospitality sector in India is about 30-35% (2006-2007). Thus the country of youth observes fast trade career advancements in this sector.

In hospitality industry one can start his career as an assistant-supervisor or directly management trainee-Assistant Manager- Senior Manager- General Manager- Director, depending upon company hierarchy. It doesn't merely provide a handsome salary and perks but also gives a good name and fame in the society. Like Sanjeev Kapoor, Tarla Dalal, Rakesh Sethi in Indian families. Day by day the number of aspirants in the field of hospitality is increasing to opt it as. a career. Food and beverage services are one of the professions with unlimited opportunities. The various sectors include hotels, Restaurants, Fast Foods, Bar, Caterers, Clubs, Hospitals, Universities, Railways, Airlines, Cruise lines and even multiplexes offer wide spectrum of opportunities.

The hospitality industry requires youth full with energy with sound health and grooming, relevant product knowledge, effective communications with expressions and action for front office. Housekeeping being an integral component of hotel operation is currently undergoing a metamorphosis. The growing demand of housekeepers globally has overshadowed the misconception of housekeeping being a underlining profession. Apart from hotels, other establishments like hospitals, service apartments, airports, metro stations, shopping malls, multiplexes and others offer exciting opportunities in housekeeping.

A professional attitude with aptitude and a flair for cooking along patience can open doors for cooking as a profession. Diversification has opened many avenues for a chef. Though the hotel industry is first option however flight catering, hospitals, food stylists, restaurants, entrepreneurs, cruise liners, demands good chefs. Other then the above mentioned there are substantial opportunities in hospitality careers in amusement and entertainment, time – share, cruise liners, concierge, wine consultancy, facility management, guest relations, travel and Tour Operations, Spa, Security, Airlines, Hospitals. In a true sense Sky is the limit.

As per the Market pulse Report (2004) of Ministry of Tourism Government of India following is the forecast for openings in Hospitality (Table-1.1 – 1.6)

Five Star, Four Star and Heritage Hotels

Table-1.1

	Employment 2010	% Trained Manpower	% Fresh Recruits	Demand 2003-2010
Front Office	5628	58	59	1926
F&B Service	17285	70	68	8228
F&B Kitchen	16247	60	56	5459
Housekeeping	12361	36	67	2981
Total	**51521**	**NA**	**NA**	**18594**

Table-1.2

	Employment 2020	% Trained Manpower	% Fresh Recruits	Demand 2010-2020
Front Office	7481	58	59	2560
F&B Service	22977	70	68	10937
F&B Kitchen	21597	60	56	7257
Housekeeping	16432	36	67	3963
Total	**68487**	**NA**	**NA**	**24717**

Three Two and One Star Hotels (Table 1.3-1.4)

Table-1.3

	Employment 2010	% Trained Manpower	% Fresh Recruits	Demand 2003-2010
Front Office	5546	34	62	1169
F&B Service	14150	26	75	2759
F&B Kitchen	14150	24	39	1324
Housekeeping	12656	7	68	602
Total	**46502**	**NA**	**NA**	**5854**

Table-1.4

	Employment 2020	% Trained Manpower	% Fresh Recruits	Demand 2010-2020
Front Office	7290	34	62	1537
F&B Service	18600	26	75	3627
F&B Kitchen	18600	24	39	1741
Housekeeping	16637	7	68	791
Total	**61127**	**NA**	**NA**	**7696**

Table 1.5: Annual Demand for Trained Manpower in Restaurants

Year	F&B Kitchen	F&B Service	Total Demand
2003	11,246	12,256	23,502
2004	11,246	12,256	23,502
2005	11,246	12,256	23,502
2006	11,246	12,256	23,502
2007	11,246	12,256	23,502
2008	11,246	12,256	23,502
2009	11,246	12,256	23,502
2010	11,246	12,256	23,502
2011	13,463	14,583	28,046
2012	13,463	14,583	28,046
2013	13,463	14,583	28,046
2014	13,463	14,583	28,046
2015	13,463	14,583	28,046
2016	13,463	14,583	28,046
2017	13,463	14,583	28,046
2018	13,463	14,583	28,046
2019	13,463	14,583	28,046
2020	13,463	14,583	28,046

Table 1.6: Projected Annual Demand vs. Supply for Trained Manpower

Year	Total Demand	Supply	Shortage
2003	29,368	11,700	17,668
2004	29,368	11,700	17,668
2005	29,368	11,700	17,668
2006	29,368	11,700	17,668
2007	29,368	11,700	17,668
2008	29,368	11,700	17,668
2009	29,368	11,700	17,668
2010	29,368	11,700	17,668
2011	39,230	11,700	27,530
2012	39,230	11,700	27,530
2013	39,230	11,700	27,530
2014	39,230	11,700	27,530
2015	39,230	11,700	27,530
2016	39,230	11,700	27,530
2017	39,230	11,700	27,530
2018	39,230	11,700	27,530
2019	39,230	11,700	27,530
2020	39,230	11,700	27,530

The above projected figures clearly represent the wide scope and opportunities in hospitality industry in India.

With unanimously accepted fact that hospitality industry has arduous working conditions. The industry is witnessing a substantial positive change. According to the survey conducted for the best companies, to work for, in India- by A BT- Mercer – INS Study published in Business Today: (November-2007 Issue Page No.- 95,124,129). Marriott Hotels India has been ranked as 11th Best Company to work for India and perhaps the best in hospitality industry to work for. The survey has revealed that Marriott hotels India has 2,502 employees with an average age of 24 years, attrition rate 32 percent, Male Female ratio 4:1, Average Career tenure- 3 years, HR cost Rs. 1.07 crore, Promotion Rate 37.6 percent, Revenues Rs 448 Crore and Gross Operation Profit Rs 240 Crore, (January-September 2007). On reviewing on qualities that made Marriott an employer of choice five key points can be observed

a) Two way communication: For new entrants; there is an event called "koffee with the G.M." to interact and share their views over a cup of coffee. For employees too shy to talk, there is the option of enormously calling up the integrity hotline, a 24×7 toll free number.

b) Employee Benefit Initiative: Employees are given size offs in a month and financial support for higher education. Each and every employee on their birthday can stay in the hotel for one day with their spouse or family and can dine anytime.

c) Knowledge Initiatives: Every Marriott hotel has a learning centre that has a collection of books and videos along with an internet connection.

d) Define span of leadership: - There is a leadership Performance process management /system which defines nine competencies which a Marriott associate should have and develop.

e) Reward System:- There are two kinds of awards for individuals or groups to recognize outstanding performance. Each Marriott property has its own awards. This is apart from an overall event involving all Marriott properties globally.

Hospitality as an Industry

Hospitality and Tourism in India is the 3rd largest foreign exchange earner, accounting for 2.5% of GDP. India has a 5000 year old history, culture, religion and alternative medicine that fascinate both budget and luxury travellers alike to enjoy the warm and courteous hospitality of India. Travel and Tourism in India, Euro monitor 2006 Report has valued hospitality travel and tourism in India at US$42 Billion in year 2005 and is expected to grow rapidly. World Wealth Report-2007 has highlited19.8% increase in the number of high net wealth Indians with assets over US$1 million, V.S. 6.5% growth worldwide which is a rising affluence to boost domestic Tourism and Hospitality Sector". Not so long hospitality was viewed into fragments and in many cases separates industry. But now it has come with lot many new things combined under one roof. Various researchers have pleaded to accord hospitality and tourism a priority Industry in India. Undoubtedly Govt. of India has been taking initiatives to strengthen and promote hospitality, travel and tourism sector, in order to provide benefits to the host population "Bed and Breakfast" plans are being promoted by Ministry of Tourism Govt. of India. In order to provide competent manpower 26 Institutes of Hotel Management (IHM's) under Ministry of Tourism Govt. of India are operational (2007) and three more are expected soon. Various Universities have introduced Hotel Management programmes in order to meet the growing demands of the Industry.

Hotel Industry

The history of the hotel industry is as old as the history of tourism and travel industry. In fact, both are two sides of the same coin. Both are complementary to each other. Hotel is an establishment, which provides food, shelter and other amenities for comfort and convenience of the visitors with a view to make profit. Hotel is a commercial establishment and intends to provide visitors with lodging, food and related services with a view to please them so as to build goodwill and to let them Carry happy memories. In general, a "hotel" is defined as a public establishment offering visitors, against payment two basic services i.e. accommodation and catering

(Ghosh, Biswanath). However, during the last few years great changes have taken place in the scope of hotel industry.

During 6th century BC, hotels were known as "inns" or "*dharamshalas*" and were providing only food and overnight stay facilities. At that point of time the standard of an inn was quite normal with earth or stone floor, common bedroom and simple food. As travel became easier, inns grew in size and number. The spirit of competition raised the standard of inns.

With the Industrial revolution and trade expansion there is an upsurge in the number of visitors crossing international border. In this era, room furnishing and catering received greater attention. Emphasis was made on accommodation with spacious assembly hall and dinning hall for organising functions and parties etc. But the real growth of the modern hotels started in the last decade of the eighteenth century with the establishment of City Hotel in New York. After that a large number of hotels of various types and grades came into existence in different countries to meet the requirements of different categories of visitors.

Modern hotels provide a number of services to the visitors. The services vary according to the aim, location, type, size and grade of the hotel. Generally, the important activities of a hotel include – (1) Direction (2) Reception (3) Provision of accommodation rooms/floors (4) Cuisine Meals and Refreshments (5) Restaurant (6) Bar (7) Bell to provide information to the guests (8) Entertainment and Recreation (9) Sight seeing (10) Transport facilities (11) Parking space(12) Swimming pool(13) Bathroom facilities (14) Lounge facilities (15) Garden (16) Shopping facilities (17) News stand (18) Tobacco and Cigarettes (19) Telephone (20) Television (21) Radio (22) Laundry and Cleaning (23) Telex service (24) Sporting installations, Tennis court, Golf and Squash (25) Installation for children (26) Banquet hall (27) Conference facilities (28) Convention facilities (29) Exhibition areas (30) Health club (31) Business centre etc. After 2nd world war, there were several distinct trends in the hotel industry. First, hotel industry became highly profitable mainly because of auxiliary services. Another feature was the growth of hotel chains. In most chain operations, some hotels are owned by the corporation while others are leased for operation to the group having experience in hotel business. The high cost of land in the heart of the city often forced a successful hotel to maintain auxiliary shops such as drug stores, flower shops, haberdashery and dress shops, beauty saloons and news stands to serve both hotel guests and the city residents who live or work near the hotel. Although such shops may be staffed and operated by the hotel but usually these are leased out to outside concerns.

Hospitality as a Support Service

The hospitality has not merely flourished in a particular sector but also supporting the travel and tourism trade. In fact Ministry of Tourism Govt. of India Report agrees to the fact "No Hotels – No Tourism". Due to the diverse nature of services the hospitality has a support function as well. Almost all the multinational companies in India are catered by hospitality Industry in terms of their food service for employees. Similarly in flight menu's, Rail meals and other such provisions are also taken are by hospitality industry. Similarly support functions in terms of service, food, beverages, accommodation comfort and care being provided in meetings, conferences, exhibitions and other such major areas. In a nutshell a society remains incomplete without hospitality.

Challenges Ahead

Globally, industry experts say that the time has come for hospitality professionals to shift their primary focus from physical assets to their patrons. This would entail broad changes for every aspect of business. Physical assets like building, restaurants, and location will fall second in the place to customer focused activities. For the marketing division of any hospitality chain, the focus will shift from Revpar (Revenue per available room) to Revpac (Revenue per available customer). Revpar is the accepted yardstick for hotels profit reflecting revenues from physical assets. As the focus shifts Revpac shall become equally significant. Experts in hospitality recognizing the current trends observe that it will be beneficial if hospitality sector including hotels shift from Standard Operating Procedure (SOP) approach to Personalised Operating Procedure (POP) one.

Downsizing is another innovative change in Indian hospitality Industry. Downsizing refers to the reduction of staff and unprofitable operations to keep overheads to an extent that it is affordable. Recently The Ashok Group of Hotels, I.T.D.C. in India has undergone downsizing. Where as other Chain hotels have started practicing Empowerment, which is a logical consequence of down sizing. Empowerment is a management policy that aims to encourage employees to control their own performance to measure business goals.

Outsourcing services, which is another strategy to manage downsizing, is being observed in many hospitality organisations in India as well. Outsourcing refers to giving responsibility of certain aspects of operations to external experts or consultants. The obligation of the organization is to pay a contracted fee and set standards as required. Various services like security, pest control, laundry; housekeeping, horticulture and even food preparation are being outsourced these days. India is a 'country of youth' and World Bank report on education (2007) says that hospitality, travel, tourism, animation, multimedia are emerging fields in the country. The youth are the future workforce. Apart from academic institutes, universities are offering formal education. Hospitality industry in India has also launched various programmers so as to get better manpower. Oberoi's has introduced STEP programme to get the youth with positive attitude by offering them earn while you learn programme. Similarly Taj has introduced Taj for youth programme in the same pattern industry collaborative programmes are being offered i.e. I.H.M. Aurangabad with Taj Group of Hotels, Welcome Group Graduate School of Hotel Management with ITC Hotels, Towers and Resorts, Apee Jay Park School of Hotel Management with The Park Hotels, Ashok

Institute of Hospitality and Tourism with the Ashok Group of Hotels (ITDC) to name a few are catering to education requirements of youth. Also various associations like FHRAI, Indian Hospitality Congress, Hotel Association of India are promoting hospitality education in India. When we see the current trends and challenges before the hospitality industry in India there is a huge gap, which is being observed in terms of industry demand. In fact the hierarchy in itself is re-positioned. The existing hierarchy in industry is projected below (Fig. 2.1)

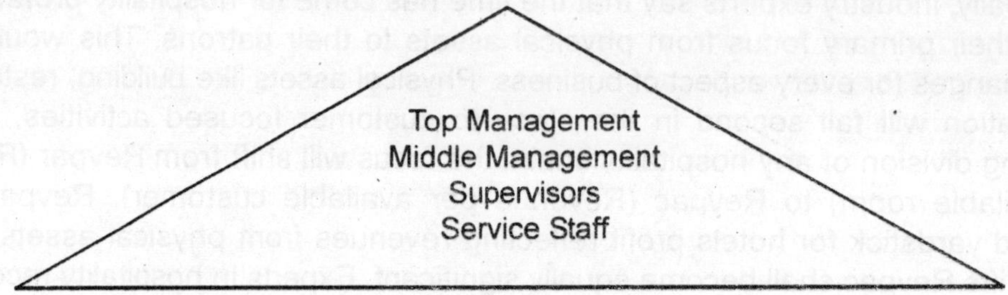

Fig. 2.1

However the new system which is cautious about guests, brand, smart choices, team building and excellence has requirements of below mentioned hierarchy-

Fig. 2.2

Thus the changing hierarchies require a change in type of workforce. The employees in hospitality Industry are expected to be Relational, Multilingual, Service Oriented, Action Oriented, Creative Problem Solvers, Techno Savvy, Physically fir. In fact "Change or move out" is the current strategy requirement of industry. Another challenge which is expected to deal with problem of Aging Manpower in industry. Although this however not a major cause of concern in Indian Hospitality Industry as the attrition rate is 30-35% annually but genuinely needs to be paid attention for the coming times.

Table 2.1 & 2.2 Hospitality and Hotel Management Interdependence and Independence

Table 2.1

Characteristics	Hospitality	Hotel Management
	Service in Nature ❆ Hetrogenity ❆ Intanagiblity ❆ Perishablity	Service in Nature
Orientation	Customer focused	Customer focussed
Products Offered	Both Tangible and Intangible	Both Tangible and Intangible
Effect	Effected by other Industries	Effected by other Industry
Abide	Abided by law	Abided by law
Facilitator	Provide a role of Facilitator	

Table 2.2

Hospitality	Hotel Management
Vast term	Confined to Hotel Services, Operations and Management.
Includes-Fast Foods, Clubs, Pubs, Youth Hostels, Hotels, Entertainment, Recreation, All form of accommodation and Service	Is more concerned with accommodation and meals is issues in respect to hotels

With this basic introduction students would get a fair concept of Hotels and Hospitality and shall come across more technicalities and details in subsequent chapters and later courses in higher semesters.

ACTIVITY

- ❖ Visit a Hospitality Service Provider in your location and identify their challenges
- ❖ Visit a star hotel and acquaint yourself with mission, vision and the blue prints to success.

QUESTIONS

- ❖ What do you understand by the term hospitality – Explain it at personal front?
- ❖ Write a note on hospitality as a business and as a career.
- ❖ What are the challenges before the hospitality industry in India?

2

GROWTH AND DEVELOPMENT OF THE HOSPITALITY INDUSTRY IN INDIA

— PAYAL[1] AND JYOTI[2]

Tourism and hospitality industry may help the developing countries such as India more in resolving the problem of employment of its ever-growing population as it is considered as highly labour intensive service industry, where the employment-investment ratio is higher than any other industry. Travel and tourism directly creates employment opportunities in hotels, restaurants, airlines, travel agencies, passenger ships, and as a result of the spread effect creates jobs in industries like construction, telecommunication, manufacturing and the retail trader. This chapter discusses the growth and development of hospitality, the problems and prospects of hospitality and tourism industry in India besides to review its different phases of development as well as significance of this industry in Indian context. The analysis shows that hotel industry is facing the problem of low profitability due to low food and beverage sales as well as low occupancy and higher taxes. Similarly, tourism industry is also not growing to its potential due to inadequate infrastructure, poor marketing strategies etc. followed for tourism promotion in India. Despite all this, there is a lot of potential for growth of hospitality and tourism industry in India and abroad due to worldwide industrial development, increased earnings of individuals, economic growth of tourists producing nations, improved transport and communication means etc.

OBJECTIVES

The main objective to study the history of the lodging industry is to understand the phenomenon in a particular society in a particular time. Therefore we not only reconstruct the past but also develop generalizations that are more useful in understanding the present nature of the tourist phenomenon. To avoid simple generalizations the data needs to be assessed carefully. In early history we have archaeological evidence of inns, hotels, villas and transport but such information is fragmentary and covers periods of thousands of years. For instance the French looked only at the key events and the factors like standard of living, free time, and cheap transport and sea side resorts and link them to the growth of industry, labour

1. Assistant Professor in Hotel Management at Graphic Era Institute of Technology, Dehradun.

2. Lecturer in Hotel Management at M.M University, Mullana, Ambala.

force, social legislation and local customs. In this the physical, economical, technical, environmental, socio-political and cultural factors are studied.

India is known for its historic past since time immemorial. Its rulers were great admirers of travel amenities and facilities. Ashoka the great constructed *dharamshalas* on highways in 3rd century B.C. such facilities can be grouped into following categories:

- *Dharamshalas*
- Road and Lanes
- Trees and other Spaces
- Wells and Tanks

With the advent of Muslim rulers, *Sarai* were introduced. In the reign of *Sher Shah Suri* and then Mughals it reached a level of perfection. Improvements in the means of transport and communication resulted in the establishment of inns and traverns.

Later with the advent of British the *Sarais* took the form of western style hotels. The credit for opening the first western style hotel goes to Pallangee Pestongee who opened a hotel under the name of British Hotel in Bombay in 1840. He is called the pioneer of western style of hotels in India.

Within the passage of time the classes of people involved in the lodging industry have changed and become more democratized. Also the natures of the facilities have become more standardized if not universal. The main periods in the history of lodging industry are:

- the ancient era
- the medieval era and
- the modern era

The following concepts were commonly used during all periods:

1) **Motivation** - the value of new experience and the transformation of travel from survival to an improvement in the quality of life. This includes:
   - *Curiosity*: moving from known to unknown
   - *Anticipation*: to look for something and evaluate every new experience
   - *Leaving a mark for posterity*: what the world offers and why you have experienced it.

2) **Holiday:** The world has two sources, religious and secular:
   - In Europe, a day was set aside at the end of a work cycle and was called for a religious ritual and this day was called the holy day. In time, certain

other observances were added to the number of holidays when no work was done and everyone celebrated.

* The secular tradition was a part of the imperial system when the state granted public holidays to celebrate imperial glory. On these holidays no work was done and the people participated in feasting and fun, public games and spectator sports were the highlights on such occasions.

In time the religious and secular combined and a day of rest became a part of all societies.

3) **Mode of travel:** Mode of travel was the state of art in terms of transport networks and routes, vehicles, cost of travel, documentation, safe passage, wayside facilities and conveniences to the traveler.

4) **Tourism impacts:** The influence of tourism is not only on the lifestyle of the people but in bringing about changes in consumption and production as well as wealth.

The chronologic growth of hotel industry can be summarised as follows:-

1282 : Rest houses were built

1312 : Hotel construction started in a true classical sense

1650 : Pascal opened a café in Paris and a coffee house in London.

1794 : City Hotel (73 rooms) at 115, Broadway, New York. First building specially made for the hotel purpose.

1829 : Tremont House. Adam & Eve of the modern hotel industry was opened at Boston (170 rooms)

1843 : Auckland Hotel was established in Calcutta.

1871 : Esplande Hotel was built in Calcutta by John Wakson.

1889 : Cesar Ritz introduced luxury hotels such as Savoy, Carlton and Hyde Park hotels in England.

1890-1899 : Fredrick Gordon and Sir Blundell Maple launched Gordon hotels and Fredrick hotels ltd.

Late 19th century : Famous Waldorf Astoria in New York.

1903 : Taj Group of Hotels came into existence by JRD Tata. The first one was Taj Mahal Hotel in Bombay.

1908 : Buffalo Statler by Ellsworth Statler in United States was considered as the birth of the commercial hotels in the world

1927 : Stevens Hotel in Chicago, later renamed as Hilton Hotel (3000 rooms).

1930 : Depression in world economy: depression in hotel industry.

1934 : M.S Oberoi became sole owner of Clarkes Hotel, Shimla and Delhi.

1949 : M.S Oberoi floated The East India Hotels Limited

1950 : Motels and international chain operations came up.

1962 : The Government of India realized the importance of tourism and when the tourist arrival dropped to 1,34,360 from 1,39,804 Hotel Corporation and Tourism Corporation were Developed.

1964 : Formation of three corporations and ITDC.

1975 : Formation of Welcom Group Division of ITC Ltd. The first hotel being the Hotel Chola, Madras.

Development of Hotel Industry in India

The concept of travel and halting facilities is quite old in India. In ancient times, people used to travel for pilgrimage or business purposes. For ages, India has been known for its hospitality. Endowed with rich historic heritage, cultural diversity, natural resources and geographical advantage, India remained a big attraction for foreigners. In ancient times, the need of travellers for food and accommodation was met mainly by hospitable householders who are still in existence in interior areas of the country. Initially it was not in an organised form. Later Buddhist monasteries provided lodging facilities to travellers. In Maurya dynasty roads, guest houses and accommodation places were developed. Universities like Taxila provided accommodation to students and faculty members. Domestic tourists were looked after by the *pandas* or priests. They used to accommodate their clients in *dharamshalas* or in their own houses at places of pilgrimage like Banaras, Haridwar, Puri and Mathura etc. In general, the attitude of the ancient Indians towards visitors was influenced by the *'Atithi Devo Bhavah'*. It means guest is like God and should be treated accordingly. These few examples amply indicate the importance which was given to guests in olden times.

Improvements in the transport and communication facilities resulted in the establishment of inns and taverns in main cities of the country. In the eighteenth century, there were plenty of taverns in the country (a tavern mean an archaic or literary inn) where travellers from long distances took shelter and food. During this period, a number of *dharamshalas* were built by Kings for encouraging travel all over the country. Apart from *dharamshalas, "Sarais"* were introduced by the Muslim rulers which provided the best possible facilities like food, accommodation etc. to travellers.

After this, the British came to India and *Sarais* took the form of western style hotels in the important cities of India like Mumbai and Kolkata. During this period, on the one hand, we find the western style hotels for foreigners and on the other,

Indian style hotels for the people belonging to upper and middle class income groups. The old type *dharamshalas* were still having their importance to serve the needs and requirements of the poor classes.

In the nineteenth century, western style residential hotels were developed in India by British and Swiss families mainly for their own use or for foreign visitors. Mr. Pallonjee Pestonjee is called as the pioneer of the western style hotel in India who opened the first – western style hotel under the name of British Hotel in Mumbai in 1840. By the end of the nineteenth century, many western style hotels were established in India. These hotels were very much popular for their efficient management, unsurpassed cuisine and the excellence of beers and wines (Negi Jagmohan).

The twentieth century may be called as the beginning of star hotels in India. In this century, big and modern hotels came into existence on account of the advent of big businessmen and new entrepreneurs. Affluent tourists also contributed a lot to the development of star culture.

The major star hotels in India are in private sector. The high profile hotels include The Indian Hotels Company Ltd., East India Hotels Ltd., ITC Hotels Ltd., Bharat Hotels Ltd., Asian Hotels Ltd., Hotel Leela Venture Ltd., ApeeJay Surendra Park Hotels and Jay Pee Hotels Ltd. etc. The only public sector enterprise is Indian Tourism Development Corporation Ltd. which runs country's largest accommodation chain, The Ashok Group of Hotels. The hotel industry in India is making a remarkable progress in private sector. The hotels have shown distinct improvement in operating techniques, catering and service.

Orissa is the first state in India, which declared hotel as an Industry in 1980 with a view of attracting investors and entrepreneurs to build more hotels, restaurants and other secondary accommodation at the important tourist centres and providing all categories of accommodation for different segment of tourists. There was a dearth of hotel rooms at major tourist centres like Bhubaneswar, Puri, Gopalpur and Chandipur due to which most of the domestic and foreign tourists could not stay overnight during the peak season. The declaration of hotel as industry coincided with setting up of Orissa Tourism Development Corporation (OTDC), which brought about a significant development in building accommodation units at Bhubaneswar, Puri, Cuttack and Barkul in due course. The OTDC in association with Department of Tourism, Government of Orissa played a major role in constructing accommodation units in different tourist centres in order to fulfil the needs of tourists. At the same time, the private hoteliers also came foreward to built different category of Hotels.

Recent Trends in Indian Tourism and Hospitality Industry

The Asian games in 1982 provided an opportunity to travel agents and tour operators to market India abroad and they grabbed it well. Encouraged by some incentives announced by government, five-star hotels began growing all over the

India. All these helped a lot in the healthy growth of tourism in our country. In fact, tourism business and hotel business go side by side and both are complementary to each other. In India, both approved and unapproved hotels are found but approved hotels have an edge over unapproved hotels in several respects. Hotels are granted approval from the Department of Tourism, Government of India at project stage and then are classified in one of the star categories. It is voluntary for a hotel to get approved status from the government, but only approved hotels cam avail the various income tax incentives, import licences and other approvals.

There were 1300 approved and 477 unapproved hotels offering 98,515 rooms in 2004 as against 1285 approved and 452 unapproved hotels offering 95,722 rooms in 2003. The Indian hotel business is focused largely on foreign tourists with almost 70 per cent business comes from this segment.

The key operating characteristics of the hotel business are the occupancy rate and the average room rate. The room rates depend on the class, location and the image of the hotel. The occupancy rate is dependent primarily on the seasonal arrivals as well as the location of the hotel. Occupancy level of 70 to 80 per cent is considered good by industry standards. Average occupancy in India was 59.7 per cent in 2004 as against 54.8 per cent in 2003 and average room rate was Rs.2689 in 2004 as against Rs.2,004 in 2003. The whole position is made clear by Table 2.1. and Table 2.1(a) shows the stastics of year 2007.

Table 2.1 Category-wise Position of FHRAI Member Hotels in India (in Numbers)

Years→	2000		2001		2002		2003		2004	
Category	Hotel	Rooms	Hotel	Rooms	Hotel	Rooms	Hotel	Rooms	Hotel	Rooms
Five-star Deluxe	57	12556	65	14959	68	15672	68	16050	74	17903
Five-star	73	9051	72	8513	72	8662	72	8669	71	8554
Four-star	92	7232	99	7791	100	7614	102	7408	104	7355
Three-star	379	19785	402	20691	413	21387	409	21098	414	21433
Two-star	244	9135	263	9958	234	9278	226	8903	221	8639
One-star	46	2253	50	2428	48	1696	44	1520	43	1480
Heritage	66	2372	73	2551	71	2492	67	2258	69	2297
Approved Unclassified	263	10560	303	12318	308	12515	297	11921	304	12058
Unapproved	493	18350	472	17757	455	17925	452	17895	477	18796
Total	1713	91294	1799	96966	1769	97241	1737	95722	1777	98515
Average occupancy	51.7		55.6		53.2		54.8		59.7	
Average Room Rate	Rs. 2123		Rs. 2046		Rs. 2058		Rs. 2004		Rs. 2689	

Source: Indian Hotel Industry Survey - 2004-05, FHRAI, Seventh Edition.

The hotel industry and the 5-star hotels in particular are concentrated in the four metros, especially in Mumbai and Delhi. As many as 75 per cent of the 5-star deluxe rooms, 47 per cent of the 5-star ordinary rooms and approx 35 per cent of all the registered rooms are in the four metros. Due to phenomenal increase in tourism activities, the hotel business has grown beyond expectations. This is particularly true about international tourism and star hotel business. At present about 789 million tourists are crossing international boarder every year and they are spending nearly 685 billion US Dollars. This figure was just 100 million in 1964. The figure is likely to swell to 1 billion by 2010 and 1.5 billion by 2020 as per projection by world tourism organisation. International tourists here in India were 3.5 million in 2004 as against 2.78 million tourists in 2003. Foreign exchange earnings from these tourists were about Rs.23,000 crores in 2004 as against Rs.16,429 crores in 2003. During the year 2005, about 4 million foreign tourists came here and India earned 5 billion US Dollars from them. In the first 6 months of the year 2006, about 2.16 million foreign tourists visited India and foreign exchange earnings from these were Rs.13,441 crores. It is expected that this growth will continue during the next couple of years if no adverse incident happens in India or the South East Region. According to an estimate of CII, the number of foreign tourists visiting India is likely to increase to 50 million by 2020. As per estimates of Ministry of Tourism, 1,50,000 hotel rooms of different categories are required to be added to the existing available rooms in the next couple of years to accommodate all the foreign tourists and this will involve an investment of Rs. 35,000 crores. Obviously, there is a good scope for hotel business all over the world including India and these estimates will boost hotel business in India.

Table 2.1(a) Category-wise Number of Hotels with Rooms in India (2007)

Years	2007	
Category	Hotel	Rooms
Five-star Deluxe	97	21314
Five-star	82	9505
Four-star	114	7606
Three-star	427	19164
Two-star	181	5148
One-star	52	2682
Heritage	85	3445
3-Star Apartment Hotels	2	110
4-Star Apartment Hotels	1	44
5-Star Apartment Hotels	1	100
Silver Incredible India (Bed & Breakfast)	2	6
To be Classified	122	7657

Source: Ministry of Tourism, Government of India, Annual Report 2006-07.

Significance of Tourism and Hospitality Industry

Tourism and hospitality industry may help underdeveloped/developing countries more in resolving their various problems as this industry today has emerged as one of the fastest growing industries in terms of capital invested, foreign exchange earnings and providing jobs. In India, it is considered as highly labour intensive service industry, where the employment-investment ratio is higher than any other industry. One of the India's biggest problems is to find ways to employ its ever-growing population. Travel and tourism directly creates employment opportunities in hotels, restaurants, airlines, travel agencies, passenger ships, and as a result of the spread effect creates jobs in industries like construction, telecommunication, manufacturing and the retail trader. According to a survey undertaken by Economic and Social Commission for Asia & Pacific (ESCAP) and Ministry of Tourism, an investment of Rs. one million in the hotel and restaurant sector may create 89 jobs as against 44 jobs in agriculture and 12.5 jobs in the manufacture sector. Investment required to create one job in manufacture is around Rs.79,000 whereas in hospitality industry it is only Rs.11,200. At present about 20 million persons are directly or indirectly employed in tourism related industry and this figure is likely to increase to 40 million by 2020. It amply proves the job potential of hospitality industry in India.

Problems of Tourism and Hospitality Industry in India

Developing countries like India have failed to develop tourism and hotel industry to its potential due to one reason or the other. Indian share in tourism business at global level is far below than its capacity to develop this industry. Data available from the World Tourism Organisation available till 2003 show France continued to maintain top slot with almost 75 million international tourists in 2003. Spain and China consolidate the second and third position having 52.5 million and 40.4 million foreign tourists respectively. Even smaller countries like Singapore, Indonesia and Thailand etc. are doing much better business than India from tourism. It is because of the number of problems faced by tourism and hotel industry in India.

The hotel industry in India is facing a number of problems such as low occupancy rate, increasing competition, high taxes, increasing cost, fuel shortage, low profitability and so forth. Similarly, on the one hand, it is alleged that there is shortage of rooms to meet the varied requirements of different categories of tourists and visitors while on the other hand room occupancy rate is very low here in India. It was 59.7 per cent in 2004 as against 54.8 per cent in 2003. Hotels are compelled to give liberal discount to the potential customers particularly during the lean period.

Further, average expenditure of those who get commercial accommodation is comparatively low due to one reason or the other. Similarly, prevailing tax rates such as service tax, excise duty and custom duty on imported luxury car, beer, liquor etc. are very high. All these factors adversely affect the profitability of the hotels. This is particularly true about 5-star hotels in India. Thus, on the one hand, heavy investment is required in hotel business while on the other hand profitability in this business is adversely affected by the aforesaid constraints. These problems can be discussed under the following heads:

1. Problem of Seasonality

Hotel is indeed a seasonal business. There is seldom 100 per cent occupancy except in peak season. In India on an average, it is 59.7 per cent. Therefore, a hotel cannot use its property fully and it accounts for low income. The problem is aggravated in case occupancy is adversely affected owing to bad weather or any other reason such as slump in business, international crisis or disturbances etc. Food cannot be stored due to its perishable nature. Similarly, hotel staff cannot be reduced temporarily at the time of poor demand of rooms. All these account for poor earnings.

2. Low Profitability

Revenue mainly comes from the rooms and sale of food and beverage in the hotel industry. Average occupancy level and average room rate have been found very low as indicated in Table 1.2. However, slight increase has been noted in both in 2003-04. But it is not sufficient to increase the profitability level of the hotel industry up to mark. Further, on the one hand food and beverage revenue is low while on the other hand food and beverage cost as well as labour cost is high as shown by Table 2.2 which affect the profitability of the hotel industry adversely.

Table 2.2 Indian Hotel Industry Position

Year	AOL (%)	ARR (Rs.)	R R (%)	F&B Rev.(%)	F&B Cost(%)	Labour Cost(%)
1994-1995	60.5	2410	49.81	37.29	35.9	18.77
1995-1996	62.3	2520	51.7	34.63	34.68	16.88
1996-1997	62.9	2560	52.41	34.36	35.93	16.97
1997-1998	56.2	2330	50.87	35.64	32.51	18.58
1998-1999	52.4	2530	48.68	36.85	33.68	21.29
1999-2000	51.7	2123	48.11	36.21	33.48	23.56
2000-2001	55.6	2046	47.63	36.95	31.95	23.17
2001-2002	53.2	2058	46.55	35.58	33	24.44
2002-2003	54.8	2004	44.44	38.34	33.47	23.79
2003-2004	59.7	2689	46.6	35.65	36.26	21.87

Source: Annual Reports, Questionnaire and FHRAI Hotel Industry Survey 2004-05.

AOL : Average Occupancy Level
ARR : Average Room Rate
RR : Rooms Revenue
F&B Rev : Food & Beverage Revenue
F&B Cost : Food & Beverage Cost.

There are some other reasons which may be held responsible for the low profitability of the hotel industry in India such as heightened competition, global uncertainty, changing technology, low efficiency, high power and fuel cost, poor sales and marketing programmes etc.

3. High Consumer Expectations

Consumer satisfaction is key to success for hotel industry. In these days, consumers are well informed and their expectations go on changing very frequently. Therefore, satisfying a consumer is a most challenging task as it depends not only on tangible but on intangible factors as well. The best of room comfort and the choicest products of culinary art fail to satisfy some people. Services have to be highly personalised in this industry. This makes the hotel industry the most difficult one from the marketing point of view.

4. High Direct and Indirect Taxes

The hotel industry is unfavourably treated from taxation point of view. Hotels do not get tax benefits as enjoyed by other industrial enterprises. Rebates in corporate income tax, service tax, custom duty, municipal taxes etc. are offered to other industries. The hotel industry does not get these benefits despite its low return on investment. Therefore, the industry cannot keep pace with inevitable changes in market trends.

5. Problems of Raising Funds

Most of the hotels are built in the heart of towns where land is very costly. Further, cost of constructing a new hotel building or renovating an existing facility is also very high. Therefore, huge capital is required to complete construction or to renovate the existing one. It is indeed very difficult to mobilise huge funds from various sources. The poor financial viability of the hotel industry has further aggravated the position.

Further, there are some problems which cannot be negotiated. For example, there is very little that can be done to help a hotel that was built on a wrong location or lost the locational advantage later on because of certain happenings. The solution of these problems needs a very high degree of managerial skill and expertise.

Similarly, there are also a number of factors which account for our failure to develop tourism in India to its potential such as:

- Inadequate tourist infrastructure at important destinations;
- Poor marketing strategies and policies for tourism promotion;
- Low priority to domestic tourism;
- Poor tourism planning and their ineffective execution;
- Faulty human resource development planning and policies in tourism sector.

Future Prospects

The prospects of an industry depend upon the economic, social, political, scientific and technological changes which are taking place in the universe. The hotel industry is very much sensitive and change in any sphere of the universe or in any branch of human activity will immediately reflect upon this industry. The techniques, ideas, modes and methods of operation undergo continual alteration in hotel business.

The emerging worldwide scenario is very conductive for the growth of tourism and hospitality industry. This is due to worldwide education and industrial development leading to greater enlightenment, increased earnings of individuals, economic growth of tourists producing nations, medical science's progress leading to longer life, improved infrastructure of communications and improved transport means etc. Similarly increase in holidays, vacations with pay policy of the government and other employers, increase in pay, extra ordinary revolution into the means of transportation including aeroplanes and steadily reduction in airlines fares have given a boost to the domestic tourism and hotel business in India.

The future of Indian hospitality and tourism industry seems to be very positive due to increased flow of business and leisure travellers. India is hosting forthcoming Commonwealth Games in 2010 and co-hosting the Cricket World Cup in 2011 and has multiple plans to promote *yoga* and meditation, rural tourism, sports tourism, medical tourism, adventure tourism etc. Thus, Indian hoteliers should try to develop world class infrastructure and facilities for games to make India the "Destination Next". India has unparalleled potential for growth and development of the tourism industry. Endowed with rich historic heritage, cultural diversity and geographical advantage, it could be developed as a leading tourist destination. India can boast of the Himalayas for mountain tourism, the 1500 km long coastline for beach tourism, temples, forts, palaces, monuments and ruins for historical tourism, over 400 national parks and sanctuaries for wild life tourism, people with diverse languages, fine arts and tradition for cultural tourism and Rajasthan for desert tourism. Foreign tourists have special attractions in India for centuries and Indian hospitality is a legend by itself. Apart from ancient culture and civilization, the diverse natural beauty of India can hardly be seen elsewhere in the world. The traditional stereotyped image of India as a cultural destination is being replaced with the image of diversified tourism products after liberalisation and tourism has been declared as an industry. Both central and state governments have identified tourism as a priority sector.

Therefore, in coming years, tourism may emerge as a major foreign exchange earner and employment generating industry. However, the hotel and tourism industry has been declared a high priority industry for foreign investment. But, to make tourism industry globally competitive there is a need to create adequate infrastructure. Government should also provide this industry the infrastructure status and income tax, custom duty, sales tax and excise duty benefits. Hugh investment is required to improve communication, transport and accommodation facilities for various categories of tourists. Therefore, apart from government investment, large-scale private investment is also required.

In a nutshell, It may be said that there is a lot of potential for the growth of tourism industry in the country and this will boost hotel business too. The demand of hotel rooms is expected to increase in future and the supply is expected to grow faster to meet the increased demand. Therefore, tourism and hospitality industry has a lot of potential for large-scale investment, employment and earnings.

ACTIVITY

1. Collect all the pictures and detail data dating form 1840 to 1975 of Hospitality Industry.
2. Find out the details on the functioning of the First Oberoi Hotel.

QUESTIONS

1. What is the objective behind studying History in Hospitality Industry?
2. Who is called as the Pioneer of Indian Hospitality Industry?
3. Bring out the detail information on the Hospitality Industry in India?

ANNEXURE 1

FACTS AND FIGURES WITNESSING THE GROWTH AND DEVELOPMENT PATTERN OF HOTEL INDUSTRY OVER A CENTURY AND THE TREND THERE IN

- 2000 - occupany - 63 %; $97 billion in sales
  - Hilton unveils plans for the first luxury hotel in space.
- 1999 - Choice Hotel International is the first chain to test making in-room PCs a standard amenity for guests. Starwood hotels and resorts takes the boutique segment mainstream with the openimg of its W brand.
- 1996 - best western celebrates its 50th anniversary, marking it the oldest continually operating brand.
- 1995 - Choice Hotels International and Promus become the first companies to offer guest "real-time" access to its central reservation system. Choice and Holiday inn are the first to introduce online booking capability.
- 1994 - First online hotel catalogue debuts - travelweb.com. Promus and Hyatt hotels are the first chain to establish a site on internet.
- 1993 - Radisson hotels worldwide is the first to introduce business class rooms.
- 1992 - Industry breakeven financially after 6 consecutive years of losses.
- 1991 - Westin is the first hotel chain to provide in room voice mail. Industry sees record losses, 61.8%.
- 1990 - occupancy - 64%; $60.7 billion in sales; total hotel rooms - 3,065,685; 45,020 properties; average room rate - $ 58.70
- 1990 - 'Loews hotel' good neighbour policy become the industry's first and most comprehensive community outreach programme.
- 1989 - Hyatt introduced a chain wide kids programme for ages 3-12 and a business centre at the Hyatt Regency, Chicago. Hampton inns is the first hotel chain to introduce the 100% satisfaction guarantee.
- 1988 - Extended stay segment introduced with Marriott's residence inns and holiday corporation Homewood suites.

- 1986 - Teledex Corporation introduced the first telephone designed specifically for hotel guest room. Days inn provides an interactive reservation capability connecting all hotels.
- 1984 - Holiday inn is the first to offer a centralized travel agent commission plan. Choice hotels introduce the concept of market segmentation. Choice hotel offer no-smoking rooms. Hampton inns is the first to offer a set of amenities. Holiday inn debuts embassy suites hotels, the first nationwide all-suite hotel chain, in overland park, Kan.
- 1983 - Westin is the first major hotel company to offer reservation and checkout using major credit cards ving card invests the optical electronic key card.
- 1980 - occupancy - 70%; $25.9 billion in sales; total hotel rooms - 2068,377
- 1979 - Hyatt names its first women general manager, Cheryl Phelps, to the former queen Marry Hyatt in long beach Calif.
- 1977 - Showtime and the movie channel debut in hotels.
- 1976 - Two Florida hotels are the first to offer HBO in guest rooms.
- 1975 - Lodging magazine is authorized as the official publication of AH& MA. Four Seasons is the first hotel company to offer in room amenities such as name brand shampoo. Hyatt introduces an industry first when it opens its regency club, a concierge. Cecil B. Day hand out wooden nickels to guest over 50, establishing the first seniors programme.
- 1974- The energy crisis hits the industry—hotels dim exterior signs, cut heat to unoccupied rooms, and ask guests to conserve electricity.
- 1973 - the Sheraton Anaheim is the first to offer free in-room movies.
- 1970 - occupancy - 65%; $8billion in sales; total hotel room - 1627473; average room rate - $19.83
- 1970 - Hilton becomes the first billion dollar lodging and Food Service Company and the first to enter the Las Vegas market. Cecil B Day opens the first day inn on Tybee Island, Ga.
- 1969 - Westin was the first hotel chain to implement 24 hours room service.
- 1967 - The Atlanta Hyatt Regency opened, featuring a 21-storey atrium and changing the course of upscale hotel design. Hyatt Hotels Corporation splits into a real-estate holding company.
- 1966 - Best Western become the first hotel company to be wholly governed by board of director made up entirely of its own member hoteliers. Inter-continental introduces retractable drying lines in guest showers business

lounges, ice and vending machines in guest corridors and street entrances for hotel restaurant.

- 1964 - Travelodge debuts wheelchair-accessible rooms.
- 1963 - AHA changes its name to the American Hotel and Motel Association desegregation in hotels has started.
- 1962- Curt Carlson buys shares of the Radisson Hotel in Minneapolis, Minn. motel 6, the forerunner of budget brands, opens in Santa Barbara, Calif.
- 1960 - occupancy - 67%; $3 billion in sales; total hotel rooms - 2400450; average room rate-$10.81; typical hotel-39 room, independent, and locally owned; average room rate - $9.99
- 1960s - Siegas introduced the first true minibar (a small refrigerator displaying product).
- 1958 - AHA sells licence for the universal travel card to American Express. Sheraton introduces reservation, the industry first automated electronic reservation system and the first tool free reservation no. Omni Hotel, originally Dunfey Hotel is founded.
- 1957 - J.W Marriott opens his first hotel, the twin bridges Marriott motor hotel in Arlington, Va and Jay Pritzker buys his first hotel, the Hyatt House, located outside the Los Angles Airport. Hilton offers direct dial telephone service.
- 1954 - Howard Dearing Johnson initiates the first lodging franchise, a motor lodge in Savannah, Ga. Conrad Hilton purchases of the Statler Hotel Company for $111 millions is largest real estate transaction in history. An inn in Flagstaff, Ariz. is the first in series of motor hotel forming Ramada a spenches word meaning “a shaded resting place”.
- 1953 - AHA buys a universal credit card. The American Hotel foundation a subsidiary of AHA is founded.
- 1952 - Kemmmons Wilson opened his first Holiday Inn in Memphis, tenn., named after a Bing Crosby movie.
- 1951 - The American Hotel Institute, later to be renamed to the Educational Institute, is the Hilton is the first chain to install TV sets in all guest-rooms.
- 1950 - occupancy; 80%; typical motel - 17 room; average room rate - $5.91
- Mid-1950s - atls hotels developed the first in-room con-fee concept.
- 1947 - Westin established hotel hoteltype, the first hotel reservation system; New York City's Roosevelt Hotel installs TV sets in all guest-rooms.

- 1946 - Westin debuts first guest credit card. Best Western is founded by MK Guertin and 54 friends. Occupancy reaches the highest ever rate 93%. The first casino hotel, the Flamingo, debuts in Las Vegas. Larrym, Wood, N.J which evolved into Loews Hotels.
- 1945 - Sheraton is the first hotel corporation to be listed on the New York Stock Exchange. Travelodge become the first economy Loding Corporation.
- 1940 - occupancy - 64%; average room rate - $3.21
- 1940 air-condition and air-cooling become prevalent.
- 1939 - quality court later choice hotel international is formed by seven motel operator as a non-profit referal system.
- 1937 - Membership in the waiters and bartenders national union, which encompasses hotel employees, exceeds 200,000.
- 1934 - The Hotel Statler in Detroit is the first to have a central system to air condition in every public room.
- 1933 - Due to the great depression, the hotel post the lowest average occupancy rate on record, 54%. Construction grinds to a halt.
- 1931 - AHA's chain hotel system debuts, later know as the Directory of Hotel and Motel Companies.
- 1930 - occupancy - 65%; AHA's hotel red book; lists 20000 hotels' typical hotel - 46 rooms; average room rate - $5.60
- 1930 - Four out of five hotels in the USA go into receivership. The standard travel agent commission is 10%.
- 1929 - Western hotels, now Westin, start with 17 hotels in the pacific northwest and established the first US hotel management company. The Oakland airport hotel become the first of its kind in the country.
- 1928 - There are more than 580,000 industry employees.
- 1927 - The Hotel Statler in Boston becomes the first hotel with radio reception; room are equipped with individual headsets to receive broadcasts from a central contract room. The American Hotel Association merges with the Hotel Red Book, first printed in 1886. The Huntington Hotel in Calif installs the first Olympic size hotel swimming pool.
- 1925 - The first road side "motel" opens in San Luis Obispo Calif., for $2.50 a night.
- 1922 - The Treadway Company has some of the first management contracts on small college inn. The first collegiate programme in hotel and restaurant management initiate at Cornell University by the American Hotel Association.

- 1920 - occupancy - 85%;
- hotel construction reaches an all time peak as thousands of room are added along the new states and federal highways
- 1920 - Prohibition begins.
- 1919 - Conrad Hilton purchases his first hotel, the Mobley in Cisco Texas.
- 1917 - The American Hotel Protective Association changes its name to the American Hotel Association (AHA) of the USA and Canada.
- 1916 - The federal road aid act spawns a new segment of lodging industry.
- 1910 - 10000 U.S. hotels; one millions rooms; 300000 employees average size - 60-75 rooms
- 1910 - The American Hotel Protective Association is founded in Chicago. The lodging industry consists almost entirely of hotel situated in urban centres and resorts near the principal vacation destinations. Electricity is beginning to be installed in new hotels for cooking purpose, as well as for lighting. However, most hotels place candlesticks, new candles and matches in every room- electric light bulb or not.
- 1908 - Gideon's international places their first bible in the superior hotel in Montana. The hotel Statler chain begins in Buffalo. All guest rooms have private baths, full-length mirrors, telephones, and built-in radios, serving as the model for hotel construction for next 40 years.
- 1904 - New York City St. Regis hotel provides individually controlled heating and cooling units in each guestroom.
- 1900 - fewer than 10000 hotels; 750000 to 850000 rooms;
- 1900 - a typical first class hotel offer steam heat, gas burners, electric call bells, baths and closets on all floors, billiard and sample rooms, barber shop and liveries. the Lenox Hotel, know today as the Lenox Hotel and suites/ village lodge, offered "fireproof lodging, unexcelled cuisine , a shower bath, roof garden and American /European lodging plans starting at $2"

Source: American Hotel and Lodging Associations.

3

HOSPITALITY INDUSTRY AND ITS ROLE IN INDIAN ECONOMY

— *PRASHANT KANDARI*[1]

The importance of an industry in a nation is recognized when it not only grows and develops itself but also leads to the growth and development of the other allied sectors, thus complementing the overall purpose that is of development of the nation. The hospitality industry is one such industry which effectively complements the other industries and sectors by creating strong forward and backward linkages in the economy. Hospitality industry has attained a respective position in Indian economy and globally due to its huge role in economic development and employment generation in the economy. Thus, it has become the world largest export industry and generating huge foreign exchange earnings. India is a land of all seasons and offers all forms and type of tourism destinations. It includes cultural tourism, adventure tourism, medical tourism (Ayurveda and other systems of Indian medicines), ecotourism, rural tourism, religious/pilgrimage tourism, spiritual tourism, and beach tourism etc.

OBJECTIVES

- ❖ To understand the linkage of hospitality industry with other sectors
- ❖ To learn the effects of these linkages on other economic variables
- ❖ To assess the contribution of the hospitality industry in an economy (India and global perspective)
- ❖ To identify the areas which has enhanced the importance of hospitality industry in Indian economy and world wide
- ❖ To study the trend of the economic contribution of the hospitality industry in Indian perspective
- ❖ To understand the working of some economic variables in context of hospitality industry

1. Lecturer in Economics at Pauri Campus, HNB Garhwal University, Srinagar, Garhwal.

A. HOSPITALITY INDUSTRY – COMPLEMENTARY TO OTHER SECTORS

Hospitality industry drives strong forward and backward linkages with the other sectors of the economy. Before discussing out the effect of these linkages it is important to understand the meaning of this term. A firm's input is another firm's output and it means that industry output is the input of the other industry than only we say that the different firms, industries or sectors are having an input output elationship or linkages. Further when the development of a sector, industry or firm is related to the development, growth of other firm, industry or sector then these different sectors, industries and firms enjoys linkages. When a firm uses the output of other firms as its inputs for carrying out its business activities then we say that this firm enjoys a backward linkage with those firms. When the output of a firm is used as an input by other firms for carrying out their business activities then the concerned individual firm enjoys a forward linkage with those firms. These linkages if created in the domestic economy it leads to the development of the country. But further the creation of the linkages in the global economy leads to the development of the global economy along with the development of the domestic economy. And the linkage of these sectors with the hospitality industry globally leads to foreign exchange earnings. Here we will briefly discuss the major forward and the backward linkages exhibited in the hospitality industry domestically and globally.

How the Hospitality Industry is Interlinked with other Businesses?

When a company is looking for a place to relocate or to grow its business, many variables are considered. One such variable is quality of life. The quality of life in urban areas is generally scaled by the: housing cost, education quality and cultural amenities existing in that region. The hospitality industry develops those cultural amenities and further provides other facilities that other companies find attractive. This favourably pulls the companies to that region and thus helps them in expanding their businesses without any troubles. The hospitality industry further supports the business activities by acting as a medium in pursuance of those activities. The companies find easier to carry out there external activities due to the support of the hospitality industry (Consider the various meetings, presentations, seminars of the companies organized in the hotels, consider the various business dealings held in it, consider the various business tours of the companies organized by the tours and travel organizations.

Consider a luxurious star category hotel opening in an area, to run that hotel, huge demand for different commodities and services will be created in it. Take for example the hotel will demand for its kitchen the huge amount of food grains, vegetables, meat, liquor etc. This will develop better earning avenues for the local vendors, who can become the suppliers for that hotel. Huge amount of clothing will be supplied to the laundry, giving local laundry workers a good business. The technical equipments (the computer systems connecting the different departments of the hotel, consider the vast electrical appliances used to decorate and facilitate the hotel services, audiovisual technology, the projection systems, lighting and sound systems used in each performance or high-tech business meeting) in the hotel, will require the repair and maintenance thus creating good opportunities for the local technicians to get work and earning source.

The different types of expenditure undertaken by hotel properties are summarised below:

- Expenditure on utilities - electricity, water, gas, etc.
- Expenditure on fresh foods - vegetables, fruits, dairy products, meat, fish, etc
- Expenditure on light manufacturing products - bakery products, alcoholic and non-alcoholic beverages, stationery, crockery, glassware, utensils, spa products, etc.
- Expenditure on construction, furniture, fixtures and equipments.
- Expenditure on services - equipment rental, custom brokerage, accounting and audit services, maintenance, transportation, etc
- Hospitality sector contributes to the economy indirectly through its linkages with other sectors like horticulture, agriculture, poultry, health, handicrafts and construction.

LINKAGE WITH AGRICULTURE SECTOR AND ITS SCOPE

Most of the local produces consumed in the hospitality industry is procured from a complex, yet unplanned network of suppliers who either purchase or credit fruits and vegetables from local farmers and then supply these foods to hotels and restaurants on a weekly basis. An important fact is, most of the foods consumed by our tourism industry are imported. Indeed, the greatest benefits that can be provided by hospitality industry will occur only when the goods and services that are consumed by that sector originate in the local economy. If a country is to maximise its benefits from tourism development, ways must be found to increase backward economic linkages, including utilizing local food products in the tourism industry. There are lots of problems in this effective linkage like, lack of communication between farmers and tourist food representatives, inconsistencies in food quality and quantity, and fluctuating food prices. These problems if sort out can help in the development of both agricultural and hospitality sector. Globally the development of the hospitality sector will help an agriculture efficient country like India to earn foreign exchange by the exports of the agri-goods. The hospitality industry provides the business to the sub-agricultural activities like - fisheries, animal husbandry, poultry etc. Further the effective linkage of the agricultural sector with the hospitality sector along with developing the agricultural sector will help it to modernize it, making it more quality conscious.

Helps in Developing the Service Sector

Transportation and Travel Sector

Transportation system is a major infrastructure that is essential for the development of an economy. The hospitality industry pushes up the need and the requirement for developing the travel and transportation system of the region. The need for developing the travel and transportation becomes more essential due to the pressure created by the hospitality industry and by the economic growth and development of the region resulted due to the introduction of the hospitality industry. The tourism and business activities in the region flourish to such an extent that they essentially require a good linkage system with other regions of the country and world wide (consider the opening of an international airport, a harbour). But this upswing comes effectively only when the government acknowledges this development and further supports it with some public investments even though private investments also starts but some areas concerning infrastructure like (construction of bridge, roads, highways etc.) are ignored by the private investors due to their low profitability. Further, the hospitality industry not only develops the travel and transportation system but also supports the new sector, i.e. travel and transportation (which flourish due to the development of the infrastructure) by giving them good business and thus an opportunity to earn huge revenue. The tour and travel sector directly serve the transportation sector by giving them good business and the hotel industry indirectly supports the transportation sector by pulling a good amount of domestic and international tourists to that region. Indeed it's not unfair to assume that with the huge development of the hospitality sector soon it will become a main support for India's travel and transport sector, which generates a huge proportion of India's total GDP (Gross Domestic Product).

Information Technology, Marketing, Maintenance, Security and so on

The other areas related to the service sector which are supported by the hospitality industry are information technology, marketing, maintenance and many others. The hospitality industry directly or indirectly drives a linkage with them and helps them by providing them adequate business. Further, it is to be noted that almost all hotels in any country has willingness to purchase more inputs locally but lack of information like availability issues, price and quality prevents them from so doing, and this develops the scope for the marketing sector in the hospitality industry.

How does it Help in the Development of the Industrial Sector?

Hospitality industry by creating huge employment opportunities not only decreases the burden of the manufacturing sector but further by generating huge employment and hence large disposable income creates indirect demand for the commodities and goods of the manufacturing sector. This newly created demand is indirect in the sense that the hospitality industry has provided the large disposable income in the hands of its employees and the other individuals who are indirectly benefited by the hospitality industry. The reasonable demand for the manufacturing goods created indirectly by the hospitality industry helps the development of the manufacturing sector. Important to add, Hospitality industry also creates the direct demand for the manufacturing sector (we have discussed it earlier).

GENERATES NEW MARKET

Apart from directly serving the local community the hospitality industry by pulling the domestic and international tourists and the other sectors in a region (due to the factors discussed earlier) generates new demand in the region. (Consider the growing population of the residents (immigrants) and the tourists in an area and there propensity to consume). How good or popular a region might be, but it will effectively attract the tourists only when the tourist finds the hospitality in that region. The hotel sector is able to extend its impact on expenditures in the local economy by encouraging and facilitating guests to visit attractions, shopping, dining and entertainment as part of their business model there by assisting with distribution of tourist spending. The growing demand due to the growing population of the residents and the visitors helps in earning good revenue which certainly increases the profit expectations (Marginal efficiency of capital) which further helps in attracting new investments in the region, thus helping in the development of the local economy.

COMPLEMENTING THE HEALTH/MEDICAL SECTOR (AYURVEDA AND OTHER SYSTEMS OF INDIAN MEDICINES)

Tourism is promoting the sectors like health and the medical. Health Tourism is a concept where a patient travels to another country for medical treatment in order to save costs, or get treatment faster or even to avail of better medical facilities.

Medical tourism has three different areas which are:

- Modern treatment,
- Ayurveda and
- Yoga.

Tourism by forming a linkage with the medical and health sector is not only promoting these sectors worldwide but also driving huge business for them in the country. Most patients from countries like U.S.A. and U.K. travel to developing countries such as India for treatment because India offers some of the cheapest pricing options of treatment, and along with offers a good holiday. The reason India is a favourable destination is because of its infrastructure and technology in which is in par with those in U.S.A., U.K. and Europe. India has some of the best hospitals and treatment centres in the world with the best facilities.

Medical Tourism companies in India have introduced several packages for patients travelling to India which include holidays and hotel stays during their travel apart from other basic requirements such as airport pickup, meetings with doctor's, post and pre-surgery etc. India has slowly developed itself as a medical tourism destination, and the state of Kerala in south India is making efforts to project itself as a health travel destination of choice.

B. CONTRIBUTION OF HOSPITALITY INDUSTRY TO INDIAN AND GLOBAL ECONOMY

After understanding the complementary association of hospitality industry with other sectors now we will discuss in detail the various important aspects related to the contribution of the hospitality industry to the Indian and the global economy.

How does it Generate Income, Investment and Employment Through Working of Multiplier in an Economy?

Before discussing how hospitality industry helps in the generation of income output and employment in an economy through working of multiplier it is important to understand the meaning of multiplier and the process of its working.

The theory of multiplier observes that the total increase in income, output and employment is manifold the original increase in investment. If the value of multiplier in an economy is 3 then an investment of 100 crore in it will lead to the generation of income up to 300 crore in that economy. The multiplier is therefore called as the ratio of increase in income due to the increase in investment. The value of multiplier in an economy depends on the marginal propensity to consume in that economy. This can be represented with the help of a formula:

$$K = \frac{1}{1 - MPC}$$

Where,

K = multiplier
MPC = marginal propensity to consume.

Now the question arises why does the increase in income is much more than the increase in investment. Suppose an investment is undertaken in an economy, this investment will become the income of the new employees absorbed by that investment. That new income earned will be spend in the economy in many other goods and services in the economy. This will increase the demand of those goods and services in the economy thus increasing the income of the suppliers of those goods and services which further result in the increase in the demand of other goods and services in the economy. This process will continue till the income increase to a multiple amount which will be decided by the value of the multiplier which is further decided by the value of the marginal propensity to consume (MPC) in that economy.

Lets understand it with the help of an example: Let's say an investment of 50 lakhs is done in the opening of a hotel, it will straight away lead to the employment generation and demand of the goods and services from its external environment. Both will lead to the generation of the income in the economy, firstly in the case of the employees of the hotel and other when the hotel will demand goods and services from the other sectors which will generate fresh revenues for them. Assume that the new income generated is equal to Rs. 50 lakhs in the economy. Consider that the marginal propensity to consume in the economy is 4/5. Thus, of the new income generated in the economy, its 4/5 part will be spend in the consumption, i.e. Rs. 40 lakhs (Rs. 10 lakhs will be saved). The spending of the Rs. 40 lakhs in the economy will further increase the demand of the other goods and services in the economy leading to more revenues and thus more income generation in the economy. The persons who will earn these Rs. 40 lakhs will further spend the 4/5th part of it i.e. 32 lakhs (8 lakhs will be saved). The process will go until the total income generated in the economy becomes a multiple of the new investment made initially in the hotel.

$$K = \frac{1}{1 - \frac{4}{5}}$$

Or, $K = 5$

Thus the initial investment of Rs. 50 lakhs in a hotel will lead to an increase in the income in the economy equal to that of Rs. 250 lakhs.

It is necessary to add that every increase in income in the economy will further lead to increase in the employment in the economy and every increase in the demand (brought in with the increase in income) in the economy will further lead to more investment and further increase in the employment in the economy.

The good thing about the multiplier that works due to the investment in the hospitality industry is that it pushes up the income and employment level not just in the one thrust (brought in by the initial investment) but the multiplier will work through the whole life of capital invested (e.g. hotel) i.e. till it exists. This will be possible due to the strong linkages created by the hospitality industry.

The hospitality industry helps generate more income, employment and investment opportunities through working of multiplier in following ways:

❖ Firstly, the expenditure done by the tourists led to the direct generation of the revenues, this is called as the direct-multiplier effect.

❖ Secondly, the individuals or groups that earns those revenues (income) because of the expenditure done by the tourists spends them in various goods and services in the economy which increases the demand of the different goods and services in the economy. This is called as the indirect multiplier effect.

❖ Thirdly, the beneficiaries of the indirect spending of the goods and services also lead to more increase in the demand of the other goods and services in the economy. This is further called as the induced multiplier effect.

Note that every increase in the demand of the goods as services lead to more investment and more production of the national output (National income) which further increases the level of employment in the economy.

The increase in the more disposable income in the economy due to the growth in the hospitality industry not only develops and grows other sectors but also results in the growth of the hospitality industry itself. It is important to note here that the tremendous growth of Indian economy has resulted in more disposable income in the hands of middle class, thereby prompting increasingly large number of people to spend money on vacations abroad or at home.

Major Generator of Direct and Indirect Employment

Hospitality industry has helped in creating huge number of direct and indirect employment opportunities (Full-time and part-time) in India and world wide. Hospitality industry (Tourism industry) is on a great boom at the moment and further India is exploiting its tremendous potential to become a major global tourist destination thus generating the huge number of direct employment in it. As per the estimates of the Department of Tourism, Government of India, total direct employment in the tourism sector in India was about 20 million during 2003-04.

Table 3. Observed and Forecasted Estimates of the Employment Levels in the Different Categories of Hotels in India

Category of Hotels	Employment intensity (Employees per under rooms)	Total employment 2002	Total employment 2010	Total employment 2020
5/4-star Hotels	174	57,000	83,000	1,10,400
1-3-star Hotels	122	52,500	63,000	83,000
Smaller hotels	58	638,000	14,05,000	32,61,500
Total	NA	7,47,500	15,51,000	34,54,900

Note: In addition, there are more than one lakh employees working in motels on state and national highways. A bulk of the employees approximately 60% are working in F&B service, Kitchen and housekeeping. Front offices of the larger hotels account for nearly 7% of the employees.

Source: *Ministry of Tourism, Department of Tourism, Government of India, Market Pulse Report, February 05, 2004.*

HOTELS IN INDIA: EMPLOYMENT PATTERN AND FORECAST

In the hospitality sector, employment intensity increases with the size of hotel. The larger Four and Five-star hotels (along with the heritage hotels) employ on an average 174 people per 100 rooms, compared to 122 in the One, Two and Three Star Hotels and 58 in the unorganized sector.

Hotel Employee Profile

Five/Four-Star Hotels: Most employees in the management/supervisory cadres in the front office, F&B service and housekeeping have hotel management backgrounds. Almost 90% of the chefs are having a hotel management degree/ diploma or a certificate from a Food Crafts Institute.

Three, Two and One Star Hotels: Almost half the managers and supervisors have either a hotel management degree/diploma or a Food Crafts Institute Certificate. A majority of those at junior levels are just graduates or even SSC pass.

Unorganized Sector: Only a few of the managers have a hotel management degree/diploma. Most of the employees consist of untrained manpower.

Almost 80% of the employees in key hotel functions such as F&B, front office and housekeeping are young; they are less than 40-year old. In the smaller hotels, more than 50% are less than 30-year old.

In addition, there are more than 1.3 million people employed in small restaurants and *dhabas* on the state and national highways. By 2020, even a 10% share for the organized sector will generate nearly 130,000 jobs for trained manpower.

More than half the employees are in key functions of F& B service and kitchen and are less than 30-year old. Almost 60% of these employed in kitchens of conventional restaurants, cafes and fast food outlets are diploma holders either from private hotel management institutions or Food Craft Institutes. Only 20% of people in F&B service are hotel management degree/diploma holders. Restaurants employ largely untrained manpower.

PROJECTED ANNUAL DEMAND FOR TRAINED MANPOWER

Category	2010	2020
Hotels	7000	10000
Restaurants	45000	45000
Total	52000	55,000

Source: *Ministry of Tourism, Department of Tourism, Government of India, Market Pulse Report, February 05, 2004.*

Key drivers of demand for trained manpower are likely to be the expansion of the organized sector, golden quadrilateral and preference for youth in the hospitality sector. Presently, 16,850 students are being trained in hotel management, annually. Only 22% are graduating from the government promoted institutes. Nearly 40% of them are pursuing alternative careers in other emerging service sectors (such as call centres). These statistics indicate that there could be a severe shortage for trained manpower by the year 2010. Along with creating direct employment opportunities the hospitality sector further generates huge number of indirect employment in the country due to its strong linkages with the other sectors in the country. These linkages results in the growth of the other sector with the growth in the hospitality sector in the country. The indirect employment opportunities in the country are created due to the working of the indirect employment multiplier whose value is fairly high in the Indian economy as is estimated to be at 1.36 during year 2003-04.

MAJOR SOURCE OF FOREIGN EXCHANGE EARNINGS

Tourism has become the world's largest export industry. The growth of the travel and the tourism sector is continuously growing globally, that is exhibited by the data given by World Trade Organisation for year 2004-05 and 2005-06. As per the World Trade Organisation, about 808 million tourists travelled internationally a growth rate of 5.6 percent over 2004 - and spent about US$680 billion. Furthermore, according to the World Trade and Tourism Council (WTTC), tourism accounted for 10.6 per cent of global GDP, 12.0 per cent of the total world exports and 8.3 per cent of global employment in the year 2005 - *Economic survey - 2006-07*. It is estimated that tourism accounts for 13 per cent of total world export and 8.2 per cent of global employment.

Travel and tourism industry is the second highest foreign exchange earner for India, and the government has given travel and tourism organization an export house status. It is not hidden that tourism is among India's important export industries. Foreign exchange earnings from tourism during 2003-04 were US $ 3,533 million (Rs 16,429 crores). During the year 2003-04, the tourism industry registered a growth of 17.3 per cent in foreign tourist's arrival compared to the modest growth of 1.0 per cent registered in 2002-03. The double digit growth in both number of foreign tourist arrivals and foreign exchange earnings there form continued for the third consecutive year in 2005-06.

Generates huge revenues for the Government

Hospitality industry earns huge revenues for the government in the form of sales tax/value added tax, corporate taxes, custom duties and taxes, entertainment taxes, etc. This huge public revenue gives the financial help to the government to carry out its development programmes in the country.

Table 3.2 Foreign Tourist Arrivals and Foreign Exchange Earnings

Year	Foreign tourists		Estimated foreign exchange earnings	
	No. in lakhs	Growth rate	Million US$	Growth rate
1996-97	23.34	6.6	2,878	6.1
1997-98	23.71	1.6	2,914	1.3
1998-99	23.97	1.1	2,993	2.7
1999-00	25.05	4.5	3036	1.4
2000-01	26.99	7.7	3,168	4.3
2001-02	24.28	-10	2,910	-8.1
2002-03	24.54	1	3,029	4.1
2003-04	29.33	19.5	3,979	31.4
2004-05	36.03	22.8	5,029	26.4
2005-06	40.53	12.5	5,931	17.9

Source: Ministry of Tourism, Government of India.

Contribution in providing business opportunities for entrepreneurs

The hotel sector in addition to its direct and indirect expenditures in the local economy actually provides direct entrepreneurial opportunities in different areas in an economy. These are principally outsourced aspects of the hotel product that are made available to external business people to operate either on the premises of the hotel or externally. The most impressive of these is the transportation. The other entrepreneurial opportunities that are created due to the development of the hospitality sector are in the activities like, restaurants, gifts and crafts shops, beauty salons and spas, water sports, adventure sports, entertainment etc.

RESTAURANTS IN INDIA

The huge demand growing due to the development of the hospitality sector and due to the burgeouning middle class and evolving lifestyle is driving the demand for quality restaurants – Conventional ones as well as fast food outlets and cafes. Our estimate is that there are at least 140,000 restaurants in urban India. Delhi and Mumbai account for nearly 15% of the restaurants. Conventional restaurants account for the largest population (30%), followed by sweet shops (16%), fast food outlets (16%) and *dhabas* (13%). Northern region already has over 10000 fast food outlets serving Chinese, Western and Indian food. (Source: *Ministry of Tourism, Department of Tourist, Government of India, Market Pulse Report, February 05, 2004).*

SUMMARY

The tourism industry in India, despite being an important component of the economy, contributed only 5.9% of the GDP in 2006/07. According to estimates of the World Travel and Trade Council (WTTC), Indian tourism demand will grow at

8.8% from 2004-13, which would place India as the third-most rapidly growing tourism market in the world after Montenegro and China. It would further result in a growth of 7.1% in total travel and tourism GDP. Tourism in the future will keep on contributing at a much higher rate to the economy indirectly through its linkages with other sectors like horticulture, agriculture, poultry, handicrafts, construction, health and many others.

ACTIVITY

1. Visit a hotel property in your locality and assess its income and linkages with other variables.
2. Estimate the budget expenditure of any restaurant in your locality.

QUESTIONS

1. What do you understand by the term linkage? Name the sectors which are closely related to the hospitality industry?
2. How does the agriculture sector is benefited with the growth of the hospitality sector? Discuss briefly.
3. Discuss the contribution of the hospitality sector to the Indian economy.
4. Explain the working of the multiplier in an economy.
5. Briefly describe the importance of the hospitality sector in the field of employment generation.
6. Discuss the different entrepreneurial opportunities in hospitality sector.
7. How the hospitality sector generated direct and indirect employment opportunities? Discuss.
8. How does the hospitality sector promotes the business activities in a country? Explain.

4

INTRODUCTION TO HOSPITALITY ACCOMMODATION

— JYOTI[1] AND PRAVEEN[2]

Food, cloth and shelter were supposed to be the basic need of the human. Now the dimension of need is revised and travel has become a major pillar of human life. This pillar has further strengthened the basic three needs, i.e. Food, cloth and shelter. As when one goes out he looks for good food, cloth (according to climate of the place) and shelter. For shelter he was dependent on friends and relatives, this limited the scope of individual to certain known places only where his or her friends or relatives were staying. But today's world has changed and people are looking beyond this limitation of destination. They are ready to spend, provided they get better place to accommodate themselves. This gives chance to businessman to use the accommodation facility and to earn from it. Earlier people use to give their houses to the visitors for some time and take certain amount of money for it. Now, we can find lodge, Yatri Niwas, Circuit House and Big Hotels providing accommodation facility to different clientele with different needs.

Thus, accommodation is the back bone of tourism Industry. The choices of destination vary as people travel not only to visit their friends and relatives (VFR) but also for business, leisure, medical treatment and to enjoy vacation. This difference in the motive for travel make the choice of accommodation differs. Say for example, if a family is going on vacation they will look for luxurious room on the other hand if an individual is going for a seminar or conference, he will look for room which can provide business facility. This difference in need for accommodation should be understood and care should be taken to provide the accommodation of guest choice rather then forcing the accommodation on them.

OBJECTIVES

- To understand different types of accommodation facility, and star categorization
- To explain the current scenario in hospitality accommodation and
- To discuss the emerging trends and issues in accommodation.

---

1. Lecturer in Hotel Management at M.M University, Mullana, Ambala.
2. Lecturer in Hotel Management at B.I.T., Mesra, Ranchi.

CONCEPTUAL MEANING

The concept of accommodation is an old age phenomena in India. However, it is now changing its face. The respect the people of this country give to their guest can be well understood by the saying *"Athithi Devo Bhava"* which means "Guest is God" and they have been providing them all what they can. With the change in time, the respect to the guest haş not gone down; surprisingly it has broadened its horizon, from guest and relatives (who were *athithi* earlier) now it is any tourist coming to their city.

As discussed earlier, people have varied needs and they decide over their accommodation requirement depending on this need only. For this reason there are number of accommodation facility available. Let us discuss some of it:-

a) Youth Hostels

The youth hostels are spread over India with excellent facilities and the main advantage of these hostels is that they are cheap compare to other accommodation facility. One can save money if they have a Youth Hostel Card; however it is not mandatory for them to have one.

b) Government Accommodation

The concept of government accommodation was initiated by Britishers for their officials visiting different part of the country, for this they made Rest Houses, Dak Bungalows, Circuit Houses, PWD (Public Works Department) Inspection Bungalows and Forest Rest Houses even at the remotest part of the country. Since these were made for the British officials, it is found often in attractive location where the Britishers need to go. However, it is still used by the government officials of the country.

c) Tourist Bungalows

State Government provides excellent facility in their Tourist Bungalows. The facility provided in the Tourist Bungalow are quite good compare to other hotels of the same tariff. Choice of rooms, good restaurant and other room amenities are some of the facilities provided by Tourist Bungalow in genuine price. One may think that Tourist Bungalow is one of the best places to stay while in India.

d) Railway Retiring Room

Railway is the major source of transportation in India. Millions of people use the facility of Indian Railway everyday. Hence, it becomes important to arrange for their accommodation when they are in transit. Retiring room facility can be compared to that of a hotel, however the only difference is that it is situated in the railway station and hence their client are the passenger with railway ticket or rail pass and those client who have to catch an early train. It is available at quite reasonable price.

e) Railway Waiting Rooms

Railway waiting room is the best option if retiring room is not available. The requirement here also is a valid reservation ticket. In many stations the waiting room for different classes is different. This accommodation is free of cost and a valid tick is only perquisite to avail this facility.

f) Hotels

In Indian Budget hotel is mostly preferred because they are quite cheap. But they raise their price as and when demand of accommodation increases due to any reason. These hotel operates on 24-Hour Check in Check out system, (that is your day will be start at the time you register in the hotel). However, some hotel still follow 12:00 Noon Check out (that is no matter at what time you registered your day will complete at 12:00 Noon). Luxury hotels in India has limited market, hence it is situated in the major tourist centres and metro cities. Luxury hotels can be kept under various star categories ranging from five stars to one star depending on the facility they provide. Various chains of hotel like Taj, Oberoi, Welcom, Centaur hotels provide these luxurious services to the customer. Most of these hotels follow 12:00 noon check out. These hotels keep proper care of the customer and provide all the facilities which make their accommodation more then mere accommodation. A sauna bath, swimming pool, gymnasium, shopping arcade is some of the essential characteristics of these luxurious hotels.

h) Home Stays

Stay with Indian to know India, this is the concept behind Home stays. These accommodations are organized in major cities of Rajasthan, Ladakh, Chennai and also in Mumbai in collaboration with the Tourism Development Corporation of the States. The tourist offices of the cities have the list of those families who are willing to offer this service.

i) Others

Beyond the above-mentioned accommodation facility, there are YMCAs and YWCAs in big cities. They are affordable and provide a god alternative for accommodation. These accommodations are generally full and hence to avail the facility reservation should be done before hand.

Though accommodation industry is expanding every day and new establishments are finding their space, then also the organization which is recognized as the major accommodation provider still remain Hotels. Layman understands hotel to be the only organization which provides facility for the visitor to stay or gives all accommodation facility name of "Hotel" only.

There are several basis on which hotels can be classified. Let us take five major basis on which the Hotels can be classified:-

Table 4.1 Typology of Hotel

Sl. No.	Basis	Type
1	Size	Small Medium Large
2	Star System	Five-Star Four-Star Three-Star Two-Star One-Star
3	Ownership	Independent Hotel Chain Hotels Management Contractual Hotels Partnership Franchise Govt. owned
4	Length of stay	Transit Residential
5	Location	Resort Motel Floatel Airport Hotels

Now let us understand the above-mentioned different types of hotels.

CLASSIFICATION ON THE BASIS OF SIZE

- *Small Hotel* : Small Hotels are those hotels in which the numbers of rooms are 25 or less than 25.
- *Medium Hotels* : Medium Hotels are those Hotels in which the number of rooms ranges from 26 to 299.
- *Large Hotels* : Large Hotels are those Hotels in which number of rooms are 300 or above.

CLASSIFICATION ON THE BASIS OF STAR CATEGORY

Five-Star: The characteristics of a five-star Hotel are its unique architecture and general construction and facade. The locality of the Hotel should be of highest standard. There should be sufficient parking space. The Hotel should have at least 25 lettable rooms with attached bathroom (with long baths or the most modern shower chambers). The public area and Hotel rooms should be fully Air-conditioned, there should be superior quality of carpet, curtains, fitting etc. Other features required are adequate number of efficient lifts, well designed lobby, ladies and gentlemen cloak room, swimming pool etc.

The facilities required at a Five-star Hotel are Reception counter, cash counter, Information counter, conference room, banquet Hall, private dining room, shopping arcade, book stall, barber shop, beauty parlour, dining room, restaurant, bar (If permissible by law), recognized travel agency, money change and safe deposit, Left luggage room, florist and a shop for toilet requisite and medicines on the premises. There should be a telephone in each room, provision of radio, TV, Personal Computer or laptop as per guest demand.

Besides, the Hotel should provide International and National cuisine to the guests with the highest standard of service by professionally skilled staff at each level of hierarchy. There should be provision of laundry, dry cleaning and 24-hour housekeeping.

Four-Star : The characteristics of a four-star Hotel are its unique architecture, general construction and facade just like Five-Star Hotels. The locality of the Hotel should be of suitable standard. There should be sufficient parking space. The Hotel should have at least 25 lettable rooms with attached bathroom. At least 50% of the bathrooms must have long baths or the most modern shower chambers, with 24-hour service of hot and cold running water. The public area and Hotel rooms should be fully air-conditioned and should be well furnished with carpet, curtains, fitting etc. Other features required are adequate number of efficient lifts, lobby, ladies and gentlemen cloak room, etc.

The facilities required at a Four-star Hotel are reception counter, cash counter, information counter, book stall, recognized travel agency, money change and safe deposit, left luggage room, dining room, restaurant and bar (if permissible by law). There should be a telephone in each room.

Besides, the Hotel should provide International and National cuisine to the guests with the highest standard of service by professionally skilled staff at each level of hierarchy. There should be provision of laundry, dry cleaning and housekeeping.

Three-Star : The characteristics of a Three-star Hotel is its very good architecture and general construction. The locality of the Hotel should be of good standard with appropriate parking space. The Hotel should have at least 20 lettable rooms, with attached bathroom with bath-tubs. At least 50% of the rooms should be air-conditioned. The furniture and furnishing should be of very good standard. Other features required are adequate number of efficient lifts, lounge, ladies and gentlemen cloak room, etc.

The facilities required at a Three-star Hotel are reception counter, information counter, book stall, recognized travel agency, money change and safe deposit, left luggage room, dining room, restaurant and bar (if permissible by law). There should be a telephone in each room.

Besides, the Hotel should provide Indian and Continental cuisine to the guests with the good standard of service by professionally skilled staff. There should be provision of laundry, dry cleaning and housekeeping.

Two-Star : The characteristics of a Two-star Hotel is its well constructed building and a suitable locality. The Hotel should have at least 10 lettable rooms out of which 75% of rooms should have attached bathrooms. For the remaining rooms there should be at least one bathroom for every four rooms. At least 25% of the rooms should be air-conditioned. The furniture and furnishing should be clean and comfortable. The hotel should have a lounge.

The facilities required at a Two-star Hotel are Reception counter with a telephone, dining room and restaurant. There should be a telephone or call bell in each room.

Besides, the staff should be courteous and efficient. There should be provision of laundry, dry cleaning and housekeeping.

One-Star : The characteristics of a one-star Hotel are its good constructed building and good surroundings. The Hotel should have at least 10 lettable rooms out of which 25% of rooms should have attached bathrooms. The furniture should be clean and comfortable.

The facilities required at a One-star Hotel are Reception counter with a telephone, dining room and restaurant. There should be a public telephone.

Besides, the staff should be courteous and efficient. There should be provision of laundry and housekeeping.

HOTEL CLASSIFICATION ON THE BASIS OF OWNERSHIP

1. Independent: Hotel — The Hotel which essentially work alone with a few employees. These Hotels are autonomous body.

Generally the single unit property comes under this category. This is also known as Solo Hotels. The advantage of this type of Hotel is that they can take the Management decision at single point. This saves times and they can easily add up with the changing market behaviour. At the same time Independent Hotels have no brand image and hence they can not attract clients from outside the locality.

2. Chain Hotel: In this category of Hotels, one organization opens its branches at different places with the same brand name for example Taj, Oberoi, ITC etc. This is the most successful type of ownership in case of Hotels as it has the advantage of centralized organization that provides good business through central reservation system, good financial strength, corporate expertise, management policies, promotional help etc. Here the power of decision making is vested with the corporate and the branch has to follow the policies made by the top level Management.

3. Management: Contractual Hotel These hotels are also a type of chain organization that operates properties which are owned by an individual or partners. Usually a long term contract is signed between the owner and operator in which generally legal and financial responsibilities are retained by owner and the operating expenses are paid by the operator. A pre-decided fees (agreed upon in contract) is given to operator by owner for operating the property. However, responsibility of paying tax lies with the owner.

4. Partnership: As the name suggest these Hotels are based on partnership which is carried on the enterprise as a joint activity. Partnership is a voluntary agreement among the partners. All the partners actively participate in the business of the Hotel. Here the risk involved in the operation is shared among the partners.

5. Franchise: The concept of franchise originated when the idea of utilizing the brand name of reputed property clicked into the mind of business people. However, they also wanted the property to be under their control. This was only possible when the organizations which already enjoy the brand image in the market agree on it. The risk involved for the organization was that if the property to

which they give their brand name does not maintain the same standard then the goodwill of the organization goes down.

The solution came by the mean of agreement in which the organization (which is known as Franchiser) agrees to give their brand name to the individual property (known as Franchisee) for which they get an agreed amount of Fees. However, the franchisee should maintain the standard as maintained by the Franchiser in their property and to ensure that a team from the Franchiser can inspect the property at regular interval.

6. Govt. Owned : There are few hotels which are directly operated by Government and are known as Government owned hotels. Here all the risks of operations are covered by the Government In India Ashok group of Hotels is example of this kind. Now due to the disinvestment policy of Government few of the Ashoka Hotels have been sold or given on lease.

HOTEL CLASSIFICATION ON THE BASIS OF LENGTH OF STAY

1. Transit Hotel: The *en route* guest are known as Transient guests and the hotels where they stay are termed as transit Hotels. They stay during their journey for very short duration. The stay may range from few hours, just for changing their clothes and taking refreshment, to a few days for business work or a whole night good sleep after a hectic journey.

2. Residential Hotel: These are hotels where the length of stay is very long; it may range from few weeks to months. These types of hotels are also known as apartment hotels. The rent is paid on monthly or yearly basis. The facilities are less than the luxury hotels; it is popular in metro cities where the clienteles of corporate sector have business engagements for long time span.

HOTEL CLASSIFICATION ON THE BASIS OF LOCATION

1. Resort Hotel: Resort hotels are located at the place where people come to enjoy their vacations and leisure time. The destination may be island, hill station, beach, exotic location etc. Now-a-days health resort and spa is also an upcoming sector of resort hotels. The other common

form of resort hotels are summer resort, winter sports resorts. In resort hotels the recreational facilities are of utmost importance. The facilities may include swimming, sailing, nature hikes, skiing, horse back riding, tennis, golf, dance parties etc. The atmosphere is more informal than other types of hotel.

2. Motel: These are the type of hotels which are located near the high way to serve the needs of the motorist. It has the facility of parking, garage, accommodation, recreational activities, restaurant, etc. Motels are generally equipped with filling and service station.

3. Floatel: These are the type of hotels which are located on the surface of water that may be sea, lake etc. It provides all the facility of first class hotels. Generally the old ships are converted into floatels. At some places like Kashmir the boats are converted into houseboats. This provides the exotic natural beauty to the guest. This is one of the booming sectors of hotel industry.

4. Airport Hotel: Airport hotels are situated near the airports and hence their clients include airline passengers or airline personnel. The stay is for very short duration, for example overnight stay. Airport hotels provide all the facilities of first class hotel with unique features of quick service and high level of comfort. The example of airport hotel in India is Centaur hotel in Delhi.

Besides the above classifications there are few other type of hotels found in the hospitality sector like suburban hotel, heritage hotel, down town hotel, retirement hotel, green hotel, casino hotel, condominium hotel and time share hotel etc.

Till now we have discussed different types of accommodation found in hospitality sector. Most of the accommodations discussed above have different types of rooms that cater different target market by providing different level of services and specialized requirements. Major types of rooms can be summed up as:-

Table 4.2: Typology of Rooms

Sl. No.	Types of Room	Description
1.	Single room	A room with a standard single bed to provide sleeping accommodation to one person (Bed size 6" x 3")
2.	Double room	A room with a standard Double bed to provide sleeping accommodation to two persons (Bed size 6" x 6")

Sl. No.	Types of Room	Description
3.	Twin Bedded room	A room with two identical twin bed separated out by a small bed side table to provide sleeping accommodation to two persons. (Bed size 3" x 6")
4.	Interconnected room	Two adjacent rooms are connected to each other by a door. The rooms may be single, double or twin bedded room.
5.	Suite	Set of two rooms – One bed room and one living room
6.	Cabana	Rooms situated near swimming pool of the hotels for changing purpose.
7.	Lanai	Rooms which have a view of scenic beauty like waterfall, garden etc.
8.	Hollywood Living room	A room with two single beds joined together with a common headboard.
9.	Studio Room	Rooms with utility furniture like sofa cum bed, roll away bed etc. that can be used for sitting purposes as well as sleeping purposes.
10.	Adjoining Room	Adjacent rooms without connecting door between them.

CURRENT SCENARIO IN HOSPITALITY ACCOMMODATION IN INDIA

Department of Tourism (MR Division), Ministry of Tourism and Culture, Government of India, commissioned the firm – Market Pulse, to conduct a research so as to assess the manpower requirement in the hotels and restaurants sector as well as tour and travel operation and to estimate the number of hotels, motels and restaurants in the unorganized sector. As per the market pulse report (2004) Ministry of Tourism Government of India there is estimated 1.2 million hotel rooms in the country. However, the star category hotels account for a mere 7% (approximately 80,000 rooms); most of the rooms are contributed by budget hotels, guesthouses and inns that cater primarily to domestic tourism. The metropolitan cities of Delhi, Mumbai, Chennai, Hyderabad and Kolkata, along with Goa account for 62% of the rooms in the five and four-star categories. The other smaller hotels are more geographically dispersed; this results from a strong correlation between hotels in the unorganized sector and domestic tourism statistics. Places of pilgrimage such as Tirupati and Haridwar have significantly lower availability of rooms – 28 and 150 rooms per lakh of tourists, respectively. It is forecasted that there will be a total of 2.5 million and 5.8 million hotel rooms in 2010 and 2020 respectively. This assumes that the infrastructure growth will keep pace with the anticipated growth in tourism. The other assumption is that the mix of hotels will remain the same; however, this might change in favour of the organized sector, if government initiatives take shape. Geographical spread might also change in favour of North-eastern states, J&K, West Bengal, Andhra Pradesh, Madhya Pradesh and Uttar Pradesh.

Table 4.3: State-wise Availability of Rooms (2004)

State	City	Total Rooms	Rooms per lakh Tourists
Andhra Pradesh		**58362**	**96**
	Hyderabad	13183	174
	Tirupati	2452	28
Tamil Nadu		**89293**	**351**
	Chennai	17577	355
	Ooty	6334	338
Karnataka		**71897**	**823**
	Bangalore	51507	962
	Mysore	4230	298
Kerala		**44049**	**759**
	Cochin	5861	559
	Trivandrum	8488	1010
M.P.		**39181**	**594**
	Khajuraho	871	594
U.P.		**295436**	**404**
	Agra	3891	175
	Varanasi	18423	558
H.P.		**53236**	**1043**
	Shimla	13202	1043
Orissa		**46683**	**1409**
	Bhubaneshwar	3467	906
	Puri	16360	1597
Assam		**10900**	**556**
	Guwahati	10900	556
Meghalaya		**2115**	**778**
	Shillong	2115	778
Rajasthan		**128823**	**1476**
	Jaipur	12874	1919

State	City	Total Rooms	Rooms per lakh Tourists
	Udaipur	5482	957
West Bengal		**17278**	**184**
	Kolkata	10709	184
Delhi		**27272**	**1540**
Uttrakhand		**17846**	**150**
	Haridwar	8000	150
Maharashtra		**51893**	**438**
	Mumbai	28682	307
	Pune	2935	NA
	Aurangabad	15060	2369
Gujarat		**60468**	**1048**
	Ahmedabad	11436	1048
Goa	**Goa**	**11924**	**747**
Punjab		**8975**	**2850**
	Amritsar	5057	2850
All India		**1171121**	**423**

ROOMS AVAILABILITY: A FORECAST (2010 – 2020)

In order to arrive at an estimate of hotel rooms in different states, the following bases have been assumed:

- The growth in star category hotels will follow the same trend as in the last 4 years.
- This trend has been obtained from the projects approved by the Ministry of Tourism in the past 4 years. If growth rate in tourism accelerates, this estimate can be treated as a conservative estimate.
- The growth in hotels in the unorganized sector will depend on the growth in tourism (domestic and foreign combined).
- The other assumption is that the 18 important states covered in the primary research will continue to represent 88% of hotel rooms in the unorganized sector.
- In 2010, there will be a total of 2.9 million hotel rooms, more than twice the numbers in 2002. Star category hotels will have almost 100,000 hotel rooms, while the balance will be present in the unorganized sector.

- The states of Andhra Pradesh, Madhya Pradesh, Uttar Pradesh, Assam/ Meghalaya and West Bengal will register the quickest growth trends. The states of Delhi, Karnataka and Gujarat might experience a stagnant phase. These are also those states that already have a high availability of hotel rooms.
- In the year 2020, there should be approximately 6.6 million hotel rooms, if the full potential of tourism is tapped.
- Market Pulse Report team feels that the contribution of North-eastern states as well as J&K, would be substantially higher than the present levels.

Table 4.4 Rooms availability in 2010 (Forecast)

State	Total Rooms	4/5 star Hotels	1/3 star Hotels	Other
Andhra Pradesh	141312	1802	5973	133537
Tamil Nadu	144250	3609	8327	132314
Karnataka	76034	2875	3159	70000
Kerala	64595	2396	7102	55097
Madhya Pradesh	114919	857	1360	112702
Uttar Pradesh	978216	3340	1779	973097
Himachal Pradesh	76769	342	372	76055
Orissa	78758	589	879	77290
Assam	45068	154	514	44400
Meghalaya	7950	50	115	7785
Rajasthan	209019	3815	3106	202098
West Bengal	83336	2421	1576	79339
Delhi	31528	9807	1721	20000
Uttarakhand	36727	323	1013	35391
Maharashtra	107952	10333	8324	89295
Gujarat	12281	732	2501	9048
Goa	21989	3035	1545	17409
Punjab	17372	975	1822	14575
All India	**2877168**	**46690**	**54867**	**2775611**

Growth in Tourist Traffic

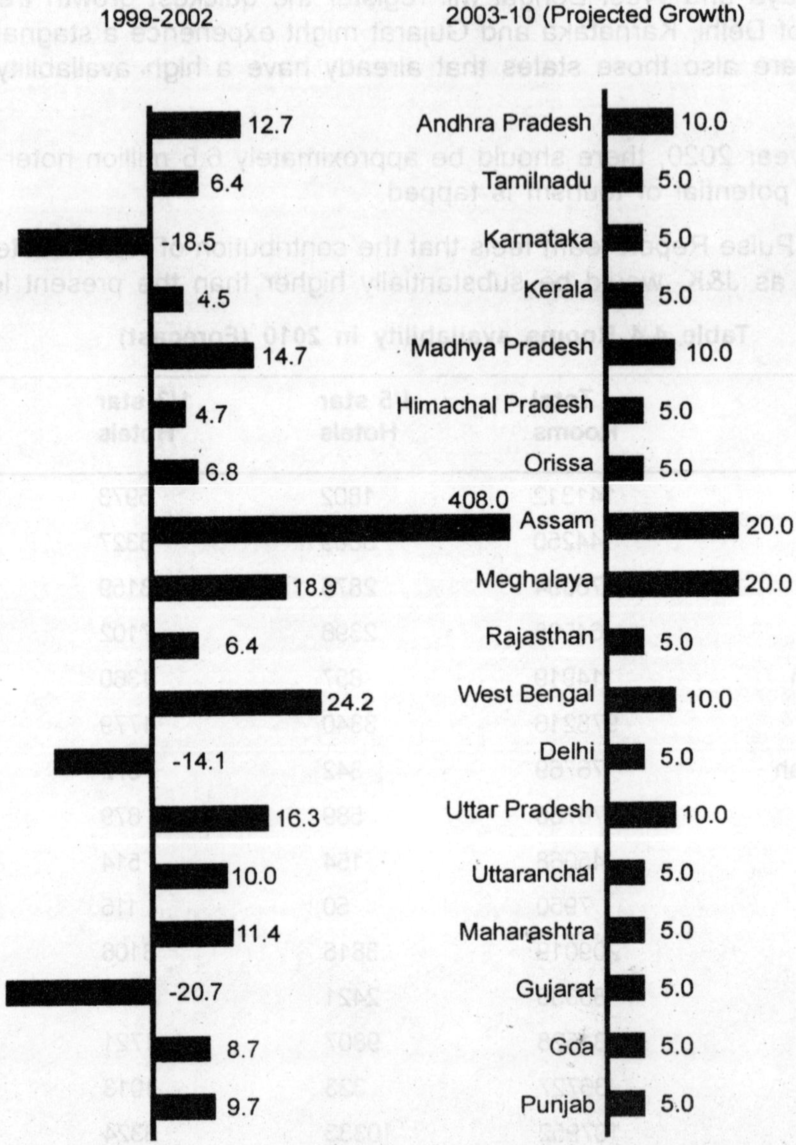

Fig. 4.1

Growth statistics pertaining to tourist traffic are based on statistics of Ministry of Tourism. For the period 2003-10, In Market Pulse Report it has been assumed that growth in tourist traffic will follow more or less the same trend as in the past. Thus, some (north-eastern state are likely to experience very quick annual growth of approximately 20%, others like Delhi, U.P, Tamul Nadu and Karnataka, where growth has already slowed down, will experience a 5% growth annually. Still others like W.B., A.P and M.P are likely to grow at 10% annually, since they have displayed robust statistics in the recent past.

Table 4.5 Rooms Availability in 2020 (Forecast)

State	Total Rooms	4/5 star Hotels	1/3 star Hotels	Other
Andhra Pradesh	355296	1802	7133	346361
Tamilnadu	231577	5082	10970	215526
Karnataka	122797	4125	4649	114023
Kerala	104671	3561	11362	89748
Madhya Pradesh	295471	1245	1908	292319
Uttar Pradesh	2530177	4385	1829	2523963
Himachal Pradesh	124699	442	372	123885
Orissa	127836	839	1099	125898
Assam	275706	154	639	274913
Meghalaya	48369	50	115	48204
Rajasthan	337082	4395	3491	329196
West Bengal	210746	3201	1761	205784
Delhi	47036	12470	1989	32578
Uttarakhand	58984	323	1013	57648
Maharashtra	169744	13798	10494	145452
Gujarat	19087	757	3591	14739
Goa	35016	4555	2103	28358
Punjab	27526	1570	2215	23741
All India	**6554019**	**49469**	**57836**	**6446714**

HOTELS IN INDIA: ROOMS AVAILABILITY IN YEAR 2007

As per Ministry of Tourism, Government of India annual report (2006-07) below mentioned are number of hotels in various categories (Table 4.6).

Table 4.6 Hotels and Rooms availability in India 2007

Category	2007	
	Hotel	Rooms
Five-star Deluxe	97	21314
Five-star	82	9505
Four-star	114	7606
Three-star	427	19164

Category	2007	
	Hotel	Rooms
Two-star	181	5148
One-star	52	2682
Heritage	85	3445
3-Star Apartment Hotels	2	110
4-Star Apartment Hotels	1	44
5-Star Apartment Hotels	1	100
Silver Incredible India (Bed & Breakfast)	2	6
To be Classified	122	7657

Emerging Concepts in Indian Accommodation

Eco Certification: India is the first country to insert an amendment into its constitution allowing the state to protect and improve the environment for safeguarding public health, forests, wildlife through 42nd amendment. The directive principle of state policy (Article 47) requires not only a protectionist stance by a state but also compels the state to seek the improvement of polluted environments. The provision that it "shall not be enforceable by any court, but it shall be the duty of the state to apply these principals in making laws" allows the directive to be an instrument of guidance for the government. The Environmental Management Certification (EMS) is also done in India through Bureau of Indian Standards (BIS). It has adapted ISO 14000 series as national standards for Environment Management System Certification. **Ecotel** concept of being eco friendly was practically non – existent in Indian Hospitality Sector earlier, but now, the Industry people are beginning to realize the benefits of incorporating green practices in their over all scenario. Orchid is the first hotel in India and in the entire continent of Asia to be labeled as eco friendly – Ecotel. **FHRAI** – has published a comprehensive environment manual for hotel and restaurant industry in India. The over all objective of this manual is to make the Indian hospitality industry more competitive and profitable through cost saving and customer satisfaction but also to reduce the adverse impacts on the environment. **Green Palm Certification** - Kerala Tourism Department has introduced an eco–certification scheme as a part of its efforts to promote eco friendly Kerala. Its scheme for **Houseboats** is green palm certification. Under it, houseboats should provide scientifically designed septic tanks and bio chemical tanks to discharge solid waste & sewage. Energy sources like solar power should be used for alternative lighting. A system for separating recyclable garbage from non-recyclable ones must also be employed. **Hospitality Giants entering Budget Segment** - is also a significant change in accommodation sector in India. Starting with IndiOne from Bangalore & then rebranding it and presenting in all together new form as ***Ginger*** Hotels by TATA's is a going to create a history in the growth and development of budget hotels with fantastic facilities or we can say "*smart basics*" – as promoted by Ginger Hotels in India. Introduction and promotion of ***Bed & Breakfast*** plan by ministry of Tourism Govt. of India may take some time to gain momentum in Indian accommodation sector but is expected to provide direct benefits to host population. More details on emerging trends have been further discussed in Chapter 13 to 15 of this book.

ACTIVITY

a) Prepare a list of hotels in your city and categories them under different heading.

b) Compare the tariff of these hotels.

c) Compare the accommodation facilities provided by them.

QUESTIONS

1. What are the basis on which hotel can be classified?
2. Discuss some of the accommodation facilities provided by the Government.
3. How will you classify hotel on the basis of locality?
4. Discuss some of the major type of rooms available in a hotel.
5. What is the difference between chain and individual hotel? Discuss the advantage and disadvantages.
6. Write a note on current scenario in Hospitality Accommodation in India.
7. What are the emerging concepts in Indian Accommodation?

ANNEXURE 1

GOVERNMENT OF INDIA

MINISTRY OF TOURISM

Department of Tourism

HOTEL AND RESTAURANT APPROVAL AND CLASSIFICATION COMMITTEE (HRACC)

QUESTIONNAIRE FOR STAR CATEGORY HOTELS

Name of the Hotel...

Questionnaire to be answered by hotels applying for 5-star category.

PART- 1

Name and address of the hotel:

In order to be assessed for 5-star category, a hotel should have the following basic features and the absences of any one of these will disqualified it from consideration for the 5-star category.

1. The hotel should have at least 25 lettable bedrooms.

   Please state the number of the guest rooms:

   a) Single

   b) Double

   c) Suite

   Total: ____________________

Note: Please furnish a list showing carpet area of each bedroom and area of bath room

2. The locality including the immediate approach and environs should be suitable for a hotel of this category

Please indicate:

(a) Distance from airport

(b) Distance from railway station

(c) Distance from main shopping areas

(d) Please describe briefly the neighborhood in which your hotel is located.

3. All public rooms and private rooms should be well appointed and fully air-conditioned (expect in hill station where there should be heating arrangements).

Please indicate

a) Are all your public and private rooms air-conditioned?

b) Is your hotel centrally air-conditioned? If so, please give the tonnage and also the total floor area/cubic space.

4. All rooms must have well appointed attached bathroom with long baths or should be equipped with most modern shower chamber. (In the case of cabana room, adequate shower facility will be acceptable).

a) Do all your room have attached bathroom? if so, how many have long baths?

b) How many fitted with most modern shower chamber?

5. The kitchen, pantry and cold storage should be professionally designed to ensure efficiency of operation and should be well equipped. Please state who designed your kitchen, pantry and cold storage and when?

6. There should be ladies and gentleman's cloakroom and the cloakrooms should be spotlessly clean and equipped with furniture and fittings of the highest standard available befitting a luxury hotel of this category.

7. Do you have ladies' and gentlemen's cloakrooms attached to the public area? If so, how many?

PART II

Maximum marks marks awarded by the committee

1. Construction

10N

The construction features and general construction of the building should have the distinctive qualities of a luxury hotel of this category.

2. Maintenance

20N

Maintenance of all section of the hotel (i.e. building, wall, gardens, surroundings, etc.) should be highest standard.

3. Parking

5D

There should be adequate parking space for car. Please state:

a) How many cars can be parked in the parking space owned be your hotel?

b) How many extra cars can locally parked in the capacity of your hotel?

c) How many cars can be parked by the guest/ visitors of the hotel when such space is most required?

4. Swimming pool

10N

There should be well designed and properly equipped swimming pool (except in hill station).

a) Does your swimming pool have its own system for filtration, chlorination and changing of water?

b) How often is the water changed?

c) What arrangements does your hotel have for heating the pool in the winter?

5. Bathroom

30E

All bathrooms should be modern in design and should be equipped with fitting of the highest quality available befitting a luxury hotel of this category, with 24 hr. service of hot and cold running water. The floor and wall should be covered with impervious material of elegant design and high quality workmanship. it is desirable that sockets for electric shaver should be provided.

a) Do the bathrooms have sockets for electric shavers?

b) Do the bathrooms have running hot and cold water for 24 hr.?

6. Reception

15N

There should be a reception, cash and information counter, attended by highly qualified, trained and experienced personnel.

Please state in details the qualification, training and experience of the personnel employed at reception, case, and information counter. (Separate sheet provided at the end of the questionnaire may be used for answering this question.)

7. Lobby

10N

There should be a well appointed lobby

Please state area of the lobby

8. Conference facilities

10N

There should be one each or more of conference rooms/banquet halls and private dinning rooms.

Please give the no. of conference rooms/ banquet halls and private dinning rooms with area of each.

9. Shopping facilities

20N

There should be bookstall, left luggage rooms, barber shop, recognized travel agency, beauty parlour, money changing and safe deposit facilities.

Notes:

1. There should be a florist in a hotel of 100 rooms and above.
2. A store selling toilet requisites and medicine should be available in the premise.

a) Is there a bookstall in your hotel?

Yes/No

b) Is there a left luggage room in your hotel?

Yes/No

c) Is there a barber shop in your hotel?

Yes/No

d) Is there a recognized travel agency in your hotel?

Yes/No

e) Is there a beauty parlour in your hotel?

Yes/No

f) Are there money changing facilities in your hotel?

Yes/No

g) Do you have safe deposit facilities for guest?

Yes/No

h) Is there a flowerist in your hotel?

Yes/No

i) Is there a store selling toilet requisites and medicines in your hotel?

Yes/No

10. Lifts

10N

There should be an adequate number of efficient lifts in buildings or more than 2 stores including the ground floor, with 24hr service.

a) How many floors are there in the building?

b) How many lifts are there in the building?

c) Please state their speed and capacity.

d) Are these available 24 hours?

11. Furnishing of bedrooms

25E

All guest-rooms should be comfortable and spacious and well furnished with good quality properly hung curtain, carpets etc. in good taste.

Note: New hotels are advised to employ the services of professionally qualified and experienced interior designers of repute in the designing and decoration of bedrooms.

12. Lighting

10N

Lighting arrangements and fixtures in the rooms/bath-rooms/public rooms/

corridors etc. should be so designed as to ensure aesthetic as well as functional excellence.

13. Telephone

10N

There should be a telephone in each room and telephone for the use of guest and visitors.

a) Is there a telephone in each room?

b) Is there a telephone?

c) How many telephone lines does your hotel have on the switchboard?

d) What is the maximum number of operators on duty and for how many hours?

(e) Separately for the use of guests and visitors?

Please use separate sheet provided at the end of the questionnaire for giving the educational background and training of the telephone operators, also starting there pay scale with allowances.

14. Radios

5D

There should provision for radios or relayed music in each room.

a) Is there a radio in each room?

b) Is there relayed music? if so, how many channels?

15. Vacuum jugs/ flask

5N

There should be a vacuum jug or thermos flask with ice cold/boiled drinking water in each bedroom except where centrally chilled purified water is provided.

16. Dining room/ restaurant

15E

There should be well equipped, well furnished and well maintained dinning room/ restaurant.

a) How many restaurants are there in the hotel?

b) Please give sitting capacity of each.

17. Carpeting

15D

All public and private rooms should have superior quality carpets/rags, which should be well kept at all times. if the floors are not completely covered, quality of the following will be assessed.

a) Are all public and private rooms carpeted?

b) Please state the areas which are not carpeted

18. linen/blanket/towels etc.

10N

There should be a plentiful supply of all linen/blanket/towels etc. which should be of the highest quality available and should be spotlessly clean. Bed linen and towels should be changed everyday.

19. Crockery

10E

Crockery, cutlery and glassware should be of the best quality available.

Note: no piece of crockery in use should be chipped, cracked or crazed. the silverware should be kept well-plated and polished at all times.

20. Bar

10N

Wherever admissible by law, there should be elegant, well equipped bar/ permit room with an atmosphere of comfort and luxury.

21. Entertainment

10D

There should be a special restaurant/dinning room where facility for dancing and provision of an orchestra are available. Hotels of this category should provide evidence that they have made a serious attempt to present specially choreographed Indian entertainment.

22. Cuisine

30N

The hotel should offer both international and Indian cuisine. (The preparation, proper seasoning of dishes and presentation to customer will be assessed).

What are the various types of cuisine offered by your hotel?

23. Food and beverage service

a) Restaurant service

25N

While assessing this item, the organisation of the dinning room/restaurant, the waiter knowledge of the menu whether in French or English, the correct laying of tables, the variety and appearance or buffet service and the method used to keep hot dishes at the right temperature will be assessed.

b) Room service

20N

The method used to ensure speedy and hot meals will be assessed.

c) Beverage service

15N

The provision and service of alcoholic and non-alcoholic beverages including methods used to service hot and cold beverage at the correct tem will be assessed.

24. Hygiene

20E

The kitchen, pantry and cold storage should be clean and organised for orderliness and efficiency, scientific and hygienic methods should be used in working and for the washing of glass, crockery, cutlery, etc.

a) Is there a dish washing machine in your hotel? if so, what's its capacity?

b) What steps are taken to keep the place safe from all types of pests?

25. Other services

10E

a) 24 hr. services should be provided for reception information and telephones.

b) There should be provision for reliable laundry and dry clean services

c) Does your hotel have its own laundry and dry clean?

d) Does the hotel accept responsibilities of the damage done in washing, dry cleaning or pressing?

26. Staff

There should be professionally qualified, highly trained, experienced, efficient and courteous staff. The overall component of trained staff will be assessed and marks given accordingly with deduction in marks if the supervision is done by untrained staff.

a) Manager

10N

b) Executive staff

10N

c) Other staff

20N

d) The staff should be in smart and clean uniforms.

10N

e) The staff coming into contact with guest should understand English and supervisory and senior staff posses' good knowledge of English. at least one member of the senior staff knowing at least one continental language should be on duty at all times.

Note: in future classification, knowledge of foreign language by some of the staff will be essential.

Please use separate sheet provided at the end of the questionnaire for giving bio-data of directors directly concerned with the operation of the hotel, general manager, department manager, executive and supervisory staff include name, age, professional qualification, on the co training and its duration and experience giving in detail the positions held and the duration of each and telephones.

27. Housekeeping

10N

Housekeeping should be of the nicest possible standard.

28. Fire

I hereby solemnly declare that the information given above is correct to the best of my knowledge and belief. in the event of any of my statement found to be untrue, I fully understanding that my application for approval/ classification is liable to be rejected.

Signature of the proprietor/
Managing Director
General Manager

5

FOOD SERVICE INDUSTRY

— YASHPAL SINGH NEGI[1]

The Indian hospitality industry's rapid growth is being derailed owing to high attrition and fickle loyalty of its most important resource The food service industry is surrounded by place like institution and companies which serve wide range of food to be eaten away from home .The industry includes food chain restaurants, schools, Hospitals, institutions, factory, cafeterias, catering operation, and many more foodies sector. In India the food service industry have started a specified beginning. The food service version is packaged in larger industry size but often lack of the colorful level design. The consumer version usually in individual size in packages with elaborated level designs for retail.

OBJECTIVES

After reading this chapter a reader should be able to:

- Understand the concept of F&B service department in a hotel.
- Know the term "Restaurant" and it's origin.
- Know the various types of restaurant.
- Know the major players in Fast – Food sectors.
- Get a know-now different catering services.

HOTEL FOOD SERVICE

The hotel food and beverage department offer food related guest service at arranged and neatly areas. Kitchen facility play a major part in determining when and how catering service demands can be met with the help of kitchen and service and well equipped with their job knowledge in relation of cooking, load and handling capacity of kitchen equipment if a kitchen is to be used to its full capacity during busy times. Storage and refrigeration facilities determine the amount of food product available at any given time. The cost of waste from food spoilage due to lack of refrigeration and freezer space could dilute the profit from additional catering business.

---

1. Lecturer in Hotel Management at HNB Garhwal University, Srinagar, Garhwal.

Currently the food service industry reeling under a manpower crunch and heightened attrition rates, which threatens to ruin its swelling fortunes. Education and training, since the inception of the hospitality industry in India, has played a secondary role, to its growth. It demands exceptional performance from employees, while promising great rewards, career opportunities and job enrichment. The skill sets required by an employee have evolved over the years, transforming their linear roles to multi-functional operations.

As per the statistics available through FHRAI 18,000 students are being trained in hotel management and food craft annually in the country. Currently, in hotels, attrition rates are at 18-25 per cent per annum, and growing at an alarming rate of 10 percent per annum. This, exacerbated by an escalating wage bill of 10-12 per annum with a five-year forecast pegged at a minimum increase of 40 per cent over current levels.

Food item for these food service areas are provided from main kitchen with the exception of large hotel attached kitchen (satellite or main kitchen) provide with extra help and support. An outlet chef supervises all the food production for there assigned food service areas where the executive chef supervises to all food production outlet chef, consulting with the manager of each food service area in addition to providing much needed cash flow during period when room sales are slow. Hotel catering services are usually classified as:

- ❖ Business
- ❖ Conference/ Convivial
- ❖ Social
- ❖ Corporate

The hotel catering service volume is available on the size and number of facilities, which can be used for banquet functions as well as availability of food production and service staff. There are three major factor based for hotel catering market

- ❖ Location
- ❖ Guest profile
- ❖ Facilities

Location

The location of hotel determinates the demands for in house catering service.In house catering service is defined as guest related food service formal social even involved with business meeting, conferences, conventions and social concerns. A hotel with remote location focuses its food catering efforts to the business looked for the hotel, resort, location often provide additional opportunities for catering services at sports facilities and landscape venues, throughout the property.

Guest Profile

The guest profile for hotel catering service is made up of both business and social clientele. Guest who uses the hotel as a location for a two or three days meeting consider meal, functions as part of the total meeting package. This arrangement not only enable guest to work within a budget that covers the entire project, but also manage with an approach to planned catering function that considers the success.

The entire function along with theme function and special event with menu planning is the responsibility of catering manager with the help of Executive-chef. The guests who plan business function on a regular basis are familiar with the services of the hotel. Their need should identify and provided. Guest who plan social event on a one time basis, however, need more personal guidance at the planning stage. Primary concern of this group is pricing.

Often a hotel will have the facilities in place to offer a limited menu of take-out items. Items have been selected from the hotel during room menu to offer to general public on a take away basis. Hotels have the advantages over many private catering companies of being able to use there own equipments. In addition food production and storage facilities are available to handle large volumes food and beverage as well as equipment. If the volume of on property business requires the use of hotel equipment, rentals can covers the additional need, with cost being charged according to the chef driven catering services with high quality services and personalized touch. Ability to consistently anticipate, meet and exceed guest expectations.

Facilities

A large volume of outside catering business is expected from a hotel with suburban or downtown location. Both are business- related and social in addition to conference and convivial. The amount of combined catering business that can be handled at any one time in hotel is based primarily on the number and size of the facilities available. The major function rooms are usually referred to as the ballrooms areas. These are complemented by a series of meeting rooms, some adjunct to the main ballroom area and some located on other areas of the hotel.

Outlets for food and beverage service can include the following:

- ❖ Specialty restaurant (lunch and dinner)
- ❖ Coffee shop (round the clock)
- ❖ Banquets (parties, conferences)
- ❖ Room service (round the clock)
- ❖ Bars (selected hour's service with snack)
- ❖ Recreational areas (24hours)

- Delicatessen (a shop selling cooked meat, cheese and other unusual eatable products or foreign prepared food)

RESTAURANTS

The restaurant is a place where guest pays to sit and eat meals that are cooked on the premises or serves prepared food and beverage to be consumed on the premises. The term covers a multifarious of venues and diversifying style of cuisine. Restaurants are sometimes distinct feature of larger complex. It is typically a place in hotel where the dinning amenities are provided for the convenience of the residents and, affini, for the hotel to maximize there potential revenue. Such restaurant should frequently open to non-residents.

ORIGIN OF RESTAURANT

An act of appearing restaurant ment in the 16th century. when a Parsi soup seller opened an establishment. The restaurant became established in France after the French revolution when they broke up catering medieval association of craftsmen and forced the aristocracy to field. Restaurant spread rapidly to the U.S in 17th century and continue on the standard approach at providing meal on the table to which would then help them selves. The modern formal style of dinning took place in 18th century where the guest are given plate with the food already placed on it is known as "Russian Service."

Till Second World War the restaurant wine not very popular in India. Only few luxury hotels existed in India such Great Eastern in Kolkata, Taj Mahal in Mumbai and Imperial in Delhi. The independent Specialty restaurant started in 1960.

Different types of restaurant

Broadly we can categorize restaurant into the following categories:

- Full service restaurant
- Bistro, Brasserie, Pub
- Fast food restaurant
- Dinning car restaurant
- Cafeteria

Full service restaurant

A variety of catering service offered in full service restaurant before any decision is made. Following important factors are normally considered before opening full service restaurant

- Location
- Concept

- ❖ Staff performance
- ❖ Cuisine and Menu

Location

Restaurant situated in rural areas with low population density can not expect immediate high volume of catering business. Areas of high density population yield a variety of catering opportunities that steadily increases in volume through referrals and reputation. The location of the physical restaurant building place a role in the type catering services to be offered. Storage facilities, expansion possibilities, and access to major transportation routes are factors important to catering service production.

Concept

The style, concept of the restaurant should be taken into consideration when planning potential catering service. All premise carting services do not necessarily have to blend with the facilities offered by the restaurant. The premises catering services should however be designed to function within the restaurant facilities.

Cuisine and menu

The primary cuisine and menu offering in a restaurant constitute one of the most important considerations for on-premise catering. Off premises catering service do not necessarily need to be the same as those offered at the restaurant for full service dinning. Purchasing and production requirements are crucial to the successful development of catering services. On premise, catering should offer menu items that duplicate the establishment menu as closely as possible in order to enhance production capabilities. Surrounding items, such as vegetables and starches are the most effective area of the menu to duplicate. Kitchen production is more efficient when the number of surrounding menu is limited. Effective purchasing for catering function requires that the ingredient for menu items be the same or similar or those on the restaurant menu.

Bistro, Brasserie, Pub

In France, brasserie is a cafe doubling as a restaurant and saving single dishes and other meals in relaxed setting. A bistro is a familiar name for a cafe serving moderately priced simple meals in an unpretentious setting. In Paris bistro have become increasingly popular among tourists. In the UK and other countries influenced by British culture, the Pub today serve a similar dual menu offering beer and other alcohol along with basic food fare. Traditionally pubs were primarily drinking places, whereas the modern pub business relies on food as well to the point where so-called gastro pubs are known for their high quality "Pub Food."

Fast Food restaurant

A fast food restaurant is a restaurant characterized both by food which supplied quickly after ordering and by minimal service. Many fast food restaurant are part of restaurant chains or franchise operation, which ship standardized food stuff to each restaurant from central location. Although fast food restaurant are often seem as a mark of modern technological cultural, they are probably as old as cities themselves with there style varying from cultural to cultural.

The American company white castle is generally credited with opening the first fast food outlet in 1921. Sellers Hambrogon. MC Donald's,are the largest fast food chains in the world and their brands are associated with term "fast food". The hot dog in San Drgo and milkshake mixer originally produced by McDonald's in the 1954. Fast food outlets introduced "drive- thru" service which allow guest to order and pick up food from their cars; but most also have as eating area in which guest can eat the food on the premises.

Most standalone McDonald's restaurants offer both counter service and drive-through service with indoor and sometimes outdoor seating. Drive-Thru, Auto-Mac, Pay and Drive, or McDrive, as it is known in many countries, often have separate stations for placing, paying for, and picking up orders, though the latter two steps are frequently combined. In some countries "McDrive" locations near highways offer no counter service or seating. In contrast, locations in high-density city neighborhoods often omit drive-through service. There are also a few locations, located mostly in downtown districts that offer Walk-Thru service in place of Drive-Thru. Especially themed restaurants also exist, such as the "Solid Gold McDonald's," a 1950s rock-and-roll themed restaurant. In Victoria, British Columbia, there is also a McDonald's with a 24 carat (100%) gold chandelier and similar light fixtures. To accommodate the current trend for high quality coffee and the popularity coffee shops in general, McDonald's introduced Mc Cafés. The Mc Café concept is a café-style accompaniment to McDonald's restaurants. Mc Café is a concept of McDonald's Australia, starting with Melbourne in 1993. Today, most McDonald's in Australia have Mc Cafés located within the existing McDonald's restaurant. In Tasmania there are Mc Cafés in every store. As of the end of 2003 there were over 600 Mc Cafés worldwide. Some locations are connected to BP gas stations/convenience stores, while others called McDonalds Express have limited seating and or may be located in a shopping mall. Other McDonalds are located in Wall-mart stores. Mc Stop is a location targeted at truckers and travelers which may have services found at truck stops.

Children's areas

Some McDonald's in suburban areas and certain cities feature large indoor or outdoor playgrounds, called "McDonald's Play Place" (if indoors) or "Play land" (outdoors). The first Play Place with the familiar crawl-tube design with ball pits and slides, with many more being constructed soon after. Some Play Place playgrounds have been renovated into "R Gym" areas. "R Gyms" are in-restaurant play area that features interactive game zones designed for children aged 4 to 12. Equipped with stationary bicycles attached to video games, dance pads, basketball hoops, monkey bars, an obstacle course, and other games which emphasize physical activity.

T.G.I.S

The Friday's restaurant chain was founded in 1965 in New York City, featuring standard American cuisine, bar food, and alcoholic beverages. The exterior featured a red-and-white striped awning, and blue paint, and the interior included wooden floors, Bentwood chairs, and striped tablecloth. The bar area added brass rails, and stained glass. The employees were young and wore wacky uniforms, and every time someone had a birthday, the entire restaurant crew came around with a cake and sang Friday's traditional birthday song. Friday's has also been used as a restaurant for hotels run by the Holiday Inn brand. Friday's has a large menu with an emphasis on alcoholic beverages. "Ultimate" drinks are served in an 18 oz. glass, and often made with top shelf and darker liquors. A section of the menu is dedicated to the "Jack Daniel's Grill", a selection of items flavored with a special Jack Daniel's sauce. Fridays formerly served Atkins approved appetizers, entrées, and desserts. Since 2006, the menu has discontinued the Atkins name and several platters were redubbed "Low Crab". The company licenses its name to Heinz for snack items and frozen foods sold in grocery stores.

PIZZA CORNER

Pizza Corner is a chain of pizzerias founded in 1996 by entrepreneur Fred Mouawad of Global Franchise Architects. Pizza Corner currently operates in Bangladesh, India and Thailand.

As its name suggests, Pizza Corner primarily focuses on Pizzas. They also serve numerous side dishes such as Garlic Bread and Chicken Nuggets. Starters like pasta and salad are becoming increasingly popular. Pizza Corner recently introduced pizza in a cone in India under the brand Conizza.

Cone-shaped pizza is a new concept which is rapidly taking up worldwide following the eating and lifestyle habits of people on the go. There are several companies delivering to the market pizza in a cone, Crispy Cones, Kono Pizza and Kornet Pizza in Europe, USA, Middle East and Australia.

WIMPY

Wimpy is the brand name of a chain of hamburger restaurants based in the United Kingdom. The restaurants were originally called Wimpy Bars and many people still refer to them by this name, despite the fact that the name "Wimpy Bar" was dropped in favour of "Wimpy" many years ago. The current owners of the Wimpy brand operate in several countries under the name of Wimpy International.

The Wimpy brand was created by Eddie Gold of Chicago in the 1930s. The name was inspired by the character of J. Wellington Wimpy from the Popeye cartoons created by Elzie Crisler Segar. Eddie Gold was running 12 restaurants by the early 1950s, when the concept of fast food came to the attention of the directors of J. Lyons.Co. Lyons licensed the brand for use in the United Kingdom and in 1954 the first "Wimpy Bar" Lyons was established at the Lyons Corner House in Coventry Street, London. Originally the bar was a special fast-food section within the more traditional Corner House restaurants, but the success soon led to the establishment of separate Wimpy restaurants serving only hamburger based meals. By the early 1970s the business had expanded to over a thousand restaurants in 23 countries.

In 1977 the business was acquired by United Biscuits. Wimpy was beginning to lose ground to McDonalds, who had opened their first UK restaurant in 1974 and so the new management of Wimpy began to streamline the business by converting some of the traditional "table service" restaurants to the "counter service" operation style of McDonalds. In 1989 the business was sold to Grand Metropolitan (now Diageo). Grand Metropolitan had acquired Burger King the previous year and they began to convert the "counter service" restaurants to Burger King restaurants. In 1990 the remaining 220 "table service" restaurants were purchased by a management buy-out backed by 3i. A second management buy-out occurred in 2002. Although Wimpy has decreased in numbers in the United Kingdom, it is still found in some towns and cities and at the Road Chef motorway services and at Mega bowl bowling alleys. However the branches at Road Chefs and Mega bowl have a counter service as opposed to a table service format.

DINNING CAR RESTAURANT

A dinning car or dinner is a rail road passenger car that serves meals or on a train in the manner of a full service sits down restaurant. It is distinct from other type of railroad food service car that do not duplicate the full service sit-down restaurant one or Dinning cars have always been priced for the way in which they exchange the familiar restaurant experiences by offering a union form of visual entertainment, namely the ever-changing views of the world outside.

CAFETERIA

A cafeteria is a type of service location in which there is no table service whether a restaurant or within an institution such as a large office building or school. A location of school dinning is also referred to as canteen. food serving counter/ stall either in line or allowing as bestiary walking path, and customer take food they requires as they walk along, placing them on tray and pay at the check out system. Due to the consumption of people, this system is rarely or never used for alcoholic beverages. As cafeterias require few employees, they are often found within a larger institution, catering to the clientele of that institution. e.g. school, colleges, department stores, museums and office building often have cafeterias.

Catering services

Independent caters and companies with a catering business on the side are two different groups provide food service at a remote side. Design and planning requirements vary from project to project, whether catering for 50 or 5000 it can be tailored services to the individual needs.

An event caterer serves food with wait staff at dining tables or sets up a self serve buffet. The food may be prepared in attached kitchen, often some combination depending on the menu and facilities. The event caterer staff is responsible not only for preparing the food but also setting up the dining area and waiting tables. This service is typically provided at banquets, conventions and weddings. Any event where all the attainders are provide with food and drinks or some time only hors d'oeuvres is often called a catered event. A catering company or specialist is expected to know not just food preparation, but how to make it attractive a weeding function requires working with entire theme or colour scheme of the wedding. Much catering is sold on a per person basis. Keeping the cost of the food and supplies below this is required to make a profit on the catering.

Contract feeding companies provide institutions such as hospital and schools, as well as business, with in house meal menu designed to meet specific needs. Food production and service is contracted for long term periods with designated budget restrictions. The growth of contract feeding segment started from 1980. Marriott international created large contracted feeding companies to service a wide range of customers. By rising a professional contract food service operator to handle this area of operation, businesses find the qualities of services increases significantly along with client and employee satisfaction. The major factors that can influence the success of catering services within a contract feeding location are:

- Catering facilities
- Customer belongings
- Off premise catering location
- Out side contractors

Independent caterers are private business offering entering service to the general public. Those caters who operate without permanent facilities of their own in which to hold functions and who operate without a formal facility must arrange for kitchen production and storage space. Their focus is on both business and social functions within a wide geographical area. In order to successfully cater to as many functions as possible simultaneously, a catering company has to be extremely well organized.

Mobile catering

Mobile catering is the business of selling prepared food from some sort of vehicle used therein. It is features of urban culture which include street car (by automobile bicycle or hand); food and beverage often served from canteens include, hot dogs and sausages, ice-cream and frozen treats, and coffee. Where the catering truck enable a vendor to sell a large volume than a cart and to reach a larger market. The mobile kitchen. "is a modified van with a built in grill, deep fryer or other cooking equipment" It offers- more flexibility in the menu since the vendor can prepare food to order.

Industrial catering

Industrial catering includes providing food for airline passenger, school prisons, factories and other institutional settings. It can include contract management of client food service facilities. Airlines often have division or hire third parties to provide food for passengers

Hospital catering

The Hospital Services has been developed to particularly meet the requirements of Multi Specialty Hospitals, Nursing hostels where quality service of highest standards is the paramount objective. Some of the high-tech Hospitals at Delhi, Kolkata, Mumbai, Ahmedabad and Chennai are already availing these services, which have elicited their approbation. Selected Health Care Management Services are there to improve quality standards, increase patient satisfaction and reduce costs.

Cafeteria

It Produces quality food by implementing standardized recipe and working procedure based on the specified menu at the appropriate timing in the appropriate manner as prescribed. It provides adequate quantity of food at the stipulated time schedule prescribed, voiding shortage and eliminating wastage on a daily basis. The cafeteria staff is there to prepare food and services as per the menu and time specified ensuring quality, reducing wastage, spillage and spoilage. It is necessary to employ staff for the cleaning of the kitchen equipments, food production area and the food service area. It is also necessary to provide them required uniform and make provision for the washing and maintenance of the same.

Private club

Private clubs offer in self contained facility that operates both full service dining rooms and private functions area with a variety of food and beverage outlets. Functioning as non profit organizations, clubs are in many places, prohibited by law from accepting or soliciting business from non members. Clubs are broken down into two general classifications private clubs and country clubs. Private clubs are generally situated in the downtown area of large towns and cities. The club facility is used primarily as a location for meeting, private dining, social and business functions.

Charcuteries and delicatessens

Charcuteries are food stores that offer take out food service along with gourmet food products. Many of these products are used as ingredients in the preparation of the food line. In some case a small seating area will be offered for eat-in customers. The trend for home-replacement food is significant to these types of operation. When customer wants something beyond fast food for a take- home meal, they turn to establishment that can provide meals that they would like to have prepared for themselves.

Delicatessens are food stores that provide a variety of food products and offer both eat-in and take -out food service. The location should be reasonable close to the targeted customer base. Menu item offering range from sandwiches, salads, and pizza to prepared meals—to-go. Take-out foodservice of prepared foods is a major business segment for these types of foodservice operation.

Delivery of in-office and at-home prepared food items can be a profitable extension of delicatessen's business. Delicatessens often provide off- premise food items on a daily basis to a wide range of customers. A delicatessen (also deli) is a type of store. A delicatessen is 'something between a fast-food restaurant and a grocery store. It offers a much wider and fresher menu than chain fast food restaurants, rarely employing fry machines and typically making sandwiches to order. A grocery store or supermarket may make its own deli food, or even have a deli on site. Like a market, a delicatessen may also offer a selection of shelved food, often of the type that is not likely to be kept for more than a day. Produçe, when present, is limited in quantity and often fresh. Delicatessens vary greatly in size, but are typically not as large as grocery stores. In areas with high rents for retail space, delicatessens are often quite small. Delicatessens can come from a variety of cultural traditions. Most delicatessens have a sandwich menu, most of which are made to order behind the counter at the time of sale. Delicatessens often sell their meats by weight as cold cuts, and prepare party trays. In addition to made-to-order sandwiches, many delicatessens offer made-to-order green salads. Equally common is a selection of prepared pasta, potato, chicken, tuna, shrimp, or other variety of "wet" salads, displayed underneath the counter and bought by weight or on a sandwich. Precooked chicken, shrimp, or eggplant products, possibly fried are found frequently, though they do not constitute the mainstay of a delicatessen. In order to provide an opportunity for a complete meal, delicatessens also offer a wide variety of beverages, usually prepackaged soft drinks, coffee, teas, milk, etc. Chips and similar products are available in some variety, though they rarely rival the selection of small package cookies and snack foods; some prepackaged, others store-made and cellophane wrapped. Alongside these primarily lunch and dinner products, a delicatessen might also offer a number of additional items geared toward the breakfast eater, including baked goods (breakfast pastries, bagels, toast), yogurt, and warm egg "breakfast sandwiches". Newspapers and small food items such as candy and mints are also usually available for purchase. Available staffs to achieve the required goals are specified.

CONCLUSION

Food Service Industry and Catering companies provide all assistance that help make special events special. They may provide simple refreshments for a film crew on a movie set or caviar and blini at a film star's party Or a buffet for a Christmas Day open-house in a private home. Or basic hors d'oeuvres at a reception for a retiring professor. Just about any sort of event you can imagine-sporting events, private parties, church functions, government events, press conferences, fashion shows and more are catered by catering companies. Some events are bare bones. Others are elaborate affairs. While many restaurants offer catering services as a sideline, many caterers are businesses completely independent from restaurants. Some caterers are small companies that mostly cater home parties and receptions. These independent businesses operate out of premises of their own equipped offices and storage space for supplies, and kitchens.

Catering involves a variety of jobs, most of them also found in the restaurant and hotel-banquet trade. Chefs and cooks prepare food and drink. Bus staff helps transport food, set up, and pick up afterwards. Kitchen stewarding staff serves Dishwashers deal with the mountains of dirty plates. Sales staff fined clients and customers. Catering companies also have staffs that aren't directly connected with cooking, serving, and cleaning up. Event designers work with customers and sales staff to plan and design events and act as liaison between customers and other catering staff. Housekeeping does Stylists select linens, table settings, flower arrangements and all the other embellishments that create a party atmosphere. Purchasing staff work with suppliers to buy goods the firm needs at the best possible price. Managers organize and manage all the others activities. In very small firms one person may do almost all of these jobs or the company may not offer all of these services. Some specialize in particular types of cuisine, like Chinese or Italian food. Still others specialize in particular kinds of events, from weddings and corporate functions.

Today, the industry is finding its feet, domestic chains re-brand and enter into each segment, only to find themselves bereft of staff in that category. To circumvent the impending dilemma of quality and quantity, the first visible change in the landscape is domestic hotel brands leaping into the hospitality education to ensure their own expansion plans don't set adrift amidst manpower shortages. Apart from that, for each employee, comprehensive training facilities are being put into place. Eventually, each organization hopes to create and retain managers for the future through internal progressions and develop their leadership skills, keeping in mind the brand, investing resources like capital, time and manpower into training. To integrate an individual into the work force and create a sense of belonging is paramount. training needs to be imparted to ensure that the agency meets the brand's set standards. To train, or not to train, there is no question.

ACTIVITY

1. Visit any tourist destination in your area and categorise accommodation properties therein.
2. Compare the cuisine and menu offering of all restaurants of your town.

QUESTIONS

1. What are the various factors to be considered before opening a full service restaurant?
2. What is the concept of "Fast-Food"? Explain about few global Fast-Food chains.
3. Write short notes on:

   a) Mobile catering.

   b) Hospital catering.

6

AN OVERVIEW OF ANCILLARY AND SUPPORT SERVICES IN HOSPITALITY INDUSTRY

— ABHINAV SHANDILYA[1]

Hotel is an organisation which includes major departments like food and beverage service, food production, front office and housekeeping. These four major departments are the one which are in touch with the customers and are busy in providing number of services to them. Yet all the services provided by major departments fulfil only the basic needs of a comfortable stay. To increase the level of services and achieve the guest satisfaction hotels provide some other services that helps in exceeding the expectation of guests. These "additional" or "extra" services are known as Ancillary services. The ancillary services include services of transportation, book shop, flowerist, chemist, airline office, beauty parlour, gymnasium, barber shop, entertainment room, etc. Also, the major departments can not run alone, they need co operation of each other and support of other departments which operate within the hotel like- security department, water supply department, personnel department, engineering and maintenance department, sales and marketing department, purchase department, accounts department, etc. These departments provide "encouragement" or "favour" or "back" up to the major departments in hotel or to the other key players in the hospitality sector and thus the services provided by them are known as Support services.

Support services are needed to run day-to-day activity of the hotel effectively and also to solve customers' problem. As guest room accounts related problem will be solved only by the accounts department, maintenance related problem will be solved by maintenance department etc. These complains, however, are not given to these department directly but by the House keeping or front office desk that receives the guest complains and passes on to the concerned department. This support service plays a major role in promoting the hotel image as if they are efficient then hotel earns a good brand name. Ancillary services on the other hand provide guest with an opportunity to avail those facility in the hotel premises for which otherwise they would have to go outside the hotel. This is an added value that attracts the guest to any particular hotel for a certain set of ancillary facilities. Guests always want their stay more and more comfortable then earlier and this can only be provided by adding some ancillary services to the core product of the hotel. It has been

1. Lecturer in Hotel Management at Birla Institute of Technology, Mesra Ranchi, Jharkhand.

noticed that provision of ancillary services and efficient support services has been always helpful in repeat business.

Every hotel provides the expected products i.e. a comfortable stay with food, transportation, some recreational facilities etc. But to take lead from the competitor in the market the hotel has to create augmented products and then further the potential products. Augmented product is the product that exceeds the customer expectation whereas potential product is the future product having all the possible augmentation and transformation. The designing of augmented and potential product for service is undertaken with the help of ancillary and support services and hence again the importance of both the services are of immense significance.

OBJECTIVES

After this unit you will be able to understand:

a) Importance of ancillary and support services.

b) Services included in ancillary services.

c) Services included in support services.

CONCEPTUAL MEANING

The ancillary and support services are not looked as one of the major department because support service is non-revenue producing department whereas ancillary services are non-operating revenue producing department. The ancillary services may be provided by the hotel directly or the hotel may give place to the service providers (like travel agency) for which they take an agreed amount as rent or a part of profit. Like ancillary service support services can also be a part of hotel operation or it may be given on contract to the contractors. In small organisation it is beneficial to give support services like maintenance on contract. On the other hand if a hotel comes under the category of a large hotel then it is advisable to have their own department which will look after these services.

Now let us understand the role of these services in the hotel. How they are managed and what is their functioning style. Let's take ancillary and support services one by one. Table 5.1 discloses the nature and sub-typology of ancillary services.

ANCILLARY SERVICES

Recreational Divison

Some of the hotels specially resorts have a special cell known as recreational division that facilitates individual or group games to the guests. It also includes other refreshing activities like gymnasium, live music, dance etc. this division is accountable for maintaining the sports ground, playing kit, indoor games room etc. and organizing the live refreshing activities. The specially organized activities under recreational decision are charged separately prior to its use by guests or as per the hotel policy.

Table 5.1: Ancillary Services

Serial No.	Type of service	Sub Type	Example
1.	Ancillary Services	Recreation division	Gymnasium Sports room Entertainment room, etc.
		Retail outlet division	Travel agency Handicraft shop Garment and jewellery Shop Beauty Saloon Chemist Book shop Flower shop, etc.

Gymnasium

Most of the modern hotels today have a gymnasium because majority of customers now-a-days is health conscious. They like to keep themselves fit and for this, they prefer the hotels which have the facility of gymnasium within their premises. Most hotels recruit a trainer who helps the customer in giving light exercise to them so that they do not go for wrong exercise. Some hotels charge for this facility, whereas some hotels allow their guest to use the Gym as a complimentary facility staying in a hotel. This facility also attracts non-resident guest who come to hotel just to avail this facility. Hotels normally extend membership facility to these non-resident guests if the policy of hotel permits.

Sports Room

Hotels do provide a sport room for recreation of the guest. When the guests have a long stay in the hotel, they do look for some sport facilities and this is provided by sports room. Sports room has various indoor games like table tennis, pool, carom, chess, squash, bowling alley and badminton etc. A trainer is accountable for the maintenance of the sport rooms with a brigade. The trainer is also the supervisor for the sport room. Generally there is a cash counter from where the tokens for different games can be taken. The guest takes token from the cash counter and gives it to the sports boys at different games, then avails the facility. This sports room has the timing and the guests are supposed to follow the timings. Some property provides this facility complimentary with the special packages offered by them to the in house guests. In resorts even the out door facilities like lawn tennis, golf etc. is also there. The person in charge of the out door games may be the same person who is in charge of sports room.

Entertainment Room

Entertainment room is a comparatively newer concept in the hotel industry. The hotel provides a separate entertainment room within the premises of the hotel which includes Video games and some puzzle games for kids. Facility of mini theatre is also there in many of the hotels. The mini theatres may be used to show the movie on demand; cricket, football hockey matches etc. The entertainment room is also used to organize live music, dance etc. for the in house guests. The entertainment room supervisor is accountable for the maintenance of the entertainment room and for organizing the live shows. The cleaning and up keep of the same is under the housekeeping department. Entertainment rooms have the facility of some light refreshments.

Retail Outlet Division

The hotels provide some space in the public or lobby area for retail outlets. The space for retail outlet is known as shopping arcade. These retail outlets include barber shop, travel agency, book shop, chemist, flower shop, handicraft shops, garment shop etc. The retail outlet are generally operated by the contractor and for this hotel gets a fixed space rental fee or a part on percentage of sale.

Travel Agency

The hotel provides a travel desk for travel agency that helps the in house guest in planning their tour and travel. The travel agency does the work of ticketing, cancellation and re-reservation for the guests. The agencies also provides the transport facility for the local movement. A new concept of "rent a car" is also being introduced by many travel agencies in India. In this the car is provided to the guest for his/her movement along with or without a chauffer. The guest can take car at one point of the city or the state and can returns it back to any other point of the city or the state. On request travel agencies do the facilitation services which includes visa, passport, insurance, immigration permits etc. The travel agents receive commission from the hotel for bringing the guests to the hotel. It is headed by the desk control supervisor. All the staff is from the travel agency and the hotel has nothing to do with the travel desk if the activities are running smoothly. The hotel administration only interferes when there is some complain regarding the services provided by the travel agencies.

Handicraft Shop

Handicraft shops find its place in the shopping arcade because it shows the speciality of the place. The tourists coming to any destination is always looking for some speciality of the destination that can be taken back to their home town and so there is always a big demand of handicraft items. These shops are the prime attraction to the tourists coming from the foreign countries as it is something which attract them. When they try to purchase the handicraft from the local people outside hotel the chances that price quoted to them will be much more is always there. This fear is not there when they purchase it from within the hotel premises as these are fixed price shop. These shops generally sale the item made by local people without use of modern machines. The handicraft shops are put in the hotel premises by the local contractor or by the state handicraft corporation.

Garment and Jewellery Shops

The garment and jewellery shops within the hotel are another facility which is provided to the guest as a part of ancillary services. This facility helps the guest to do the purchasing without stepping out from the hotel. Since these shops provide branded garments and jewellery, it provides a standard outlet for the guest to purchase from. The guest feel comfortable while purchasing from these shops as there is minimal bargaining, the environment is safe and the guest feel as if he is purchasing sitting in his own room.

Beauty Saloon

Currently beauty saloon is the most demanding and not only women but men are also sparing time to go to saloon. The desire for men to look smart has increased and hence the demand for the saloon has risen. This made the hotels to include these shops in their shopping arcade. Business personnel would like to have a decent look before going for meetings; similarly other guest coming to the hotel would like to have a fresh look before going out. Wives of business executives accompanying their husband during business travel, have ample of time to visit the saloons. It is managed by the professionals who receive specialized training for the same.

Chemist

The chemist shop is becoming a must as the medicine may be required by guest at any time. The hotels have a resident doctor for the medicinal need of the guests and these chemist shops act as a supplement to it. These shops are quite beneficial at the time of emergency as most of the lives saving drugs are available.

Book Shop

The book shop provides ample opportunity for the book lovers to purchase books. These shops provide books of various choices. Novels, informative books, city guide, children books, railway time table, newspaper, women's magazine are available in the shops.

Flower Shop

The flower speaks the language of heart. Guest does like to celebrate special occasion in the hotel and an occasion can not be celebrated without flowers. Birthday, anniversary, New Year, Christmas are some of the occasions which needs to be celebrated with flowers. Guest look for flowers to celebrate the occasion and find it convenient when they find a flower shop within the hotel premises. The flower choice ranges from a single flower to a bouquet of flower with varying prices.

SUPPORT SERVICES

Support services have their own significance. Table 5.2 gives the detailed examples of support services.

Table 5.2: Support services

Sl. No.	Type of service	Example
1.	Support Service	Engineering and Maintenance Department Security Department Human Resource Department Sales and Marketing Department Accounts Department Purchase Department etc.

Engineering and Maintenance Department

This department is concerned with the civil works, electrical works, mechanical works and computer works of the hotel. The operations of the department can be divided into two sub-groups, i.e. providing utility services and performing repair and maintenance work. Utility services include the day-to-day services of electricity, sanitation, hot water, steam, air-conditioning etc. Repair and maintenance work includes the preventive maintenance to reduce the break down of the heavy equipments and periodic repair and up keep of furniture and fixture of the hotel. The importance of this department is of great use due to the complexity of mechanical and electrical system in modern hotel. Not all engineering and maintenance work is handled by the hotel's staff, often some problems or projects requires outsourcing for example – to set fire extinguishers and test and adjust building fire alarm.

The maintenance and engineering department has the control desk which registers all complains made by the house-keeping or the front office. The desk attendant is responsible for registering all complaints, communicating it to the shift in-charge, following it up till complaint is attended and informing the final status to the department from where complaint was received. The front office and house keeping must communicate complaints of the guest at the earliest to maintenance division. If maintenance department is given the responsibility to repair a room not fit for sale then they should inform the front office and house keeping when the room is ready for sale again.

The maintenance and engineering department is headed by the chief engineer and he is the accountable person for all the operations. The department has a brigade which executes the tasks. The size of the brigade depend on the size of the hotel, it includes AC mechanic, plumber, mason, blacksmith, painter, carpenter, polisher etc. Maintenance work has been divided into four types for proper execution of the operation. These types of maintenance work are routine maintenance, preventive maintenance, scheduled maintenance and break down maintenance. Routine maintenance refers to the activities related to upkeep of the property. It includes cleaning guest-rooms, washing floors, replacing bulbs etc. Preventive maintenance refers to the activities that help to prolong the life of equipments and minimize the incidents of break down. It includes checking, oiling and overhauling of the equipments. Scheduled maintenance refers to the activities that take place after a regular interval to delay the occurrence of any problem. Break down maintenance is the emergency services to the sudden failure of any equipment. It is the costliest maintenance because until the equipments restart there is potential loss of revenue to the hotel.

Security Department

Security department is responsible for surveillance of the hotel. This department ensures that safe and secure surrounding is provided to guests, visitors and employees. The security of the hotel is not only the responsibility of this department but also of the employees working in a hotel. Many hotels train their staff as how to verify guests, how to deal with suspicious activities taking place anywhere in the premises and to report the security staff in case of any doubt.

Hotel security involves security of guest room, public area, boundaries, etc. Many hotels now-a-days follows card key system in which a guest is given a magnetic card which is used to open the guest room door. Public area security is of prime concern since it is accessible to people. Close Circuit TV are installed in public areas to monitor the activities taking place in these areas. Boundary security is achieved by providing sufficient light, hedges, wires and also some time electrified fencing.

The guest who stays in the hotel is always concerned of his belongings especially when his room is cleared by housekeeping staff. A strong security programme will ensure that staff is not able to take any item outside the hotel premises. For this in most of the hotels security programme include physical checking of staff before they leave the hotel premises. Since the staff cannot take any item outside the premises of the hotel it will be useless for them to steal the guest's belongings. Also, the executive housekeeper prepares the room cleaning schedule in such a way that two or more people are involve in the cleaning of a single room.

The security system not only protects the hotel from outside anti-social elements but also from the hotel employees and guest. The guest may damage hotel's property intentionally or unintentionally. If the damage has been done intentionally by the guest s/he may be charged by the hotel management. However, if it is unintentionally it may be overlooked by the management. Theft by the guest is also noticed as few guests have a peculiar habit of taking hand towel, face towel, pillow cover, bed sheet, shampoo etc. provided by the hotel, along with them at the time of check out. In view of this house-keeping staff should be trained to check the guest-room at the time guest check outs. Any missing item should be reported to front office immediately. The front desk staff should then handle the situation cleverly. If any item being taken out by the guest is not of much value then it may be overlooked. However, in case of costlier items the front desk staff should politely ask to the guest whether he has unintentionally packed any belonging of the hotel. Guest should be asked to open his luggage only when the hotel management is confirm that guest has packed the hotel belonging.

Security department also deals with various situations like bomb threat, fire in hotel, death in a hotel, accident in a hotel etc. In majority of security programmes the hotel staffs are given mock drill of how to deal with these situations. The fire exit plan is framed at back of all guest rooms door so that the guests are aware of which route to follow in case fire accidents. If the hotel security department is active the guest gets the feeling that they are at a safer place and prefer to stay in same hotel at their next visit, hence increasing the hotel business.

Human Resource Department

A skilled staff will always bring revenue to the organisation by showing his technical and communication skill. Guest generally complains about the technical skill of the staff or about their behaviour. Both these complains can be minimized if proper recruitment of staff is undertaken. The human resource department is responsible to recruit the staff and train them so that they can perform to the expectations of guests.

Human resource department is headed by Human Resource Manager who estimates the manpower requirement for present operations and future expansion of the organisation. The major functions of the department are recruitment, orientation or induction, training, motivation and counselling of the staff. The recruitment process starts with the advertisement in the newspaper and its ends when new entrants are on the job. The recruitment may be from internal or external source. Orientation or induction is the process by which the new entrants are made familiar with organisation and its culture, their job and post in the hierarchy. If required, proper training is given to the staff to increase their efficiency while they are performing their routine work. Some hotel organizes development programmes with a vision to enrich their staff to fulfil the strategic plans. Motivation and counselling are the tools by which the morale of staffs is boosted and a career path is shown to them. When any staff leaves the organisation the human resource department takes an exit interview. The main purpose of the exit interview is to take the feedback from the employee that can be used for the benefit of the organisation. This helps to reduce the employee turn over.

Now the human resource is considered as an asset to any organisation and the hotel is not an exception. The hotel provides services where the role of staff is linked to the service. And hence the importance of Human resource is obvious. For example when a steward is serving meal to the guest, the guest is not only consuming the meal but he is also experiencing the attitude and behaviour of the steward as a part of the meal. The same meal can be served in different ways and in each case the guest satisfaction level will be different.

The experience of the guest when he talks to the hotel staffs can be said to as moment of truth i.e. the guest builds an image of the organisation when he is in conversation with the staff. This moment of truth is based on how the staff helps in making guest comfortable. If the guest finds staff to be courteous, humble and polite then he will develop a positive moment of truth else a negative one. Positive moment of truth always help in the repeat business.

Sales and Marketing Department

Sales and marketing are the tools that are used to increase the revenue of the hotel. Sale is a product oriented concept, whereas marketing is a customer oriented concept. In sales we offer the products and services of the hotel whereas marketing is related to the research work which includes finding of new market place, competing products, guest expectations and future demand. These all can be developed by some of the marketing methods like advertisement, public relation program and survey or by giving feedback forms. The guest gets information of different hotels from the advertisement in news paper, magazines, television etc. These advertisements give information to the guest about various facilities being provided by the hotel. Hence, it is important for hotel to market them in such a way so that they can attract maximum clients. All this becomes successful when there is a proper coordination between the front office staff and other division of the hotel because these are the staff that directly communicate with the guest and can inform the sales and marketing department about guest needs and expectations.

The prime goal of this department is to promote the sale of hotel products and services. This can be achieved only if the personnel involved in this division are efficient and able to find out what actually the guest needs and expectations are. They should also posses the quality to predict the future demands and scenario so that they may inform the other division to cope up with the changing hospitality needs.

The size of this division may vary from one part time person to more than a score of full time employee. In a smaller hotel, an employee looks after sales and marketing activity whereas in large hotel every personnel has to play a different role in achieving the set targets of sale of services and products of the hotel. Front office staff may also act as a sales person when they are interacting with the guest either at reception or in the back office at reservation.

Accounts Department

This department is responsible for the financial activities of the hotel. It includes the paying of outstanding invoices, maintaining the cash register and also accountable for making of employee's payroll and salary slips. Accounts department compiles the annual financial statement like balance sheet, profit and loss statements, trial balance etc. through which one can understand the present financial status of the hotel. Accounts department is responsible for making cash deposit and securing cash loans. The accounts division's success depends on co ordination with the front office staffs which provide the guest's bill for settlement. The most common financial activity handled by the front office like receiving cash payments, credit card, debit card, verifying personal check and maintaining guest account statements.

The accounts department also plays a major role in smooth relation of purchase department and supplier by verifying and settling the bill of supplier on time. The account department is also responsible for the settlement of Non guest account, i.e. settlement of those guests' accounts who are non resident or those resident guests who left the hotel without settling his/her bill in full. The follow up for the same is the responsibility of the accounts.

Purchase Department

Purchasing is process of searching, selecting, receiving and storing a commodity as per the hotel's policy. The main objective of the purchase department is to put a control on the purchasing process and to ensure that the commodities are of standard quality and the supply is regular. Each department of hotel gives their requirement to the purchase department on daily, weekly and on a monthly basis. Purchase department maintains at par stock of each and every commodity.

Purchase department plans their purchase in advance and floats the tenders for various items in the market. The tenders clearly mention the specifications required for example in case food items size, quality, quantity, rate etc. After receiving the tender from different suppliers it is open and one which matches with organisation need is selected. Then hotel sign the contract with supplier in which both agrees on the rate, quality, quantity and time of delivery. If any party breaches the contract then it can be sued by another party. There are two types of purchasing contract-specific period contract and the quantity contract

The principle suppliers are wholesale supply houses, manufacturers and packers, local farmers and producers, municipal markets, cooperative associations and retail food stores. The department selects any one or the combination of the suppliers after gathering the full information about the firm and the range of items they supply, recent price list, trading terms, the other hotels taking supply form there etc. For selecting supplier, the three performance criteria used are price, quality and delivery. The purchase is done by many methods like cash and carry, weekly quotation list, fortnightly quotation list etc.

ACTIVITIES

a) Find out the various ancillary services provided by some of the A Grade or classified property hotels in your locality.

b) List the importance of support services for the smooth running of hotel.

c) Find out the various support services provided by the hotel near your locality.

QUESTIONS

1. Discuss the role of security department in a hotel.
2. How Human Resource Department can help in repeat business of a hotel?
3. What is the difference between ancillary and support services?
4. How ancillary and support services are helpful in increasing the occupancy in a hotel?
5. Discuss the function of purchase department in a hotel. How the malpractices in the purchase department can affect the business of hotel?

7

HOSPITALITY ORGANISATIONS

— ABHINAV SHANDILYA[1]

Since the beginning of the human civilization organizations have existed in one or another form. As organizations emerge and exist in the society and therefore they affect the society and the changes in the society affect them. Let us define organization:

Organization is the group of two or more people who work for attaining an objective with the combined efforts. Organizations are deliberately constructed and reconstructed to attain the specific goals. Organizations include the identification of job dividing it further in to smaller units, grouping responsibilities and authorities among the staff, determining the relationship amongst different activities and different staff.

An outsider might never guess the complexity of the hospitality sector but one single service offered to the guest is the outcome of the proper co-ordination between the key role players of the hospitality sector. To attain the set goal of the hospitality, to run effectively and efficiently each and every key role player has to perform its function up to the standard. Team work is the key to success in Hospitality sector. Every key player works to improve the quality of service and this is the uniqueness of Hospitality Organization. Like other organizations the hospitality organization also defines its mission statement. It may be in terms of providing safe and secure accommodation, comfortable guest rooms, professional and friendly services, convenient transportation, achieving the guest satisfaction etc. The next step after defining mission statement is determining the goal. It is more specific and for a specific period of time. It can be measured in term of achievements.

Once the organization has been formed, it is time to chalk out the plan which will help in fulfilling the mission and achieving the goal and because of this formulation of plan; we can further divide our long-term goal in numerous short-term goals. To achieve these goals department or division establishes strategies and tactics which define how goals will be achieved. Tactics are day to day operating procedures that implement successful strategies. It is important that goals and strategies are set at the departmental or divisional level, so that every one can recognize easily what role he has to play in achieving the over all goal of the organization.

1. Lecturer in Hotel Management at B.I.T, Mesra, Ranchi Jharkhand.

Every organization has a structure to establish the relationship among the various components or the department of the organization. The work is divided among the departments or members or key players of the organization and then to perform effectively, powers and authorities are also spelled out. The main benefit of the organization structure is that it establishes the co ordination and also the action of different players can be monitored effectively. The pictorial representation of the organization structure is known as ORGANISATION CHART. The structures may be classified as formal and informal structures but in hotel industry generally the formal structure is preferred. The three component of the organization structure are complexity, formalization and centralization. The complexity is the degree to which activities within the organization are differentiated. Formalization is the degree to which rules and procedures are utilized. Centralization defines where the decision making authority lies.

OBJECTIVES

After reading this chapter you will understand:

- The meaning and concept of an organization and its organizational structure
- The different types of organization structure
- The major role players in hospitality organization

MEANING AND CONCEPTS

Hospitality organization is a broader unit and new sector are clinging to it every now and then. However, the major sector of hospitality still remains hotel, travel agency and tour operator. These three components cater to the majority of guest needs. However, the task is different. Hotel deals with the accommodation and food of their guests, tour operator plans the tour and make arrangement for the same and travel agency manages the ticket for various travel requirements. Before going into the detail about the organization of above three key role players of a hospitality organization, let us understand about the organizational structure prevailing in hospitality industry.

- Product service base structure,
- Spatial base structure,
- Conglomerate structure and
- Matrix structure.

Product Service-based Structure

This type of structure is found in those organizations which offer a variety of products and services. The structure is based on the different products and services provided to the consumers. Here the activities are structured in accordance with the services and products. For example, in a restaurant we have two major activities that are production of food and service of food so that structure can be divided as food and beverage production and food and beverage service. Further, food and beverage production can be classified in different sub-sections like Italian, Mexican etc. and the services can be divided under table service, assisted service, etc.

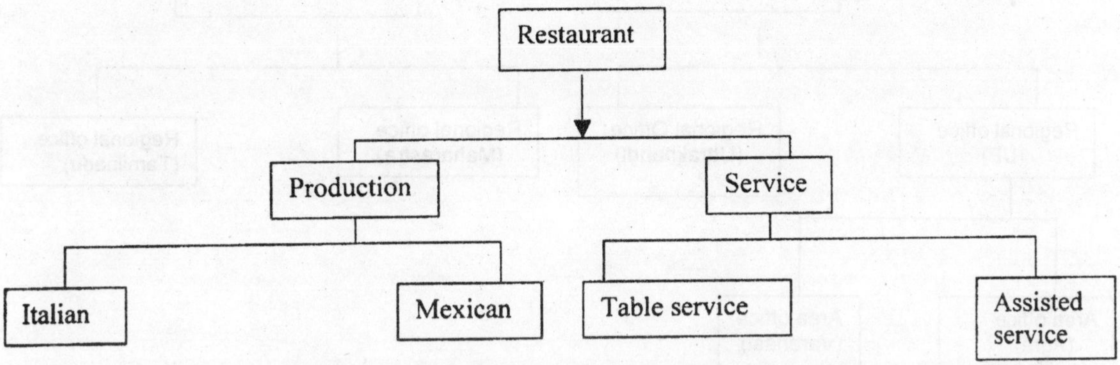

Fig 6.1: Product service-based organisation chart

Spatial Base Structure

In this category the structure is based on the customer or regional basis. The organizations divide its activities by structuring on geographical lines through a network of regional offices. For example – travel agency have different zonal offices to provide the services as per the requirement of the customer of that zone. Further the zones are divided into regions and then areas.

Conglomerate Structure

In conglomerate structure the business or companies are acquired and maintained as subsidiaries. However, subsidiaries work under parent company policies and strategies and the line of communication is work between them and power of control is vested with the parent company. Delegation of authority takes place in this system. For example: an individual hotel in a town may be acquired by a reputed hotel and hence it will work under its name on their terms and condition.

Matrix means an array of vertical column and horizontal rows. In this type of structure an employee works under dual authority. The first line of command is based on divisional or functional and second one is project based approach in a specialized area. It means that a person is accountable to two heads at the same time. For example: a cook is accountable to the kitchen supervisor at the same time he may be accountable to a specialty chef who is taking care of that particular cuisine, this may be for a limited time period as for food festivals.

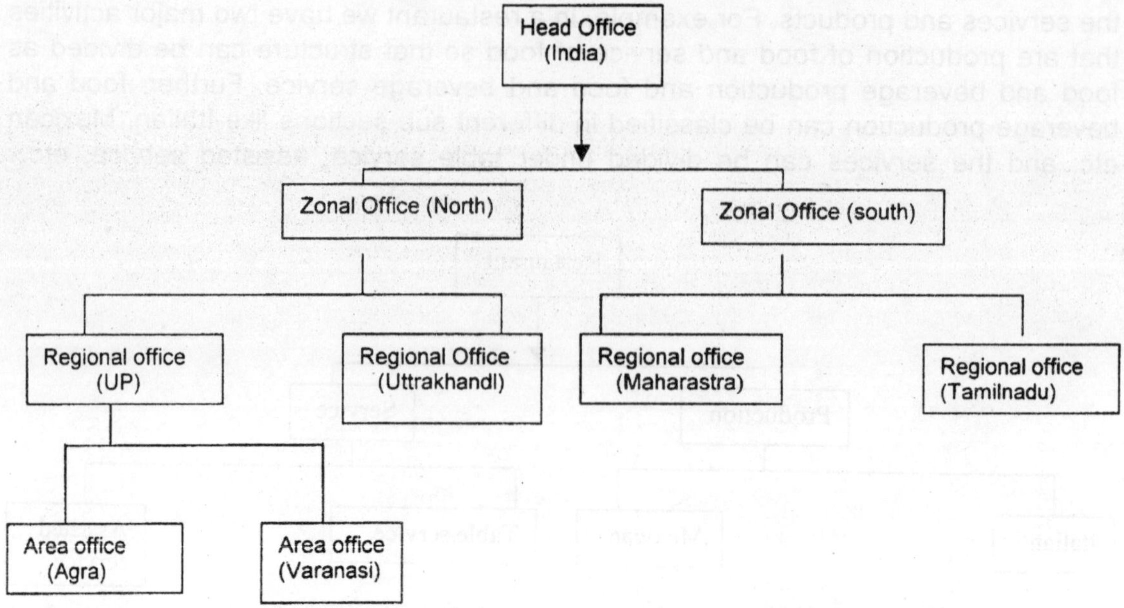

Fig 6.2: Spatial base organisation chart

The above structures have its distinctive characteristics and the same structure may be best suited for one organization but not for other. The structure of the organization is determined by their size, type of product to be offered and the target customer. Besides the above classification the structure may also be broadly classified as **mechanistic structure and organic structure**. The former structure is based on high complexity and formalization. Here in this structure mostly downward communication channel has been used. It means all the levels of management have to follow the instruction give by top level management. Lower level members have little participation in decision-making process. However, in organic structure it is low in complexity and formalization, two way communication channels is used and lower level employees can also communicate their ideas and views. Any organization structure falls under one of these two structures. Now, let us discuss about the organizational structure of the three key players in the hospitality industry:

MATRIX STRUCTURE

Hotel

Hotel is an organisation as it is a business set to attain profit by achieving certain pre-decided goal. Hotel involves in providing food and accommodation to the guest. Providing food includes preparation and services and accommodation includes booking a guest room, receiving the guest and making the guest stay in the hotel a comfortable one. So we can say that on the basis of revenue generation, the hotel organisation has four main divisions i.e. food and beverage production, food and beverage service, house keeping and front office.

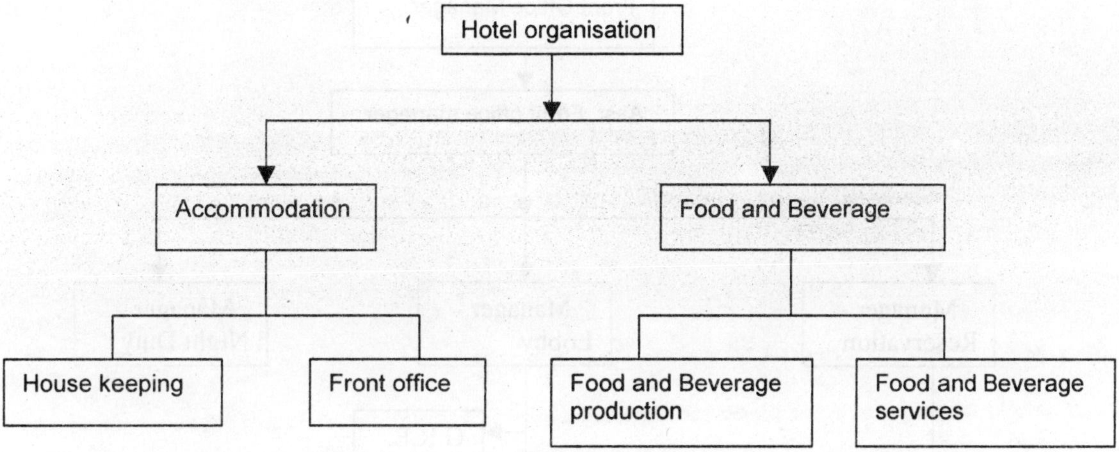

Fig. 6.3: Organisation chart of a Hotel

ACCOMMODATION

Accommodation department of hotel industry takes care to provide comfortable stay to its guests. As depicted in the chart above, this major department is divided into two sections. First is housekeeping department, this department deals with up keeping of the rooms and the public places of the hotel. It maintains the cleanliness and hygiene of the entire property. Also laundry, flower arrangement, lost and found etc. comes under this department. Second is front office department which reserves the room for the guest. It also includes the guests dealing with the help of its different sub sections like concierge, guest relation cell, business center, cash counter, central reservation system etc. Accommodation department is headed by the Accommodation Manager, he directly reports to the general manager.

FRONT OFFICE

This department is the face of the hotel and remains in touch with guests all through their stay i.e. the first call made by a guest for a query to reserve a room to the settlement of the bill at the time of check out. The major functions of the front office include reservation, registration, answering to the guest query, maintaining relation with guest, settling guest account, handling foreign exchange of guest, taking guest calls, mails, faxes etc. and to ensure that the guest stay is comfortable.

The front office department is headed by the front office manager. He is accountable for the smooth running of the front office. He does the administrative job and whenever require take helps from the assistant front office manager. Assistant front office manager acts like Front office manager in his absence and accountable for the execution of departmental operations. He delegates his work amongst difference section head like reservation manager, front desk manager, concierge manager, business centre manager, guest relation manager and receptionist etc.

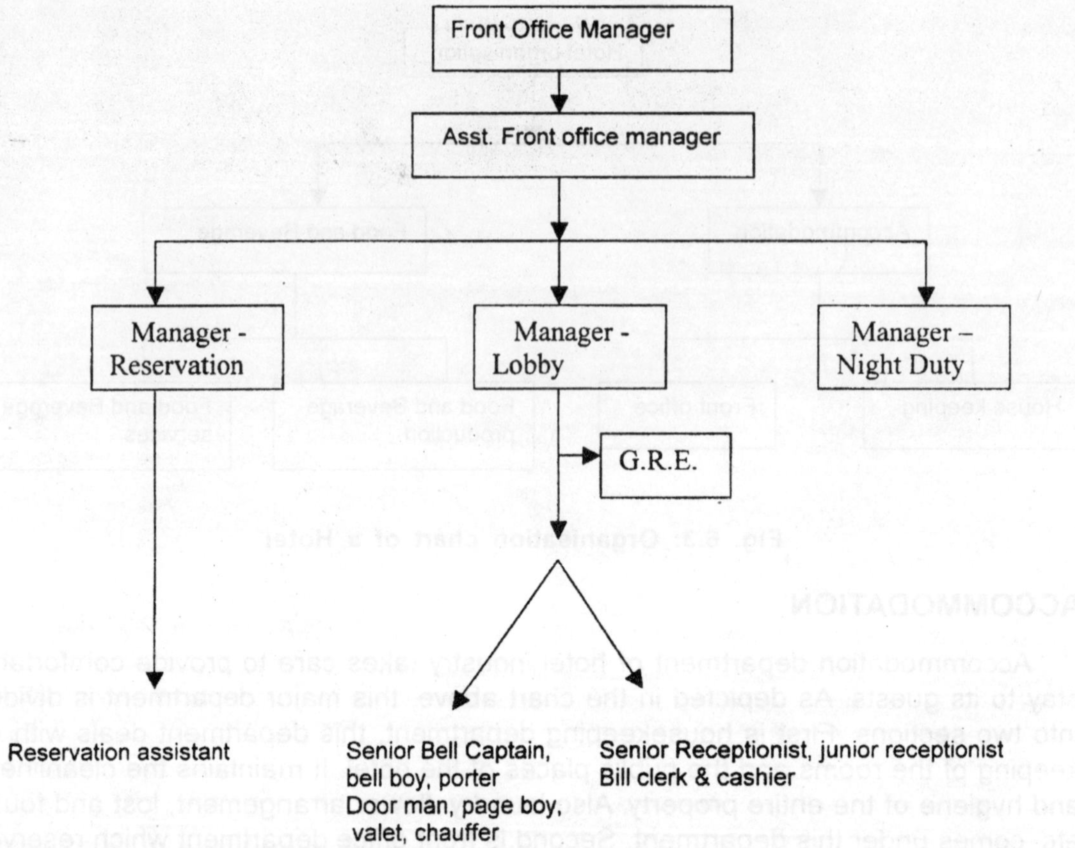

Fig.6.4: Organisation chart of Front Office Department

HOUSE-KEEPING

This department is the back-bone of the hotel and is involved in cleanliness, maintenance and aesthetic upkeep of the property. It helps to provide a clean, comfortable and safe stay to the guests. The major functions of the housekeeping include cleaning of rooms, public areas and back house; providing laundry facility; attending calls at house keeping desk and sorting the problems; arranging flowers to rooms and public areas; maintaining the lost and found register; co ordinating with the architects during renovation and refurbishing etc.

The house-keeping department is headed by executive house-keeper. He is accountable for the smooth functioning of the housekeeping. The Executive house-keeper is responsible for the administrative jobs of the department. He takes help from the assistant house keeper for the execution of entire jobs. Assistant Housekeeper delegates the work amongst different section in-charges who execute the daily operations of their respective sections. The section in-charge are floor supervisor, public area supervisor, Linen room supervisor, laundry supervisor, Horticulturist etc. The center in-charge takes help from attendants to get the work executed.

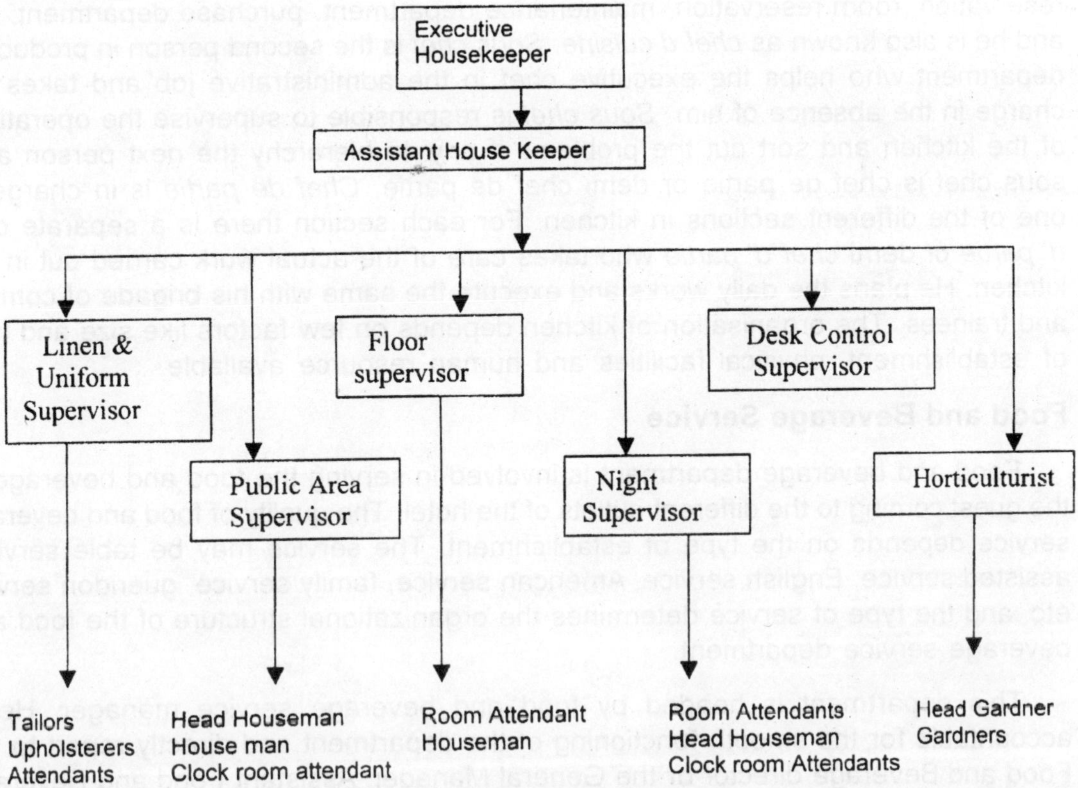

Fig. 6.5: Organisation chart of House-keeping Department

FOOD AND BEVERAGE

Food and beverage department of hotel industry takes care for providing variety of food and beverages to customers. As discussed earlier, this major department is divided into two sections. First is food and beverage production department, this department deals with preparation of food and beverage. Hotel has kitchen which prepares the variety of food, some hotel has more than one kitchen, which cater to the specific needs of the customers. Second is food and beverage service department which serves the food made by kitchen to the guest at restaurant, coffee shop, at room etc. Along with the food, variety of beverage is also served by the department. The food and beverages department is headed by the Food and Beverages Director.

Food and Beverage Production

The food and beverage department of any hotel is engaged in preparing food for the guest. This department is headed by the executive chef who is the accountable person of production department. Executive chef is more a manager then culinary skilled personnel. He looks after all the administrative work of the production department, his prime job includes coordination with other departments like Banquet reservation, room reservation, maintenance department, purchase department, etc. and he is also known as *chef d cuisine*. *Sous chef* is the second person in production department who helps the executive chef in the administrative job and takes the charge in thè absence of him. *Sous chef* is responsible to supervise the operations of the kitchen and sort out the problems if any. In hierarchy the next person after sous chef is chef de partie or demi chef de partie. *Chef de partie* is in charge of one of the different sections in kitchen. For each section there is a separate *chef d' partie* or demi *chef d' partie* who takes care of the actual work carried out in the kitchen. He plans the daily works and execute the same with his brigade of commis and trainees. The organisation of kitchen depends on few factors like size and type of establishment, physical facilities and human resource available.

Food and Beverage Service

Food and beverage department is involved in serving the food and beverage to the guest coming to the different outlets of the hotel. The quality of food and beverage service depends on the type of establishment. The service may be table service, assisted service, English service, American service, family service, gueridon service etc. and the type of service determines the organizational structure of the food and beverage service department.

This department is headed by food and beverage service manager. He is accountable for the smooth functioning of the department and directly report to the Food and Beverage director or the General Manager. Assistant Food and Beverage manager helps in executing the activities of the department and act as the in-charge of service department in the absence of the manager. In hierarchy next come the outlets managers who are responsible for the execution of daily operations of their respective outlets. The outlets manager may be a restaurant manager, specialty restaurant manager, coffee shop manager, room service manager, bar manager, banquet manager etc. The outlets managers have a brigade which helps them in day to day work. The brigade includes senior captain, captain, steward, trainee, and apprentice.

In the above organisation chart we have taken six section of the kitchen, the number of section may vary as per the size of establishment and accordingly the CDP (chef de partie) will change.

In the above organisation chart we have taken six sections of the food and beverage services; however the number of sections may vary as per the size of establishment and accordingly the outlet manager will change.

TRAVEL AGENCY

Travel agency is involved in providing the travel needs of tourist/traveler. The agency is the link between the traveller and the principle supplier like airline, railways, transport operator etc. The major operation of the travel agency is ticketing, booking and cancellation, facilitation etc. Ticketing involves booking of domestic and international tickets, booking and cancellation is done when the amendment is required in the pre set schedule, facilitation involves necessary support require for passport, visa insurance, immigration permit, etc.

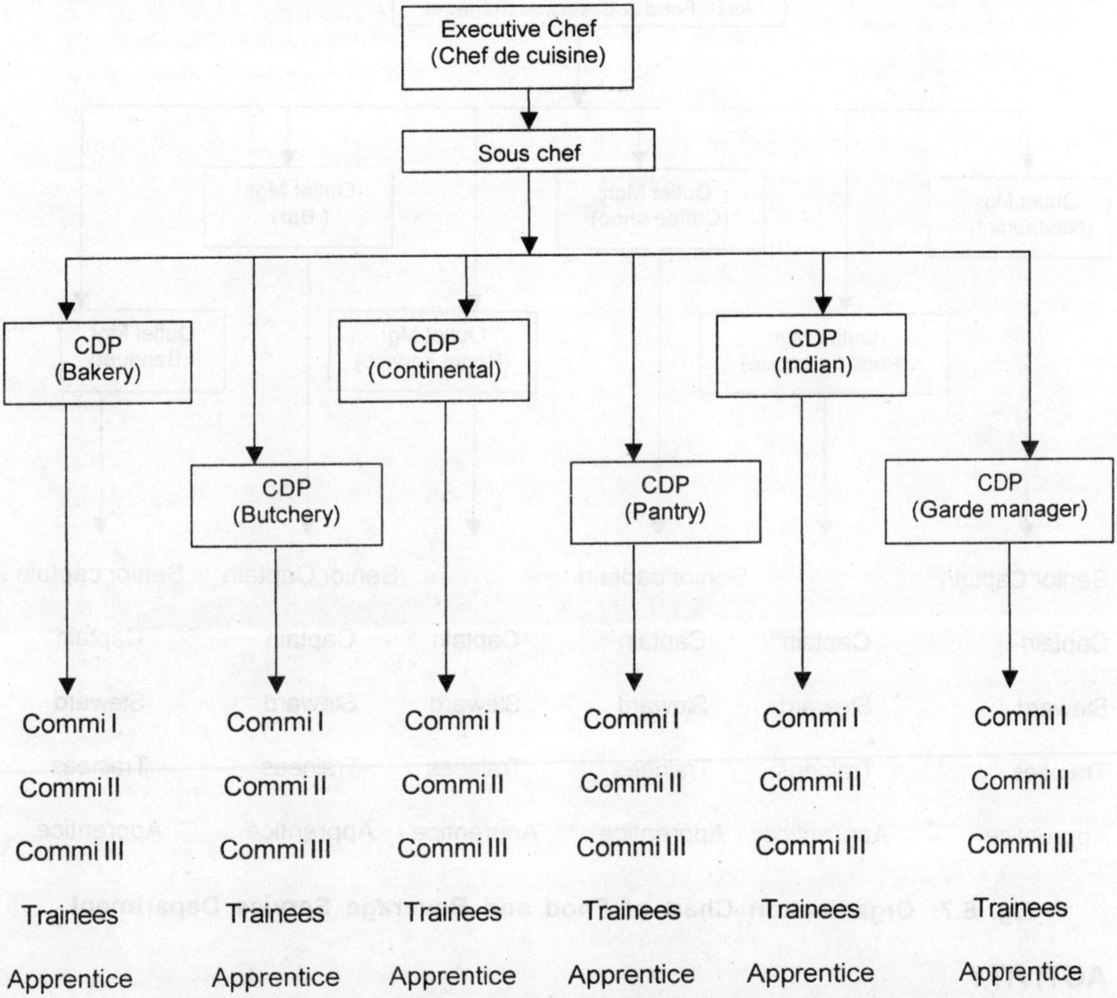

Fig. 6.6: Organisation Chart of Food Production Department

The travel agency is headed by the Managing Director who is accountable for the smooth functioning of the agency. Managing director delegates the work to the different functional head like manager (tour), managers (reservations), Manager (administration). All the functional heads have their own brigade to perform the task.

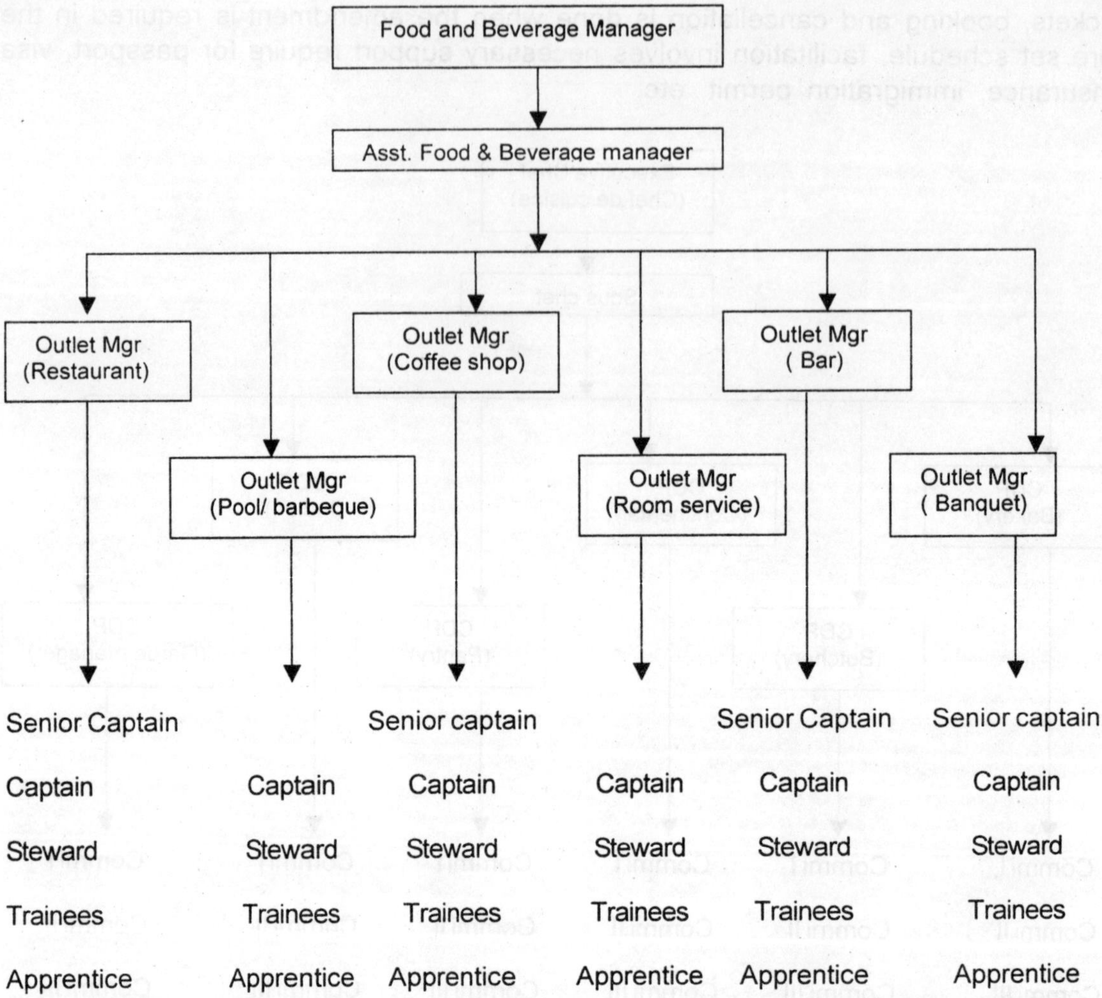

Fig. 6.7: Organisation Chart of Food and Beverage Service Department

ACTIVITY

1. Find out some travel agents in your city and evaluate facilities provided by them to tourists.
2. Visit a hotel in your town and prepare a list of services provided by them.
3. Compare the organisation structure of the two leading hotels of your city and discuss their strengths and weaknesses accordingly.

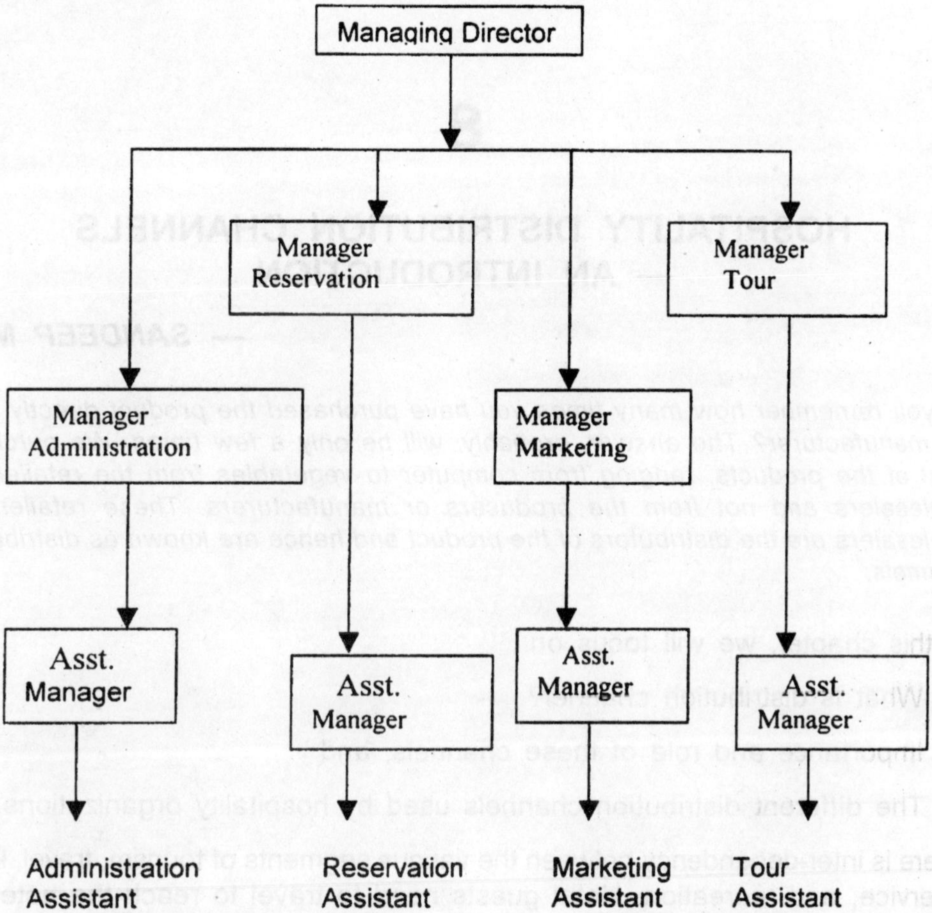

Fig. 6.8: Organisation Chart of Travel Agency

QUESTIONS

1. Define the terms organisation and organizational structure.
2. Briefly describe the different types of organisation structures found in hospitality organisation.
3. What is the difference between mechanistic and organic structure?
4. Discuss the organisation set-up of a Travel Agency.
5. Draw the organisation structure of food and beverage production department, of a classified hotel property.

8

HOSPITALITY DISTRIBUTION CHANNELS — AN INTRODUCTION

— SANDEEP MALIK[1]

Do you remember how many times you have purchased the product directly from the manufacturer? The answer, probably, will be only a few times. We purchase most of the products, ranging from computer to vegetables from the retailers or wholesalers and not from the producers or manufacturers. These retailers or wholesalers are the distributors of the product and hence are known as distribution channels.

In this chapter, we will focus on:

❖ What is distribution channel?

❖ Importance and role of these channels, and

❖ The different distribution channels used by hospitality organizations.

There is inter-dependency between the various segments of tourism, travel, lodging, food service, and recreation. Hotel guests need to travel to reach the hotel. They eat in nearby restaurants and visit attractions. Each segment is, to some extent, dependent on other segments for business. Unlike physical goods, it is not possible to bring our hospitality products at the place of tourists origin. Effective distribution is especially important in the hotel sector, as the accommodation product is extremely perishable. Revenue from an unsold hotel room is lost forever, and thus selling each room each night at an optimum price is critical to profitability. As a result, the efficiency of a hotel's set of channels of distribution is critical. Hotels have thus traditionally used a variety of simultaneous channels to help maximise their sales. These include distributing through other properties within their brand, joining consortia or other types of associate organisations, joining representative companies, using intermediaries such as travel agents, tour operators or incentive houses, and making use of an increasingly important portfolio of electronic channels. In each case, the objectives are to make information about the product conveniently available to customers and to make it easier for them to reserve that particular property.

---

1. Lecturer in Hotel Management at Kurukshetra University, Kurukshetra, Haryana.

Hospitality organisations also need distribution systems to make their products available to consumers. In contrast to physical products, with hotels the intermediary rarely takes possession of the product to be distributed. The concepts of product flow, ownership flow and title transfer are not always applicable where intangibles are being distributed. Although the consumer must come in contact with the firm to receive the service, there is often little tangible evidence of the transfer of ownership or title. Instead it is information – about availability, prices, qualities and convenience – that is transferred, communicated and manipulated (Poon 1993).

Chart-7.1: Hospitality Distribution Channel System

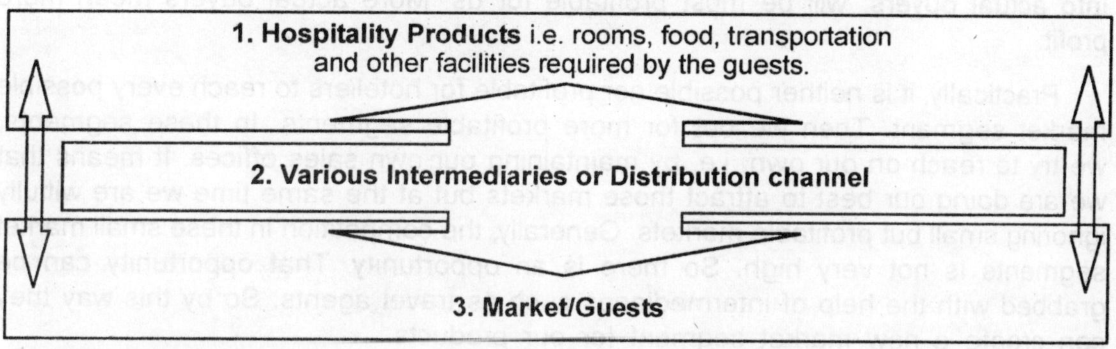

1. **Hospitality products** i.e. rooms, food, transportation and other facilities required by the guests.
2. **Various Intermediaries or Distribution channel** which help in distribution of the product.
3. **Market/Guests** are the buyers who buy the products.
4. Represents those guests who approach directly to the hotels and other hospitality organizations.

Importance and Role

Everyone agrees that hospitality industry is known for a highly seasonal business which means that there are two seasons i.e. *peak season* when there negative occupancy as the demand exceeds supply and *lean season* when we have more staff members then guests. Here we can make use of these channels to balance these situations. Let's take an example of a hotel in Rajasthan, a large number of tourists travel to Rajasthan in winters, due the harsh climate in summers, making the availability of rooms next to impossible where as in summers profitable or valuable tourists are hard to find and a large number of tourist facilities go waste and hoteliers loses a large sum of money in the form of inventories. Here comes the role of distribution channels, in summers they can divert the conference tourists to Rajasthan. They have two good reasons behind this; first, very good facilities are available there, and second, conference tourists remain indoors in day and they generally go out in evening or night by that time climate become pleasant. But here the role of these channels will become very important as they have to convince the clients. In this way, they help in providing a steady progress in tourist flow.

Good distribution channels can convert potential buyers into actual buyers with a higher rate of success. Potential buyers are those buyers who wish to buy our products. They may or may not buy our products because of certain factors. Where as actual buyers are those who actually buy our products. How many of potential buyers graduates to become actual buyers, will tell us about the success rate of a particular distribution channel. The one, who can convert maximum potential buyers into actual buyers, will be most profitable for us. More actual buyers mean more profit.

Practically, it is neither possible nor profitable for hoteliers to reach every possible market segment. Then we opt for more profitable segments. In these segments, we try to reach on our own, i.e. by maintaining our own sales offices. It means that we are doing our best to attract those markets but at the same time we are wilfully ignoring small but profitable markets. Generally, the competition in these small market segments is not very high. So there is an opportunity. That opportunity can be grabbed with the help of intermediaries such as travel agents. So by this way they can create a new market segment for our products.

These channels help in increasing revenue for hotels in a number of ways. They market our products at their own cost. This saves on our marketing costs, of course we have to pay them on an agreed commission. The amount paid as commission, in any case, is much lower than the cost involved in maintaining and training a sales workforce and infrastructure.

The intermediaries are specialists in distributing products. So they work with much more effectiveness and efficiency than the hotel marketing personnel. Incidentally they may not be as loyal and committed as the staff. This can overcome by working out an affordable higher rate of commission paid to intermediateries. By this they may sell our products effectively and also create niche market for the hotel.

Different Intermediateries

Many specialized intermediateries are available to hospitality and travel organizations. These are:

- travel agents and tour wholesalers
- travel corporations
- corporate travel manager
- certified travel counsellors
- destination management companies

- hotel representatives
- government tourist associations
- consortia and reservation systems
- global distribution systems
- the Internet;
- concierges
- unorganized taxi operators

Travel Agent and Tour Wholesaler

The concept of a travel agent emerged with Thomas Cook who organized the first tour by rail from Leicester to Loughborough. Travel agent is a person who has full knowledge about tourist product destinations, modes of travel, climate, accommodation and other areas of service sector. He .acts on behalf of product providers/principals and in return gets commission. Technically, a travel agent is the owner or manager of an agency, but other employees are responsible for advising tourists and selling package tours/individual component of travel product. Travel agents typically deal with a diverse range of tasks, including:

- Making reservations
- Planning itineraries
- Calculating fares and charges
- Buying tickets
- Advising clients on destinations, resorts, airline companies and a wide range of travel products
- Communicating with clients verbally and in writing
- Maintaining accurate records on reservations
- Ensuring racks are well stocked, or supplies are kept in-house
- Acting as intermediaries when customer complaints occur.

Travel agents are also known as image builder of a country. A travel agent may be an individual/firm or corporation that run a travel agency. An agency means office of the travel agent or organisation where all travel goods and services are assembled and coordinated for the smooth conduct of travel agency business. It is a travel agency which packages and processes all the attractions, amenities and ancillary services of a country or destination for tourists. Presently there are more than 70,000 travel agencies operating throughout the world. However, the maximum number of travel agencies are in USA.

The travel business in India started with setting of 'The Travel Agents Association of India' (TAAI) in Mumbai' in 1951. Before that there were two major foreign companies - Thomas Cook and Sons and The American Express with their main branches; and Indian Companies - Jeena and Co., Lee and Muirhead India Pvt. Ltd., and N. Jamnadas and Co. Ltd., operating in India. However, the bulk of International tourists were handled by Thomas Cook and Sons and The American Express. In 1920 Jeena and Company, the First Indian Travel Agency organised group tours abroad and in India for Indian travellers and it handled the first group of foreign tourists in 1950. However, Jeena and Company and the other two Indian travel agencies were merged into one composite travel company known as 'Travel Corporation of India Ltd.' (TCI) in 1961. After this there were a number of travel companies established in India such as SITA (1963), Thomas Cook India Ltd., American Express, Cox and Kings, Ind. Travel and so forth.

Presently, there are around 500 travel agencies/companies on the approval list of Department of Tourism, Ministry of Tourism and Culture, Government of India.

Types of Travel Agency

- ❖ Retail Travel Agencies
- ❖ Wholesale Travel Agency

Retail Travel Agencies: A retail travel agency sells tourist products directly to the public on behalf of the product suppliers and in return gets commission.

Wholesale Travel Agency: A wholesale travel agency purchases tourist product components in bulk and designs package tours. Sometimes, a wholesale travel agency buys travel components from a vendor in bulk and re-sells them to another travel business organisation.

Wholesale travel agencies assemble package holidays and sell them to the clients by retail travel agencies. A package tour includes - transportation tickets, accommodation, and other desired services, such as entertainment, sightseeing and sports activities etc. These packages are referred as 'package tours'. Most of these tours include the services of escorts but a few are sold to people who wish to travel independently. Now the question arises - How a wholesale travel agency generates profit? Generally a wholesaler receives volume discounts from the principal suppliers because a wholesaler might agree to purchase a large number of seats from a particular airline or reserve a large number of rooms at a particular hotel and resort.

Travel Corporations

Travel Corporations provide same services as provided by the travel agents. The largest travel corporation is American Express Travel Services. American Express (AMEX) is a corporation that has a travel services division with locations worldwide.

Each is licensed and bonded with the guidelines of International Air Transportation Association (IATA), it provides travel services and tickets through the corporation. The travel services division provides other services, including foreign exchange, AMEX traveller's checks in different currencies, and gift-checks. Currently, the travel services division is trying to promote foreign currencies to increase revenues.

The majority of American Express Travel Services' revenues are generated through corporate accounts. The airlines give the travel agency an override to portion with the corporate client. The business contract is individually set up, based on annual travel expenses. For example, if IBM's annual travel expenses are $1 million, the airline will give AMEX a 1.4 per cent override commission to split with IBM. AMEX chooses their airline vendors according to who gives the largest override percentage and whose negotiated rates are most appealing. The same policy applies to other vendors in the industry, such cruise lines. Every travel agent, whether in-house or off-premise, receives commission from a vendor, based on their annual sales volume. Usually, this commission varies, but the standard is 8 to 10 per cent of the sale.

Travel managers for AMEX function as national account managers. Their pay is based on their grade level, region, and market. Their salary also depends on who they service. A small, local clientele generates a lower salary and a broader-service centre provides a higher salary. Depending on whether they are on or off-site, a travel manager's salary for AMEX is between $60,000 and $95,000 for corporate clients. The salary range for general public leisure travel is between $40,000 and $65,000. Each travel manager is hired internally, and pay is based mostly on seniority.

American Express Travel offers its services on the Internet and one can search for the best ticket price or the most convenient flights in the same reservations systems used by thousands of travel agents. In a snap, users can check out the price or search for other options and then book their own reservations online. Users can view descriptions of packages to sunny, snow-filled, cultural, or just plain fun destinations, along with full-colour photos and a list of amenities. These packages may not be booked online. A toll-free number is listed at the site or consumers may visit an American Express Travel office. Visitors to the site currently have three options: They can book airline tickets, they can view vacation offers, and they can look up the most convenient American Express Travel office. In addition, card members may take advantage of special travel, retail, restaurant and entertainment offers and shop for a variety of merchandise on another Internet site called Express Net.

Corporate Travel Manager

A corporate travel manager is a type of entrepreneur working within the frame work of a large corporation. For example, Mitsubishi Electronics, in California, was spending about $4 million for travel and entertainment. The total expenditure for travel and entertainment was $11 million. Then they recruited John Fazio, to improve efficiency and reduce costs. Fazio invited interested agencies to submit proposals based on

Mitsubishi's travel needs. The fifteen initial proposals came out of these two were asked to submit their last quotes. These offers were evaluated based on Mitsubishi's criteria: technological capabilities, locations, and ability to give personal service. By this way they not only lower down the cost but also the efficiency in the process.

An interesting trend in corporate travel is agent less booking via electronic mail (e-mail). Travel is initiated at the keyboard, not at the switchboard. Increasingly, technologically savy corporations are making travel bookings via e-mail.

Certified Travel Counsellors

In USA, leading experts in the travel industry worked together to form an Institute of Certified Travel Agents (ICTA). The ICTA offers specialized professional studies; for those seeking higher proficiency in the travel industry. The professional designation of CTC is awarded to individuals who have successfully passed examinations and who have 5-year full-time experience in a travel agency or in the marketing and promotion of travel.

Destination Management Companies (DMC's)

A destination management company is a service organization that offers a host of programmes and services to meet clients' and group needs. The needs of such groups may range from an airport pickup to an international sales convention with theme parties. The DMCs work closely with hotels; sometimes DMCs book rooms and does everything, including airport greetings, transportation to the hotel, VIP check-in, theme parties, sponsoring programs, organizing competitive sports events, and so on, depending on budget.

Hotel Representatives

These are the hotel representatives who sell hotel products at the location where it is not possible for the hotel to maintain its own staff and office. They hire locals to sell their product in a distant market. Apart from financial consideration, social differences are main reasons to go for this kind of intermediaries. These help in selling the product and understanding the market in a better way. These representatives may or may not represent more than one hotel but these hotels must be of different categories. The payment made to them can be in the form of commission or salary or a combination of both. The most important point that should be of great significance is that they should have complete knowledge of hotel products and taste of market.

Government Tourism Corporations

In a country like India, where all most all of the tourist attraction are in the hands of government. And the government has maximum infrastructure facilities i.e. ITDC and other tourist corporations. The authorities at different level can easily sell their products to the wide category of tourists within the country and abroad. They sell their product to other countries through their overseas offices. Their biggest positive point that they considered as the true representatives of their countries.

Consortia

Consortium is a *Latin* word, meaning 'partnership, association or society' and derives from *consors* 'partner', itself from *con-* 'together' and *sors* 'fate', meaning *owner of means* or *comrade*. A consortium is an *association* of two or more individuals, companies, organizations or governments (or any combination of these entities) with the objective of participating in a common activity or pooling their resources for achieving a common goal. Each participant retains its separate legal status and the consortium's control over each participant is generally limited to activities involving the joint endeavour, particularly the division of profits. A consortium is formed by contract, which delineates the rights and obligations of each member.

In hospitality industry, consortium is a group of hospitality organizations that is formed for their mutual interest. Marketing is often the reason why these are formed. The largest consortia are:

- Utell
- Superanational
- Logis de France
- Leading Hotels of the World, and
- Golden Tulip.

Utell, primarily a reservation service, represents more than 1.3 million rooms from 6500 member hotels. It is also linked to all major global distribution systems and it also has its own website. It is linked to TravelWeb, Travelcity and Expedia. One feature of its Website is UtellVision, a system that allows reservation agents throughout the world to see pictures of a property on their computer terminals. It also operates the Hotel and Travel Roadshows. This organization markets include hotel to the incentive market, conference planners, tour operators, corporate meeting planners, travel agents and wholesalers. Logis de France is an association of more than 4000 small one, two-, and three-star hotels in France.

These organizations have proved to be the major marketing agents of the hotel and tourism industry products. The use of information technology has also lead to their success.

Reservation Systems

A computer reservations system (CRS) is a computerized system used to store and retrieve information and conduct transactions related to travel. Originally designed and operated by airlines, they were later extended to travel agents as a sales channel. They provide a central reservation system for hotels. A few CRS are:

- Loews Representation International
- Steigenberger Reservation Service

They allow the hotels to sell their rooms through a central reservation system.

Global Distribution System (GDS)

It provide a list of products i.e. room, tickets etc. to various intermediaries. The major GDS are:

- Amadeus
- Abacus (Asia/Pacific)
- Travelsky (China)
- Infini (Japan)
- Galileo International
- Axess (Japan)
- Worldspan
- Sabre
- Apollo
- Navitaire
- Atraxis (ex-swissair now EDS)
- Topas (Korea)
- Fantasia (South Pacific)
- SITA's Gabriel.

Amadeus is a computer reservations system (or global distribution system, since it sells tickets for multiple airlines) owned by the Amadeus IT Group with headquarters in Madrid, Spain. The central database is located at Erding, Germany. In addition to airlines, the CRS is also used to book train travel, cruises, car rental, and hotel rooms. Amadeus is a member of IATA and SITA, and its IATA airline designator code is 1A. Amadeus was formed in 1987 by an alliance between Air France, Lufthansa, Iberia Airlines, and Scandinavian Airlines System. Today it holds the position of leader in terms of number of bookings worldwide. Through the Amadeus System close to 90,270 travel agency locations and over 29,660 airline sales offices around the world are able to make bookings with:

- More than 490 airlines, representing more than 95% of the world's scheduled airline seats.
- Some 75,280 hotel properties.
- Some 22 car rental companies, serving over 36,000 locations.

- Other travel provider groups (ferry, rail, cruise, insurance companies and tour operators.

Besides this Sabre (Semi-Automated Business Research Environment) is another computer reservations system/global distribution system (GDS) used by airlines, railways, hotels, travel agents and other travel companies. Sabre GDS is a unit of Sabre Travel Network division. Currently North American hosted carriers include Alaska Airlines, American Airlines, Cape Air Nantucket Airlines, Frontier Airlines, Hawaiian Airlines, Mesa Airlines, and Midwest Airlines are availing its maximum services. Its current IATA code is 1S. However some internal areas are still under 1W.

Internet

Internet is becoming an effective distribution channel. Many international chains such as Hilton, Marriott are getting a large number of reservations through this channel.

Restaurant companies are also using the Internet as a distribution channel Pizza Hut developed PizzaNet, an on-line ordering system in California. TerraNet was developed in Boston for customers wanting home delivery of restaurant meals. The database allows the user to search by restaurant name or type of food. The Internet user then gets information on the menu, including colour photos of the dishes. The customer can select either takeout or delivery. After they have made their selection, they will get the amount owed, including any delivery charges.

Some of the advantages of the Internet are:

- It is 24-hours open.
- It has worldwide coverage,
- Easy to use
- You can actually see the product.
- Less costly
- Less inconvenient.
- Time saving for both host and guest.

The most important factor is having a well-designed site. Easy to operate and understand, it is very important to update the site regularly as wrong information may be given to the guests which will lead to dissatisfaction.

Unorganized Taxi and Autorickshow Drivers

This is probably the least admired and acknowledged channel of distribution. These are the main sources of business in small towns and for low category of hotels in cities without any cost. Though their sole motive is to earn commission but still they provide business. Every hotel fixes their commission and they get this at the time of check-in of the guest. They are very good source of business if handled properly and hotel should try to formulate policies regarding these booking agents.

CONCLUSION

The distribution channels are too important in the hospitality industry. Not only the new distribution channels but also the traditional hotel product distribution channels are equally important for the achievement of dream of all seasons. It may be quite possible that not all channels favour all the producers but it does not mean that they are not good. The case may be that under those particular circumstances one channel may be less profitable than other. It is the management who has to decide which the most profitable channel for the property. A combination of these channels can be used to achieve the organizational objectives. For example: a hotel may have its own sales force and signed to GDS and also market through travel agents. The use of high speed internet services by guests has also benefited the hotels as they can easily market through net with less cost. This may be a factor in the phenomenal growth of Web based channels, which now generate significant numbers of reservations for the chain hotels, particularly when considered collectively. Thus it's likely that most hotel companies will have to make use of an increasing number of multiple simultaneous routes to the customer in the future. While this in itself is beneficial as it increases the likelihood of the company's product being placed in front of the right customer, it does raise issues in terms of management, control and cost. Maintaining descriptive information, room rates and availability data in multiple databases is administratively challenging and error prone, and failure to actively manage such data results in inconsistencies and customer dissatisfaction. A probable solution to it is creating industry standards which will benefit both the guests and the producers.

ACTIVITY

- Visit travel agents and tour operators of your locality and understand their reservation systems.
- Visit the tourism corporation of your state and analyse their products and services and ways they sell them to customers.

QUESTIONS

1. What is the role of travel agents and tour operator in the distribution of hotel products and services?
2. What is the significance of distribution channels in hospitality industry?
3. Write short notes on (a) Consortia (b) Reservation Systems (c) Global Distribution systems.

9

FUNCTIONS AND LEVELS OF DISTRIBUTION CHANNELS

— *SANDEEP MALIK*[1]

Distribution channel and various channels used by the hotel industry have been discussed in length by a number of scholars. It appears to be very simple that an organization can pick up any channel and market its products but the case is not so simple. This is due to various reasons as channels play different roles and functions, difficulty in managing these etc.

In this chapter, we will focus on:

- ❖ Channel functions
- ❖ Channel levels
- ❖ Distribution strategy
- ❖ Designing channels
- ❖ Channel behaviour and organization

As we have discussed in earlier chapter that the distribution channels are of prime importance in the hospitality industry. They are the main deciding factor in selling. These channels, such as tour operators, travel agents, representatives etc., are now playing very important role in deciding sales policies of the hotels. Hotel guests normally prefer one roof shopping and lower price etc. Technology has also played a great role in the success of these channels. CRS and GDS are the best examples of this.

This is only the greener part of the picture. These channels can be double edged sword where one edge will always point toward us. The careful management of these is extremely important otherwise it will lead to monetary and goodwill loss. In this chapter we will discuss, various aspects of managing the distribution channels. The channels perform various functions such as information dissemination, product promotion, contacting the guests on behalf of the organization etc. There are different levels of any channel each level performs certain functions. The number of channels

1. Lecturer in Hotel Management at Kurukshetra University, Kurukshetra, Haryana.

will depend on many factors. There may be times when the channel member will lock their horns due to some conflicts. So their selection criteria become very important.

FUNCTIONS OF DISTRIBUTION CHANNELS

A distribution channel performs the following functions.

- Collect information about potential and current guests, competitors, and other actors and stakeholders in the business environment.
- Helps developing the marketing medium to inform guests about the product.
- Enter in contract on price and other terms with the facility providers.
- Inform the suppliers about the possible demand in advance.
- Acquire the funds to finance inventories at different levels in the marketing channel.
- These help in customizing the available product according to the needs of the guests.
- They bear financial risks in case their inventories are not sold.

Some functions such as promotion constitute *a forward flow* of activity from the company to the customer; other functions (ordering and payment) constitute *a backward* flow from customers to the company. Other functions like information, negotiation, finance, and risk taking occur in both directions.

CHANNEL LEVELS

It means how much number of intermediaries remains present in the distribution. More the number of intermediaries more will be the number of levels. For example: a zero-level channel will have no intermediaries where as a three-level channel will have three intermediaries.

The following are the levels of various channels:

- Zero-level Channel
- One-level Channel
- Two-level Channel
- Three-level Channel.

Zero-level channel (also called a direct marketing channel): It consists of a manufacturer selling directly to the final customer. The major examples are door-to-door sales (Eureka Forbes), home parties (Tupperware), mail order (Otto Burlington), telemarketing (ICICI Bank cards), TV selling (Asian Sky Shop), Internet selling (Amazon, Indiatimes), and manufacturer-owned stores (Bata, Indian Oil/Bharat Petroleum petrol pumps).

Table 9.1: Levels of Various Channels in Accommodation Industry

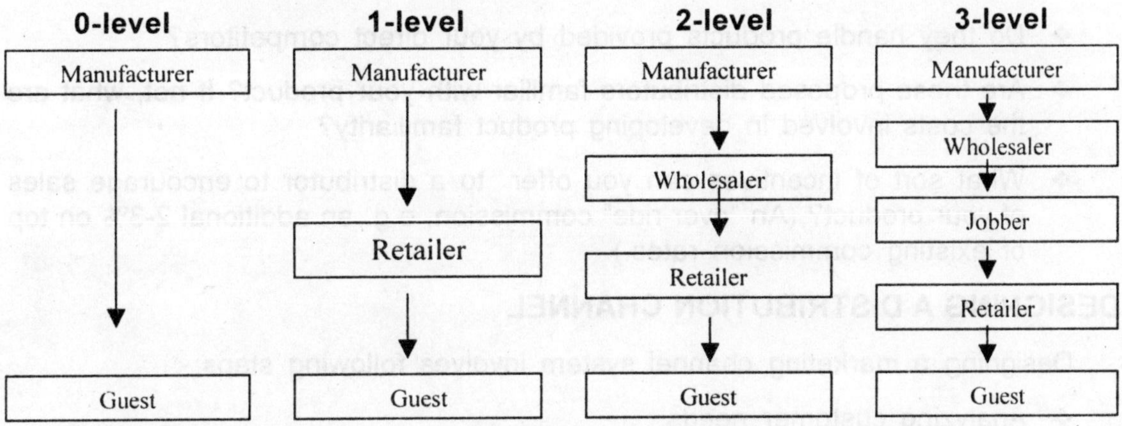

One-level channel contains one selling intermediary.

Two-level channel contains two selling intermediaries. These intermediaries could be retailers, distributors, a system-house or a combination of stockists/ wholesalers and retailers, distributors and dealers, or distributors, agents, and dealers.

Three-level channel contains wholesalers, jobber and retailers between the producer and the consumer.

Longer marketing channels also exist. As the number of levels increase, the level of difficulty of information sharing and coordination also increases. However, the cost of a channel system is not necessarily proportional to its length/levels. Channels normally describe a forward movement of products from source to uses which, are important in the following cases:

- to reuse products or containers
- to refurbish products (such as computers) for resale;
- to recycle products (such as paper); and
- to dispose off products and packaging (waste products).

Compiling a Distribution Strategy

It is very difficult to analyse which distribution channels will be the most profitable to be on an effective distribution strategy. Major considerations should include:

- How do your target markets currently purchase your products and how do you go about establishing a relationship with them?
- What distribution methods have you in mind that appeal to and reach your identified audiences?
- What sort of costs will be incurred by using these particular distributors?

- ❖ Are these proposed distributors enthusiastic about your product, and are potentially good sales ambassadors?
- ❖ Do they handle products provided by your direct competitors?
- ❖ Are these proposed distributors familiar with your product? If not, what are the costs involved in developing product familiarity?
- ❖ What sort of incentives can you offer to a distributor to encourage sales of your product? (An "over-ride" commission, e.g. an additional 2-3% on top of existing commission rates.)

DESIGNING A DISTRIBUTION CHANNEL

Designing a marketing channel system involves following steps:

- ❖ Analyzing customer needs,

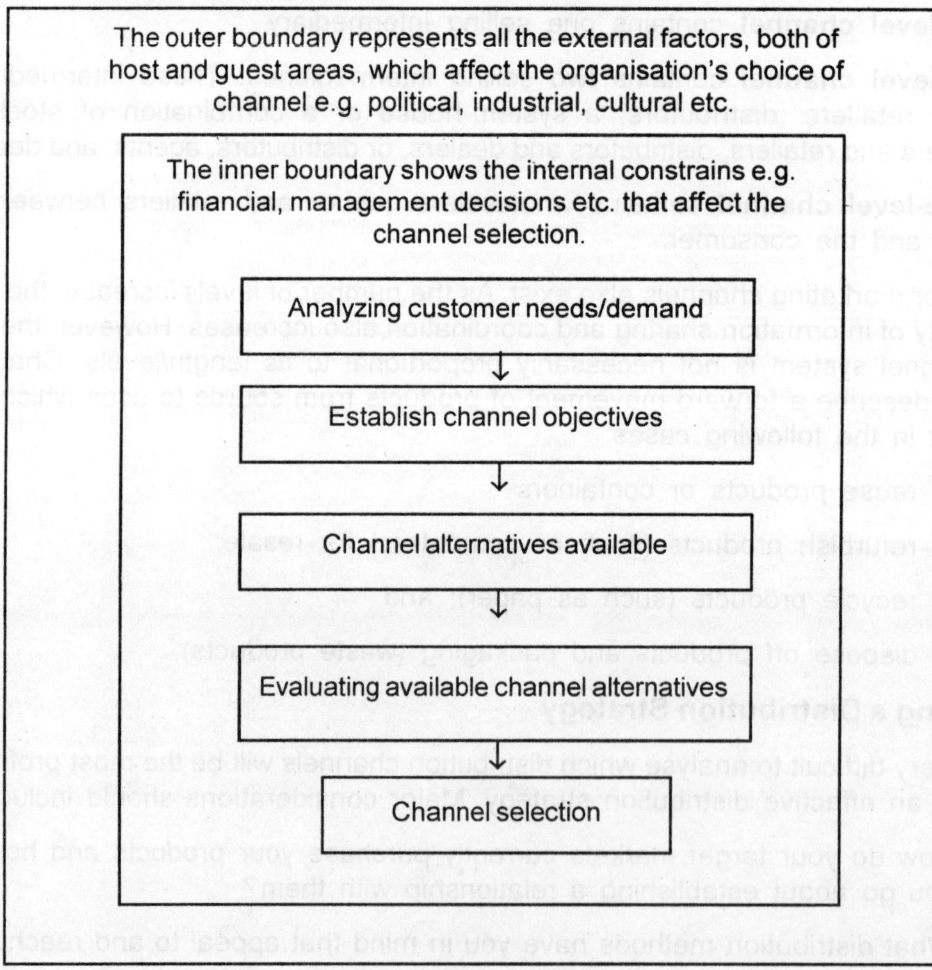

Box 9.1

- establishing channel objectives,
- identifying major channel alternatives, and
- evaluating major channel alternatives.

ANALYZING CUSTOMERS NEEDS

In designing the marketing channel, the marketer must understand the need of customers. The guests have certain expectations from channel, these are:

- The number of units: The channel permits a typical customer to purchase specific units on an occasion. A guest expects a larger size from the channel member.
- *Time*: It means waiting and delivery time. Faster the delivery, more preferred will be the channel.
- *Convenience*: The degree to which the marketing channel make it easy for cus-tomers to purchase the product. More convenient it is more preferred it will be.
- *Product variety*: More the number of products, more preferred channel will be.
- *Service back-up*: The add-on services (credit, delivery etc.) provided by the channel. The greater the service backup, the greater the work provided by the channel.

The marketing-channel designer knows that by providing these services will enhance the reliability. Greater service output means increased channel costs and higher prices for customers.

ESTABLISHING OBJECTIVES AND CONSTRAINTS

Channel objectives should be stated clearly. Under competitive conditions, channel institutions should arrange their functional tasks to minimize total channel costs. Usually planners can identify several market segments that want different service levels. Effective planning requires determining which market segments to serve and the best channel for each.

Channel objectives vary with product characteristics. Perishable products, require more direct marketing. Bulky products such as building materials require channels that minimize the shipping distance and the amount of handling. Products requiring installation or maintenance services such as heating and cooling systems are usually sold and maintained by the company or by franchised dealers. Channel design must take into account the strengths and weaknesses of different types of intermediaries. Channel design is also influenced by competitors' channels. Channel design must adapt to the larger environment, i.e. legal regulations, taxes, labour laws, etc.

IDENTIFYING MAJOR CHANNEL ALTERNATIVES

Companies can choose from a wide variety of channels for reaching customers from sales forces to agents, distributors, dealers, direct mail, telemarketing, and the Internet.

Each channel has unique strengths as well as weaknesses. Sales forces can handle complex products and transactions, but they are expensive. The Internet is much less expensive, but it cannot handle complex products. Distributors can create sales, but the company loses direct contact with customers.

The problem is further complicated by the fact that most companies now use a mix of channels. Each channel hopefully reaches a different segment of buyers and delivers the right products to each at the least cost. When this does not happen, there is usually channel conflict and excessive cost. A channel alternative is described by three elements:

- The types of available business intermediaries,
- The number of intermediaries needed, and
- The terms and responsibilities of each channel member.

The types of available business intermediaries: A firm needs to identify the types of intermediaries available to it. Out of these one or more may be selected. Sometimes a company chooses an unconventional channel because of the difficulty or cost of working with the dominant channel. The advantage is that the company will encounter less competition during the initial move into this channel. Companies have to decide on the number of intermediaries to be used at each channel level. Three strategies are available:

- Exclusive distribution,
- Elective distribution, and
- Intensive distribution.

Exclusive distribution means severely limiting the number of intermediaries. It is used when the producer wants to maintain control over the service level and outputs offered by the resellers. Often it involves exclusive dealing arrangements. By granting exclusive distribution, the producer hopes to obtain more dedicated and knowledgeable selling. It requires greater partnership between seller and reseller and is used in the distribution *of* new automobiles and some major appliances.

Selective distribution involves the use of more than a few but less than all of the intermediaries who are willing to carry a particular product. It is used by established companies and by new companies seeking distributors. The company does not have to worry about too many outlets. It can gain adequate market coverage with more control and less cost than intensive distribution. Disney and Titan Watches are good example of selective distribution.

Intensive distribution consists of the manufacturer placing the goods or services in as many outlets as possible. This strategy is generally used for items, such as tobacco products, soap, snack foods, and gum, products, for which the consumer requires a great deal of location convenience.

The producer must determine the rights and responsibilities of participating channel members. Each channel member must be treated respectfully and given the opportunity to be profitable. The main elements in the "trade-relations mix" are

- price policies,
- conditions of sale,
- territorial rights, and
- specific services to be performed by each party.

EVALUATING THE MAJOR ALTERNATIVES

Each channel alternative needs to be evaluated against economic, control and adaptive criteria. Economic criteria mean that each channel alternative will produce a different level of sales and costs. Different sales channels can be arranged in sequence of increasing cost but decreasing added value. The sequence is- internet, telemarketing, travel agents, sales force. Producers can also lure customers to the cheaper distribution channel that is by offering them discounts. This will benefit both the producer and the customer.

Control and adaptive criteria*:* Hotels have little control over travel agencies. As they are independent firms seeking to maximize their profits, where as hotel sales representatives work for their hotel only. So the extent of control must be kept in mind while designing the channels.

Apart from control, adaptability is another reason which must be looked after while designing a channel. Many factors, such as competition and technological changes, have necessitated that the channel should be such that it provides high adaptability.

Typology of Distribution Channels, region with market share and owner airlines

Region	CRS System	Market Share*	Owner Airlines
North America	Sabre	22%	American
	Worldspan	10%	Delta, Northwest, TWA
	System One		Continental
	Gemini	N/A	Air Canada, Canadian

North America/ Europe	Galileo International	22%	United, US Air, British Airways, Swiss Air, KLM, Alitalia, Olympic, Air Canada, Aer Lingus, Austrian, Air Portugal
Europe	Amadeus	27%	Air France, Lufthansa Iberia, SAS (merged with Continental's System One)
Asia-Pacific	Abacus Infini Axess Topas Southern Cross Fantasia	Combined 9%	Cathay Pacific, Singapore, Malaysia, Philipine, Royal Brunei, China Airlines All Nippon Japan Airlines Korean Airlines Australian, Ansett Airlines Qantas Airlines
Africa, Eastern Europe	Gets	N/A	Founded by SITA (aviation telecom company) to serve Africa, Eastern Europe & Latin America

CHANNEL BEHAVIOUR AND ORGANIZATION

A distribution system consists of many dissimilar firms that have come together for their common good. These associations may range from informal to formal types. In some way or another they are balancing to each other and their success lies in their working together. Each channel member is dependent on others, playing a role in the channel and specializing in performing one or more functions. In this kind of situation, they must work for mutual benefits rather than benefits of individuals. But the case is not so, often it is seen that the member work for their own goals and profits. This leads to frequent channel conflicts. These are of two types:

- Horizontal Conflict, and
- Vertical Conflict

Horizontal conflict is conflict between firms at the same level of the channel. For example, some restaurant franchisees may complain about other franchisees cheating on ingredients and giving poor service, thereby hurting the overall image.

Vertical conflict, which is more common, refers to conflicts between different levels of the same channel. The conflict between travel agent and hotel is example of this.

These conflicts up to some extents are required so that a healthy competition keeps the channel alive. But again if these are not managed properly, they can lead to disastrous effect on the entire channel.

CHANNEL SYSTEM

The types of channel system are:

1. Conventional Marketing system
2. Vertical Marketing System
   - Corporate
   - Administered
   - Contractual
3. Horizontal Marketing Systems
4. Multi-channel Marketing Systems

Conventional Marketing system

A conventional distribution channel consists of one or more independent producers, wholesalers, and retailers. Each is a separate business entity seeking to maximize its profits, even at the expense of profits for the system as a whole. No channel member has much control over the other members, and no formal means exist for assigning roles and resolving channel conflict. For example most hotels pay a commission to travel agents. No formal contract is signed be-tween the hotel and travel agent. The hotel simply communicates its policy and can, if it wishes, make rooms unavailable to travel agents on a temporary basis.

Vertical marketing system (VMS)

It consists of producers, wholesalers, and retailers acting as a unified system. One channel member owns the others, has contracts with them, or has so much power that they all co-operate .The vertical marketing system can be dominated by the producer, wholesaler, or retailer. VMSs were originally developed to control channel behaviour and manage channel conflict. Another major benefit is economies through size, bargaining power, and elimination of duplicated services. The VMSs have become dominant in consumer marketing, serving as much as 64% of the total market.

There are three main types of VMS: a *corporate VMS* is attained through common ownership at different levels in the channel. The company owns all the channel levels and roles and responsibilities are well defined. Every channel member has to follow the same goals and objectives. For example a hotel may have its own garden which supplies the required vegetables.

In an *administered VMS,* the size and power of the members decides the coordination. The strongest among the members decides the roles and responsibilities.

In a *contractual VMS*, there are contractual agreements among channel members. And every member is bound by the law to follow the roles and responsibilities assigned to them. An important form of contractual VMS is franchising.

FRANCHISING

"Franchising is a method of doing business by which a franchisee is granted the right to engage in offering, selling, or distributing goods or services under a marketing format which is designed by the franchisor. The franchisor permits the franchisee to use its trademark, name, and advertising." Franchising has been the fastest-growing retailing form in recent years which involves comparatively low cost (in form of fee) and more benefits. The advantages of the franchise to the franchisee (person or organization buying the franchise) are:

- Recognition of brand
- Less chance of a business failure
- National advertising, pre-made advertisements, and marketing plans
- Faster business growth
- Help with site selection
- Architectural plans
- Operational systems, software, and manual to support the systems
- National contracts with suppliers
- Product development
- Consulting
- Help with financing

The disadvantages of purchasing a franchise are:

- Fees and royalties are required.

- ❖ It limits the products you sell and the recipes you use.
- ❖ You are often required to be open a minimum number of hours and offer certain products.
- ❖ A poorly operated company can affect the reputation of the entire chain.
- ❖ The franchisor's performance affects the profitability of franchisees.
- ❖ Some franchisees may not benefit from national advertising as much as other franchisees often a source of conflict.

One of the reasons that companies decide to franchise is that it allows for increased distribution of their products. The franchisee's money expands the business, while the franchisor collects an initial fee and royalties. Franchising is not effective for all companies. The company must be able to offer the operational systems, management support, and a good business concept. For new businesses it requires time and money to provide a good franchisee package. Smaller chains often franchise to people who are close to business. For example, franchising is used in smaller restaurant chains to help them re-tain managers. It is difficult for a small chain to compete with opportunities that a large chain offers its managers. Some small chains combat career opportunities the large chains offer by helping their best managers get their own store through franchising. This allows the chain to keep managers who might otherwise grow bored and unchallenged. The advantages of franchising for the franchisor are as follows:

- ❖ Receives a percentage of gross sales
- ❖ Expands brand
- ❖ Support for national advertising campaign
- ❖ Negotiating support for national contracts with suppliers.

The disadvantages of a franchise for a franchisor are as follows:

- ❖ There are limits on other options of expanding distribution; for example the ability to develop alliances may be limited if the alliances may violate the territorial agreements of the franchisees.
- ❖ Franchisees must be monitored to ensure product consistency.
- ❖ There is limited ability to require franchisees to change operations;
- ❖ Franchisees want and need to have an active roll in decision making.

Alliances: Alliances are another form of contractual agreement. Alliances are developed to allow two organizations to benefit from each other's strengths. Thus both partners benefited from the alliance. Alliances by two or more non-competing firms are a popular and effective way of expanding markets. For example, restaurants are developing alliances with convenience stores and hotel properties to distribute their products. Airlines are developing alliances to access customers in other parts of the world and to provide their customers with new destination opportunities.

Horizontal Marketing Systems

Another channel development is horizontal marketing systems, in which two or more companies at one level join to follow a new marketing opportunity. By working together, companies can combine their capital production capabilities, or marketing resources to accomplish more than one company can working alone. For example, many restaurants have combined to open large food outlets.

Multichannel Marketing Systems

In these types of marketing systems, the companies go for different type of channels at the same time. Today, with the proliferation of customer segments and channel possibilities, more companies have adopted this distribution. Such multi-channel marketing occurs when a single firm sets up two or more marketing channels to reach one or more customer segments. For example, McDonald's sells through a network of independent franchisees but owns more than one-fourth of its outlets. Thus the wholly owned restaurants compete to some extent with those owned by McDonald's franchisees.

The multi-channel marketer gains sales with each new channel but also risks offending existing channels. As the existing channels may feel threatened unless it limits competition or repays them in some way.

CONCLUSION

No matter how impressive your product, its success relies on customers knowing you exist in the marketplace. Choosing the most effective distribution system to reach and then sell to your target audiences will help you succeed. An efficient product distribution strategy should facilitate product sales in advance of their actual use. Different distribution channels have different functions in the system. It becomes important that every channel member must function as per its role. These functions are assigned to the channel members at the time of making a distribution channel and strategy. If it is not done at the earlier stages then there will conflicts among members. To avoid these most of the organization likes to have formal agreements so that everyone's interests can be protected without compromising on profits. Many new innovative and profitable systems are coming up which can solve these problems. In the last, it can be said as the old proverb stands true "united we stand, divided we fall." Every channel member must try to act in such manner that every member gets their share of profit.

ACTIVITY

- ❖ Visit a distribution channel agency of hotel products and find out its distribution strategy.

QUESTIONS

1. What do you understand by distribution channels? Write a brief note on its functions.
2. Enlist some points that you consider appropriate for a distribution strategy.
3. Write note on channels behaviour and organizational setup.

10

MAJOR HOSPITALITY DISTRIBUTION CHANNELS-II (Reservation System, Global Distribution Systems and Internet)

— *SURJEET KUMAR*[1]

The tourism and hospitality industry is a thriving sector of world economy in present time and in India too this sector is growing very fast. Hospitality meets boarding, lodging and recreational needs of people in different areas. In India, it is one of the booming sectors. Year 2006 has been the best year so far in term of foreign arrival, which reached a record 4.5 millions. Currently this sector is growing at the rate of 10-15 per cent. This is one of the vital sectors for Indian economy, since it contributes to 5.9 per cent of the GDP and provides employment to 41.8 million people.

Distribution channel plays a very important role in promotion of hospitality services to customers. In the previous unit you have already studied few important distribution channels such as travel agents, tour operators and consortia. In the continuation to that, we will explore few more distribution channels equally important for hospitality industry.

OBJECTIVES

After completion of this unit your will be able to know more about hospitality distribution channels, such as:

a) Reservation System

b) Global Distribution Systems

c) Internet.

RESERVATION SYSTEMS

Reservation has a very broad meaning but when it comes to hospitality industry it is generally referred to an agreement between a supplier and customer. Hospitality industry includes three important components, such as lodging, food and beverage

---

1. Lecturer in Hotel Management at Kurukshetra University, Kurukshetra, Haryana.

companies and travel and tourism services. So, for a travel and tourism it can be referred as "An agreement reached between a supplier and a traveller or travel agent or a clerical or electronic process whereby a seat, a room, a berth or other accommodation is withdrawn from sale and set aside for the use of a specific person, often on payment of a deposit."

Same way, reservation in the context of the front office of a hotel means "the booking or reserving of a bedroom by a guest and involves a particular type of guest-room being reserved for a particular person or persons for a certain period of time". When a reservation or room booking is made at a hotel it is expected that the hotel will honour its commitment in accepting that reservation and guarantee that a room will be available when a guest arrives.

This is same with other components of hospitality industry too, which can be any entertainment centres or restaurants etc.

Broadly, the reservations have been classified into following:

1) Confirmed Reservation: (where the supplier confirms the reservation.)
2) Unconfirmed Reservation: (where the supplier does not confirm the reservation.)

Reservation system is man-made system which main objective is to aid the customer in making the reservations from anywhere at anytime. Today it is very important for hospitality and tourism industry to grow. Now-a-days it is acting as a fuel for growth of hospitality industry. Take an example of hotels, one of the impotant components of hospitality industry, where an in-house reservation system can keep close track of reservations. Systems can tightly control room availability data and automatically generate many reservation-related reports. Automated systems can also generate reports summarizing reservations by room type, guest profile, and many other characteristics. The biggest advantage of a reservation system is the unproved accuracy of room availability and rate information. Some reservation systems are programmed to automatically suggest alternative room types or rates, or even other nearby hotel properties. System can be programmed to itemize room availability for future periods and may display open, closed, and special event dates for an extended period of time. Special event dates can be programmed to alert reservations agents that a convention or large group is expected to occupy the hotel either before, during, or immediately following a caller's requested day of arrival. In addition, many reservation systems have a management override feature which enables overbooking. This override provision should be exercised with extreme care.

Computer Reservation Systems (CRSs) have had the most crucial contribution to the tourism industry in the 1980s and have dominated the industry. Essentially computerized systems assist tourism enterprises with handling their inventories profitably and with facilitating the tourism products distribution. The CRSs are normally operated by tourist producers such as airlines, hotels and tour operators and are distributed nationally or globally, via computerized or videotext systems. They normally use mainframes and extensive networks to support many remote terminals in travel agencies or other tourism enterprises. Reservation systems originally appeared in the early 1960s, aiming to offer an efficient tool for handling and managing inventory. The rapid growth of both tourism demand and supply in previous decades had demonstrated that the industry could be managed only by powerful computerized systems. Airlines were the pioneers in introducing this technology, as they replaced their manual booking systems with electronic databases. Soon, international hotel chains and tour operators realized the potential and followed suit by developing centralized information and reservation systems. The CRS is often used as an umbrella term to include the entire variety of systems used. The CRSs can provide important strategic tools for both enterprises and destinations, while they can also form autonomous strategic business units (SBUs) and act as a new independent tourism distribution industry.

Computer Reservation Systems are drivers for the globalization of tourism and hospitality. This can be understood in terms of four drivers, that is cost drivers (helps in increasing efficiency, low distribution cost, low communication cost, low labour cost, minimize the waste factor, and act as flexible pricing), market drivers (helps in satisfying sophisticated demand, flexibility in time of operation, support specialization and differentiation, provide last minute deals, accurate information, support relationship marketing strategies for frequent customers, quick reaction on demand fluctuation, market research), government and regulatory drivers (helps in deregulation, liberalization, government support) and competitive drivers (help in managing networks of enterprises, value- added skill building, flexibility, knowledge acquisition, strategic tool, barrier to entry.) so one say that they are the driving force of both tourism and hospitality industry.

GLOBAL DISTRIBUTION SYSTEMS (GDS)

Global Distribution System

A computer reservation system, typically owned jointly by airlines in different countries, that includes reservation databases of suppliers in many countries. This term has largely replaced by "computerized reservation system (CRS)" as the term of choice within the industry. The CRS is Worldwide-computerized reservation network used as a single point of access for reserving airline seats, hotels rooms, rental cars, and other travel related items by travel agents, online reservation sites, and large corporations. The premier GDS are Amadeus, Galileo, Sabre, and World span owned and operated as joint ventures by major airlines, car rental firms, and hotel groups. It is also called automated reservation system (ARS) or computerized reservation systems (CRS).

The largest and best known GDSs include SABRE, Galileo International, Amadeus, and World-Span. Each GDS is owned by an airline or consortium of airlines. GDSs provide worldwide distribution of hotel reservation information and allow selling of hotel reservations around the world. GDSs also provide distribution of airline tickets, automobile rentals, and other services required by travellers.

Selling hotel rooms is usually accomplished by connecting the hotel company reservation system with the GDSs. Most travel agents around the world have terminals connected to one or more of the many airline reservation systems to book airline travel. By having hotel accommodations and automobile rentals available in the computer system at the same time, most GDSs provide single source access to most of the travel agent's selling requirements. In one transaction, a travel agent can sell an airline ticket, hotel room, and automobile rental.

With over 200,000 terminals around the world, GDSs have become a powerful force in hotel reservations. Nearly 37 million of America's more than 162-million active Internet users have already purchased travel online. Online travel bookings exceeded $23 billion in 2001. The airline industry created the first GDS in the 1960s as a way to keep track of flight schedules, availability, and prices. Although accused of being "dinosaurs" due to their use of legacy system technology, the GDSs were actually among the first e-commerce companies in the world facilitating B-2-B electronic commerce as early as the mid 1970s.

Currently, there are four major GDS systems:

- Amadeus
- Galileo
- Sabre
- Worldspan

In addition, there are several smaller or regional GDSs, including SITA's Sahara, Infini (Japan), Axess (Japan), Tapas (Korea), Fantasia (South Pacific), and Abacus (Asia/Pacific) that serve interests or specific regions or countries. Let us know more about these Major GDS systems.

Amadeus

Founded in 1987 by Air France, Iberia, Lufthansa, and SAS, Amadeus is the youngest of the four GDS companies. Amadeus is a leading global distribution system and technology providers serving the marketing, sales, and distribution needs of the world's travel and tourism industries. Its comprehensive data network and database, among the largest of their kind in Europe, serve more than 57,000 travel agency locations and more than 10,500 airline sales offices in some 200 markets worldwide. The system can also provide access to approximately 58,000 hotels and 50 car rental companies serving some 24,000 locations, as well as other provider groups, including ferry, rail, cruise, insurance, and tour operators.

Galileo International

Galileo International was founded in 1993 by 11 major North American and European airlines: It includes Aer Lingus, Air Canada, Alitalia, Austrian Airlines, British Airways, KLM Royal Dutch Airlines, Olympic Airlines, Swissair, TAP, Air Portugal, United Airlines and US Airways. It is a major player in the GDS business mailny in North America, Europe, the Middle East, Africa, and the Asia/Pacific region. Galileo International is a diversified and global technology leader. Its core business is providing electronic global distribution services for the travel industry through its computerized reservation systems, leading-edge products and innovative Internet-based solutions. Galileo is a value-added distributor of travel inventory dedicated to supporting its travel agency and corporate customers and, through them, expanding traveller choice.

In 1997, Galileo International became a publicly traded company, listed on the New York and Chicago Stock Exchanges. In October of 2001, Cendant Corporation acquired Galileo International for approximately $1.8 billion in common stock and cash. Currently, the company is represented in 116 countries, and serves travel agencies at approximately 45,000 locations. Other travel suppliers include 500 airlines, 227 hotel companies, 33 car rental companies, and 368 tour operators.

Galileo's competitive strengths include market share, well balanced and global presence, relationships with diverse groups of travel vendors, technologically advanced information systems, highly skilled personnel, and a stable product line. Compared to other GDS companies, Galileo is a cautious follower when it comes to technology.

Sabre

For more than 40 years, Sabre has been developing innovations and transforming the business of travel. From the original Sabre computer reservations system in the 1960s, to advanced airline yield management systems in the 1980s, has touched all points of the travel industry. Sabre, represented in 45 countries, is a leading provider of technology for the travel industry and provides innovative products that enable travel commerce and services, and enhance airline/supplier operations.

Headquartered in Southlake, Texas, Sabre connects more than 60,000 travel agency locations around the world, providing content from approximately 400 airlines, 55,000 hotel properties, 52 car rental companies, 9 cruise lines, 33 railroads, and 229 tour operators. In addition to being one of the leading GDS companies, Sabre also provides a broad range of products and services that enhance travel agency operations and their ability to serve the traveller. Sabre-connected travel agencies use Sabre web-based technologies and low-fare finding solutions to create new sales opportunities, drive operational efficiencies, and improve customer service. Among the company's recent innovations Sabre Virtually There is a personalized web site service that automatically gives travellers up-to-the-minute details about itineraries, while also providing a wealth of information about their destinations.

Worldspan

Founded on 7th February, 1990, Worldspan was originally owned by affiliates of Delta Air Lines, Inc., Northwest Airlines, and Trans World Airlines, Inc. It is currently owned by affiliates of Delta Air Lines, Inc. (40%), Northwest Airlines (34%), and American Airlines, Inc. (26%). Since its 1995 advance into the world of Internet technology for the travel industry, Worldspan has successfully developed the strategies, solutions, and services to ensure the company's long-term success in the new web-based world of travel distribution. Worldspan provides worldwide electronic distribution of travel information, Internet products and connectivity, and e-commerce capabilities for travel agencies, travel service providers, and corporations. Worldspan currently serves 20,021 travel agencies in nearly 90 countries and territories. Headquartered in Atlanta, Georgia, Worldspan connects approximately 421 airlines, 210 hotel companies, 40 car rental companies, 39 tour and vacation operators, and 44 special travel service suppliers.

Internet

The Internet, sometimes called simply "the Net," is a worldwide system of computer networks - a network of networks in which users at any one computer can, if they have permission, get information from any other computer (and sometimes talk directly to users at other computers). It was conceived by the Advanced Research Projects Agency (ARPA) of the U.S. government in 1969 and was first known as the ARPANET. The original aim was to create a network that would allow users of a research computer at one university to be able to "talk to" research computers at other universities. A side benefit of ARPANet's design was that, because messages could be routed or rerouted in more than one direction, the network could continue to function even if parts of it were destroyed in the event of a military attack or other disaster.

Today, the Internet is a public, cooperative, and self-sustaining facility accessible to hundreds of millions of people worldwide. The most widely used part of the Internet is the World Wide Web (often abbreviated "www" or called "the Web"). Its outstanding feature is hypertext, a method of instant cross-referencing. In most Web sites, certain words or phrases appear in text of a different colour than the rest; often this text is also underlined. When you select one of these words or phrases, you will be transferred to the site or page that is relevant to this word or phrase. Sometimes there are buttons, images, or portions of images that are "click able." If you move the pointer over a spot on a Web site and the pointer changes into a hand, this indicates that you can click and be transferred to another site.

Now, it is the era of e-commerce, the Internet is also very widely used as a mode of business tourism and hospitality industry is not an exception, Many airlines, hotel companies, and car rental firms offer online reservation services through their Internet site. This enables travellers from many different market segments to use their personal computers to book flights, reserve hotel rooms, and select rental cars. Vacation travellers, business travellers, corporate travel offices, international visitors—all are able to use the World Wide Web to arrange for their own travel and accommodation needs. The variety of potential guests accessing Internet sites to place reservations has prompted travel and hospitality companies to develop simple, user-friendly reservation procedures.

While making reservation through Internet, following process has to be followed:

- ✳ Users first identify the area where he has to travel and fits to its travel needs
- ✳ The dates of travel.
- ✳ Then it selects the hotel, after selecting it, users input the necessary reservation information.
- ✳ They can guarantee their reservations by providing personal or corporate credit card data.

In addition to providing a user-friendly reservations process and securing transactions. Online systems also perform important functions like:

- ✳ Marketing services for the hospitality company.
- ✳ Reservation features of many Internet sites enable users to access detailed pictures of individual hotels. Some enable users to download multimedia presentations of the features and benefits of the hotel chain and of individual hotels—complete with a "walk through" of the property and a virtual tour inside the various rooms and services offered offered.

CASE STUDIES

Royal Orchid Group

Royal Orchid Group, earlier known as Balajee Hotels, The Group's properties include Hotel Royal Orchid, Royal Orchid Central, Royal Orchid Harsha and Royal Orchid Resort in Bangalore; Royal Orchid Metropole and Royal Orchid Brindavan Garden in Mysore; Royal Orchid Central, Jaipur and Royal Orchid Golden Suites, Pune has been expanding aggressively across India in the last few years. However, the rapid growth and expansion posed new challenges for the group as it could not maximize its revenues as the group had manual bookings system in place, owing to which it was becoming increasingly difficult to optimally manage nearly sold out capacities. The case was more to do with offering rooms at right rates instead of serving on a first come first serve basis to maximize revenue. Also managing last minute cancellations and co-ordinations with property and the guests were becoming tedious and time consuming. Since the group has multiple properties, their objective was to offer alternate accommodation at other properties in case rooms were not available in the desired property.

Fortune Central and Fortune Enterprise

Fortune Enterprise is a complete Property Management System, designed to empower, improve productivity, performance for full-service hotels and hospitality enterprise operations. It is built around the most contemporary technologies, for properties looking at integrating their entire operations. It is a comprehensive system with the capability to address all the computing needs of a modern hotel or resort.

Fortune Central is the best of its class; end-to-end Central System that has the capability of delivering customized functionality and superior scalability from mid size to large segment hotels, resorts and property chains. Integrating Fortune Central with Fortune Property Management System extends the ability to provide enhanced customer service and pilot better operating efficiencies centrally.

IDS

Headquartered at Bangalore, IDS currently has more than 1200 clients in around 20 countries. IDS has offices at Mumbai, Delhi, Kolkata, Hyderabad, Chennai and Goa in India and several offices globally. IDS specializes in comprehensive and integrated software solutions under the brand name 'Fortune' for the entire spectrum of the hospitality industry. IDS technology team has a combined domain experience of over 600 man years. The company's development and global support centre at Bangalore offers support to its customer on a 24 x 7 x 365 basis. Its customers include Fortune Suite powers Sarovar Hotels and Resorts, ITC Fortune Park Hotels, Pride Group of Hotels and Club Mahindra Holidays to name a few.

ACTIVITY

- Explore various Global Distribution System (GDS) used by star category hotels and approved travel agents in India.
- Visit any hotel or tourism organization Internet site and take out the information about them.

QUESTION

1. How GDS is an important hospitality distribution channel? Comment.
2. What are the benefits and burdens through internet reservation.

11

MAJOR PLAYERS IN HOSPITALITY INDUSTRY – AN INTERNATIONAL SCENARIO

— *VINAY RANA*[1]

With the marked improvement in the aviation industry and the arrivals of Boeing jets and jumbo jets, the international travel became an enormously growing phenomenon in 1958. The upsurge in international business and tourism called for the need for large international hotel chains. By the 1960s the international hotel chains like Sheraton, Park royal, Hilton, Holiday Inn, Ramada Inn, Marriotts, and Intercontinental group emerged as the key players in the hoteliering industry. This mobility transformed the industry from small, wholly owned, and independently operated properties to the concept of development by franchising, partnership, leasing and management contract.

OBJECTIVES

After this unit you will be able to learn:

- ❖ The growth and development of International hotel chains.
- ❖ The need for expansion of hotel chains in the present globalization scenario.
- ❖ Various hotel chains and their affiliates.

THE EMERGENCE OF HOTELIERING IN THE AGE OF PROSPERITY

The first quarter of the twentieth century was outlined with the emergence of hotel properties. King Alphonse XIII was intent on having a luxurious hotel in his capital at Madrid, as a result the Hotel Ritz was inaugurated in 1910. Barcelona, not to be left behind, inaugurated its own Ritz in 1919. It offered an unheard of luxury at that time, bathrooms with hot as well as cold water. In the same era many other luxurious hotels were built namely, the Ritz and Savoy in London, the Beau Rivage Palace in Lausanne, le Négresco in Nice, the Plaza in New York, the Métropole in Brussels, the Plaza-Atheneé and l'Hôtel de Crillon in Paris, the Taj Mahal in Bombay and so on. The hotel Taj Mahal was renovated in 1972 by the Inter-Continental chain.

---

1. Assistant Prof. at Kukreja Institute of Hotel Management, Dehradun, Uttarakhand.

The economic growth in nineteen-twenties saw a marked boom in the hotel industry. Numerous hotels were established in this decade. In 1923, the architects Marchisio and Prost constructed a hotel in some wonderful gardens in the heart of Marrakech in Morocco, and for decades it was considered the most beautiful hotel in the world: La Mamounia. Winston Churchill helped to forge its reputation by becoming a frequent guest. Hotels not only came in cities, but also in the mountains. The first ski resorts in Switzerland (Saint-Moritz, Gstaad, Montana, etc.) welcomed tourists (often English ones) to some very renowned establishments. The worldwide economic crisis led to depression in 1929, but it did not prevent the construction of the famous Waldorf Astoria in New York. This stood as the greatest hotel edifice of those troubled times.

After the end of second world war, the fifties saw the second boom in the hotel industry. The Club Méditerranée (G. Trigano) created the now famous, but then revolutionary concept of the club village. The first casino hotel came up during this period. This was also the time when the airline companies began to develop their own hotels. In the sixties, new tourist resorts flourished around the Mediterranean. From Spain to Greece and from the Balearics to Yugoslavia, numerous city and beach hotels opened their doors to summer guests hungry for relaxation and a good dose of sunshine. Portugal and the Scandinavian countries soon followed their lead.

EMERGENCE OF INTERNATIONAL BRANDS

1970 saw the beginning of the construction of hotels for business people. This movement of buissness travel was supported by several factors. There was the sudden economic boom, due to black gold the crude oil, of Middle Eastern countries which attracted business people from the entire world. This forged a business travel trend - not limited to this region alone - which resulted in the development of hotels primarily designed for business travellers in Middle-Eastern cities like, Abu Dhabi, Dubai, Riyadh and Jeddah, to mention only the most important.

Hotel chains, in accordance to customer's expectations, started to offer an increasingly varied range of services. Their rooms became more spacious and the cuisine more refined. Gradually various first class hotels (among them former palaces and city centre hotels) which had fallen into disrepair began systematic renovation programmes. The end of the seventies, when China opened its doors to foreign tourists, also saw the first congresses of international hotel experts.

The eighties defined the third hotel industry boom - The third boom in the hotel industry began in 1980, marked by more inventive marketing and the development of hotels increasingly adapted to a particular type of clientele. This trend prompted the construction of hotels near airports, hotels for conferences, health hotels, ski holiday hotels, holiday villages and marina hotels. The first Property Management Systems (Fidelio, Hogatex, etc.) appear in the hospitality market.

In 1984, work began on the renovation and transformation into a hotel of the prestigious sultans' residence, the Ciragan Palace in Istanbul. The resulting hotel is no less prestigious than the Ciragan Palace was. Managed by the Kempinski chain. It opened its 322 rooms to guests in 1991. In the eighties, too, the Far East began to prepare itself to welcome both business people and the tourists who were beginning to discover the countries of the rising sun, such as China, South Korea, Thailand and Japan. The international chains (American for the most part) prepared expansion plans for Europe, the Middle and Far East which were mainly aimed at congress participants and business people.

The nineties saw the impact of technology on hoteliering - The early nineties were defined by a recession in the hotel business, caused by reductions in multinationals' travel budgets and the growing crisis in the Gulf. The Gulf War helped to create great insecurity for both individuals and business. 1991 was considered to be the black year of the hotel trade. It forced hoteliers to become more creative in finding ways of attracting guests (special programmes, offers for "frequent travellers", high performance reservation systems) and thus emerge from the crisis with the minimum damage. For the first time, the environment and energy conservation played an important role in the marketing activities of numerous chains (thanks in part to the green movement) and even helped to win the loyalty of numerous clients while safeguarding assets at the same time.

Reservation systems became more efficient and offered the hotelier a new dimension in the creation of customer loyalty, the database. The records of each guest's individual history have helped to create individualised marketing programmes and have enabled hotels to satisfy a guest's personal needs from the moment of his arrival. Hotel Adlon Berlin from its opening in 1907, until it was destroyed in 1945, was a symbol of Berlin. Now it has been rebuilt (1997) on its original site, the corner of Unter den Linden and Pariser Platz, facing the Brandenburg Gate. Outside, it is a virtual replica of the original; inside it is testimony to what smart hotel operators (in this case the Kempinski group) can accomplish with an investment of $260 million. The hotel's 337 rooms and suites are the ultimate in luxury. Interiors, designed by England's Ezra Attia and Sweden's Lars Malmquist, dazzle with marble, sandstone, stained glass, gold leaf, stuccowork, cherry wood panelling, and damask draperies. This hotel is today equipped with the most advanced technology with regards to the Room Management System communicating with the Property Management System.

Since 1992 technology has started to take its rightful place in hotel administration (simplification of check-in and check-out procedures, global reservation systems, marketing management etc.). In 1995, the first Hotel Room Management System is launched at the European level. It is linked to the most popular Property Management Systems to make the front desk more efficient and near to the guests.

Since 1990 hotel chains had been searching for alliances and some of them. For example: Holyday Inn, Intercontinental, and Crown Plaza have merged to form

Six continents hotels Chain; Marriot absorbed Renaissance and Ramada International; Sol Melia opened a new line of Boutique hotels, Accor signed several joint ventures in the East and the Far East, etc.) Forte acquired Méridien to reinforce its global position. Starwoods (Sheraton) absorbed the Italian Ciga chain and Westin.

The main expansion zones for the hotel industry in 1994 remained Asia (particularly China and India), the Middle East (above all, the United Arab Emirates and Egypt) and Latin America. In Europe, hotel enterprises in the eastern countries (Russia, Croatia, Slovakia, etc.) decided to renovate dilapidated palaces built at the turn of the century. All the European capitals started to invest in preparations for the major event of this fin de siècle period, that is, the celebration of our entry into the third millennium. Capitals throughout the world were busy developing the necessary infrastructure to welcome the millions of tourists for the celebration of this event.

Major hotel chains are drawing up development plans in almost all parts of Europe. These plans primarily involve the renovation of numerous prestigious hotels in both western and eastern European countries. Gradually, the great capitals of Europe have been endowed with hotels boasting three, four and five stars, offering quality services, innovative architecture, style, charm, and interior design (city Boutique hotels). Specialised hotels offer wellness programs including health and beauty centres, personalised services and treatments, anti-stress, revitalising, regenerating programmes, etc.

In 1995 construction began in Dubai of one of the most ambitious and prestigious tourist complexes in the region, the Jumeirah Beach Hotels (Jumeirah Beach hotel, Burj Al Arab, etc.). These comprise several establishments capable of satisfying the needs of average tourists, business people and those who can afford real luxury. The talk now is of six- and seven-star hotels, a surprising designation which is nevertheless perfectly justified by the luxury of the bedrooms and the facilities they offer, the impeccable service, the high degree of modern technology, as well as the beauty of the surroundings and the high-quality environment.

A BRIEF PREVIEW OF SOME PROMINENT INTERNATIONAL BRANDS

Accor

With 145,000 associates in 140 countries, Accor is the European leader and one of the world's largest groups in travel, tourism and corporate services, with two major international activities: (1) Hotels: 3,500 hotels (400,000 rooms) in 90 countries, travel agencies, restaurants and casinos. Accor's hotel brands worldwide include: Sofitel; Novotel; Mercure; Ibis; Etap Hotel; Formule 1; Red Roof Inns; Motel 6; Suitehotel; Coralia; and Thalassa International and (2) services to corporate clients and public institutions: each day, 12 million people in 31 countries use a broad range of services (Food Vouchers, People's Care, Expenses Management, Social Services, Incentive/Events) engineered and managed by Accor.

art'otels (by Park Plaza Hotels Europe)

art'otels are stylishly decorated 4-star modern hotels whereby each hotel is dedicated to a famous contemporary artist. art'otels are well-known for their "art'rageous" service and cater to those who live and travel "artfully". art'otel brand characteristics: (1) an inspiring fusion of travel, architecture and contemporary art, (2) individual service in a relaxed atmosphere offering all modern guest facilities and (3) stunning design and great original artwork appeals to both leisure and business travellers.

Banyan Tree Hotels and Resorts

The corporate mission of Banyan Tree Hotels and Resorts is to develop and manage upmarket luxury boutique resorts, which are steeped in Asian traditions and are environmentally sensitive. Banyan Tree offers an intimate retreat experience featuring its own signature blend of romance, rejuvenation and exotic sensuality. The philosophy behind the resorts is based on providing a place for rejuvenation of the body, mind and soul—a Sanctuary for the Senses. Banyan Tree's multiple award-winning resorts are currently located in Phuket, Thailand, the Maldives and in Bintan, Indonesia. The company is embarking on a rapid expansion plan with Banyan Tree Seychelles opening in early 2002, Banyan Tree Pokhara, Nepal after 2002 and Banyan Tree Mexico in 2003.

Best Western

Best Western is the world's largest hotel chain. The company had 4,065 hotels in 82 countries and territories. It is a membership association of independently owned and operated hotels that provides marketing, reservations and operational support to its members.

Boutique Hotel Group LLC

Boutique Hotel Management Group LLC operates a collection of boutique hotels that offer personalized services, superior locations and distinctive architectural designs. The gracious residential quality of each hotel makes it the address of choice for leading corporate travellers, designers, entrepreneurs, media and fashion executives, and leisure guests.

Bristol Hotels and Resorts

Bristol Hotels and Resorts is the largest owner of full-service hotels in North America and the largest Holiday Inn franchisee in the world.

Carlson Hospitality Worldwide

Through the operations of Carlson Hospitality WorldwideSM, Carlson Companies, Inc. is a major force in the world's hotel, resort, restaurant and cruise ship industries. Specific companies include Radisson Hotels WorldwideSM, Regent International

Hotels,Country Inns & Suites By Carlson, Friday's Hospitality Worldwide Inc., and Radisson Seven Seas Cruises.

Cendant Corporation

Cendant Corporation was a New York-based provider of business and consumer services, primarily within the real estate and travel industries. On 15th September, 2004, Cendant purchased the Ramada International Hotels & Resorts unit from Marriott International. At the time, Ramada was primarily a franchised brand of 204 hotels operating in 26 countries and territories. Earlier in 2004, Cendant acquired the trademark rights to the Ramada brand in the United States, where there are 819 franchised properties. It also owns the Canadian rights. On 31st July, 2006, both the Cendant Real Estate division as well as the Cendant Hospitality division were spun-off and became separate companies under the names Realogy and Wyndham Worldwide, respectively. Realogy was subsequently bought by Apollo. Wyndham Worldwide diversify into following brands:-

- Amerihost Inn
- Days Inn
- Howard Johnson
- Knights Inn
- Ramada
- Super 8 Motels
- Travelodge
- Wingate Inn
- Wyndham Hotels and Resorts
- Baymont Inn and Suites

Conrad Hotels and Resorts (by Hilton)

Conrad Hotels and Resorts is the contemporary luxury brand of the Hilton Family of Hotels, with 18 properties in cosmopolitan destinations across the US, UK, Ireland, Belgium, Egypt, Turkey, Hong Kong, Singapore, Thailand, Indonesia, Japan, Australia and Uruguay.

Country Inns and Suites (by Carlson)

Country Inns & Suites by CarlsonSM is a highly successful mid-tier lodging chain offering excellent value with over 395 locations worldwide. The chain boasts of welcoming guests with traditional furnishings that blend rich woods and elegant floral-patterned fabrics. Guests may borrow a book from the in-hotel lending library and return it on their next stay at any Country Inns & Suites location in the U.S. and Canada. Based on the number of books returned, the brand makes a donation to a non-profit literacy organization.

Dusit Hotels and Resorts

The leading Thai-based international Group of Hotels & Resorts, for both the business and leisure markets. The Dusit Thani, Bangkok, the Group's flagship property, opened in 1970. The Dusit Group has expanded in the deluxe sector throughout Thailand, to include hotels and resorts in all of the key city centers and top leisure resorts in the country.

Four Seasons Hotels and Resorts

With a history spanning four decades and a portfolio that now extends to six continents, Four Seasons Hotels and Resorts is the world's leading operator of luxury hotels, currently managing 51 properties in 22 countries, and continues to expand, with over 20 projects in development stages in choice locations around the world.

Global Hyatt Corporation

Hyatt Corporation opened its first hotel on 27th September, 1957. Hyatt's first property at Los Angeles International Airport was originally named Hyatt House. The owner of Hyatt House was a local entrepreneur by the name of Hyatt R. von Dehn. Hyatt hotels expanded aggressively along the West Coast during the next decade. However, it wasn't until 1967, when Hyatt Corporation opened the world's first atrium hotel that the Hyatt name became known worldwide. The hotel's 21-story atrium tower lobby and dramatic departure from traditional hotel architecture changed the course of the lodging industry. The challenge to hotel architects was no longer to eliminate extra space; rather, to create grand, wide-open public spaces.

By 1969, there were 13 Hyatt hotels in the United States. That year, a subsidiary of the newly formed Hyatt International Corporation opened the first international hotel, the Hyatt Regency Hong Kong.

Hyatt Regency hotels are the core brand of Hyatt Hotels & Resorts, offering guests opportunities to broaden their horizons and rejuvenate. Lobbies and rooms are designed to reflect the best of the local cultures, the food and beverage outlets are inventive, and exceptional technology, meeting, and fitness facilities are available

There are 212 Hyatt hotels and resorts (over 90,000 rooms) in 43 countries around the world, operating under the Hyatt, Hyatt Regency, Grand Hyatt and Park Hyatt brands. Currently, there are an additional 28 Hyatt hotels and resorts under development, including 10 new hotels in China. Hyatt Corporation (domestic U.S., Canada and Caribbean hotels) and Hyatt International Corporation (international properties) are subsidiaries of Chicago-based Global Hyatt Corporation. Global Hyatt

Corporation is also the owner of Hyatt Vacation Ownership, Inc. (timeshare), Hyatt Equities, L.L.C. (hotel ownership), and U.S. Franchise Systems, Inc. (which franchises Hawthorn Suites, Microtel and Best Inns).

Golden Tulip Top Hospitality Group

Golden Tulip is one of the leading European franchisers of three and four star Hotels in Europe. At present, the Golden Tulip portfolio comprises some 30,000 rooms in approximately 300 hotels in 240 cities across 42 countries, with 240 hotels being located in Europe. The franchising operation markets two brands: Golden Tulip Hotels are Superior First Class hotels in business destinations and the better resort areas (four-star), whilst Tulip Inns are comfortable three-star establishments and Superior Tourist Class Hotels (three-star), also catering to the corporate and the leisure traveller. Each hotel maintains its individuality and local character.

Hilton Hotels and Resorts (by Hilton)

The Hilton brand features approximately 231 full-service hotels and resorts in cities throughout the United States. This includes 55 owned and/or managed hotels, 170 hotels under franchise agreements, one leased property, and 5 joint ventures. Flagship properties include the Waldorf Astoria, Hilton Hawaiian Village Beach Resort and Spa and the Palmer House Hilton, among others.

Hilton Worldwide (all brands)

Hilton Hotels Corporation is recognized internationally as a preeminent hospitality company. The company develops, owns, manages or franchises approximately 1,900 hotels, resorts and vacation ownership properties. Its portfolio includes many of the world's best known and most highly regarded hotel brands, including Hilton, Conrad, Doubletree, Embassy Suites Hotels, Hampton Inn, Hampton Inn & Suites, Harrison Conference Centers, Hilton Garden Inn, Hilton Grand Vacations Company, Homewood Suites by Hilton, and Red Lion Hotels & Inns.

InterContinental Hotels Group (I.H.G)

InterContinental Hotels Group can be traced back to 1777 when William Bass began a brewery in Burton-upon-Trent. 1989 the British Government limited the number of pubs brewers could directly own, so Bass began to grow their small line of hotels. In 1990 they purchased Holiday Inn International from Kemmons Wilson, expanding themselves into North America. In March 1998 they acquired the InterContinental brand, expanding into the luxury market.

In 2000 the company changed its name to Six Continents PLC. IHG was created in 2003 after Six Continents PLC split into two daughter companies: Mitchells and Butlers PLC, to handle restaurant assets and IHG to focus on hotels and soft drinks. IHG is primarily engaged in managing hotels owned by other parties and in franchising its hotel brands. As of 2007 it franchises over 3,200 hotels, manages over 510 and owns only 24. The owned hotels do however include many of the key properties of company's flagship InterContinental brand

- InterContinental
- Crowne Plaza
- Holiday Inn (Holiday Inn Select, Nickelodeon Family Suites by Holiday Inn, Holiday Inn Resorts and Holiday Inn SunSpree Resorts, Holiday Inn Express known as *Express by Holiday Inn* outside North America).
- Staybridge Suites
- Candlewood Suites
- Hotel Indigo.

Jin Jiang International Management Corporation (China)

Jin Jiang Holdings Co Ltd. is one of the major actors in the hotel and tourism industry in China. Hotels, tourism, car hire, real estate, entertainment, trading, finance, etc. are its main activities. Jin Jiang International Management Co Ltd, a subsidiary of Jin Jiang Holdings Co Ltd, owns a chain of 53 hotels (14,127 rooms) in 14 regions of China. Jin Jiang is the best-known brand name in the Chinese hotel industry.

Jumeirah International

Jumeirah International properties are regarded as among the most luxurious and innovative in the world and have won numerous international travel and tourism awards. The Dubai based luxury hospitality group encompasses the world renowned Burj Al Arab, the world's most luxurious hotel, the multi-award winning Jumeirah Beach Hotel, Emirates Towers Hotel, Offices and Boulevard, The Jumeirah Beach Club Resort and Spa, Madinat Jumeirah, The Arabian Resort – Dubai, and Bab Al Shams Desert Resort & Spa. The group's activities are however, not restricted to hotel and resort management. The Jumeirah International portfolio also includes Wild Wadi, regarded as one of the premier water parks outside of North America Jumeirah International has also expanded internationally and manages The Carlton Tower and The Lowndes Hotel in London's Belgravia. Building on this success, Jumeirah International has become a member of Dubai Holding, a collection of leading Dubai based businesses and projects.

JW Marriott Hotels & Resorts (by Marriott)

Most elegant and luxurious Marriott brand. Provides business and leisure travellers a deluxe level of comfort and personal service-on their terms. 20 JW Marriott Hotels worldwide; 8 U.S., 12 international.

Kempinski Hotels & Resorts (Germany)

Kempinski Hotels & Resorts' prestigious portfolio comprises 40 luxurious properties in Europe, the Middle East, Africa, South America, Asia and Australia.

Le Meridien

Le Meridien, part of Starwood Hotels & Resorts, consists of a portfolio of more than 120 luxury and upscale hotels in 52 countries worldwide. Starwood Hotels & Resorts is one of the leading hotel and leisure companies in the world with approximately 850 properties in more than 95 countries and 145,000 employees at its owned and managed properties. Starwood Hotels is a fully integrated owner, operator and franchisor of hotels and resorts with the following internationally renowned brands: St. Regis, The Luxury Collection, Sheraton, Westin, Four Points by Sheraton, W, Le Meridien and the recently announced Aloft. Starwood Hotels also owns Starwood Vacation Ownership, Inc.

Mandarin Oriental International Limited

Mandarin Oriental Hotel Group is the award-winning owner and operator of some of the world's most prestigious hotels and resorts, currently operating 21 luxury hotels with a further six under development in Hong Kong and Tokyo (opening 2005), Prague and Riviera Maya, Mexico (2006), Boston (2007) and Chicago (2008). In total, Mandarin Oriental now operates, or has under development, approximately 8,000 rooms in 14 countries with 12 hotels in Asia, ten in The Americas and five in Europe.

Marriott International, Inc

Marriott International is a leading worldwide hospitality company with over 2,600 lodging properties in the United States and 68 other countries and territories. Marriott International operates and franchises hotels under the Marriott, JW Marriott, The Ritz-Carlton, Renaissance, Residence Inn, Courtyard, Towne Place Suites, Fairfield Inn, SpringHill Suites and Ramada International brand names; develops and operates vacation ownership resorts under the Marriott Vacation Club International, Horizons, The Ritz-Carlton Club and Marriott Grand Residence Club brands; operates Marriott Executive Apartments; provides furnished corporate housing through its Marriott ExecuStay division; and operates conference centers. The company is headquartered in Washington, D.C.

Nikko/JAL Hotels

JAL Hotels (JAL Hotels Company Ltd.) is the only Japanese-owned global hotel chain. JAL Hotels' mission is to deliver the highest standards of service through a unique blend of renowned Japanese hospitality and local custom

- ❖ JAL Hotels has been a hotel management company since its establishment in 1970 as a subsidiary of Japan Airlines Co. Ltd.
- ❖ On 1st July, 1996, Japan Airlines Development Ltd. was renamed to "JAL Hotels Company Ltd." to further establish its business description as a hotel operator.

- On 1st April, 1999, a merger with "Japan Airlines Hotel Co. Ltd." resulted in JAL Hotels taking over the management of the "Ginza Nikko Hotel" and "Kawasaki Nikko Hotel". This was a welcome addition to the JAL Group's business enterprise and created a strong base for the JAL Group.

Operating under the "Nikko Hotels International" (NHI) and "Hotel JAL City" (HJC) brands, JAL Hotels manages 67 properties worldwide, with a total inventory of 21,406 guest rooms.

- **Nikko Hotels International (Hotel Nikko)** has established a nationwide and worldwide network as they strive to fulfill their guests' needs. Hotel Nikko properties are placed in cities throughout the world, covering all the major tourist and business districts. Also, their affiliation with Japan Airlines allows them to provide travel packages to customers.
- **Hotel JAL City**: Accommodation specifically designed with the business traveler in mind, Hotel JAL City properties are either placed around airports or the business districts of major cities. The rooms come complete with all the modern conveniences the busy travelling executive requires. In-house restaurants, conference centers, and business centre facilities are also available.

Oberoi Group of Hotels

The Oberoi Group is one of Asia's leading hospitality companies. Founded in 1934, The Group owns or manages 37 luxury and first class international hotels in seven countries. The Group is also involved in Airline Catering, Airport Bars and Restaurants, Delicatessen Products, Travel & Tour Services, Corporate Air Charters, Limousine Services and Project Management. The market capitalization of the flagship company of the Group, EIH Limited, currently exceeds US$ 700 million.

Park Plaza hotels (by Carlson)

Park Plaza Hotels and Resorts is positioned in the mid-scale segment of the full-service hotel category and is known for its great value and customer-focused service culture. These hotels are generally 125 rooms or larger and located in downtown, suburban and airport commercial locations. There are currently more than 40 Park Plaza locations worldwide.

Quality Inns, Hotels, and Suites (by Choice International)

Quality is a mid-priced brand competing in the mid-scale with food and beverage market segment. With over 900 locations, it is known around the world for its friendly, professional service and clean, safe accommodations.

Radisson Hotels and Resorts

Radisson Hotels and Resorts is one of the world's leading, full-service hotel companies, Radisson Hotels and Resorts currently encompasses more than 405 properties in 64 countries.

Raffles International Hotels and Resorts

Raffles Hotels and Resorts is a collection of 13 luxury hotels located in major cities around the globe. The collection of includes Raffles Hotel and Raffles The Plaza in Singapore, Raffles L'Ermitage Beverly Hills in the US, Raffles Hotel Vier Jahreszeiten, Hamburg, Germany and Raffles Le Montreux Palace, Montreux, Switzerland. Raffles Taimana Resort Tahaa, French Polynesia is the latest addition to the portfolio.

Renaissance Hotels and Resorts (by Marriott)

Renaissance Hotels and Resorts is an upscale brand providing full-service accommodations to business travelers, group meetings and resort travelers. Generally located in commercial or airport districts of major cities. The system currently encompasses 36 hotels in the United States and 54 international properties.

Starwood Hotels and Resorts Worldwide

Starwood Hotels and Resorts Worldwide, Inc. is one of the top hotel companies in the world. The company owns and operates hotels under leading brands such as Sheraton, Westin, St. Regis, Four Points, and its recently developed W brand. The majority of Starwood's hotels are owned by franchisees, and the company directly owns or leases about 170 of its approximately 750 hotels worldwide. Close to 500 of the company's hotels are in North America. Starwood also runs hotels in some 80 countries in Asia, Europe, Africa, and South America, including a chain of prestigious European palaces called the Ciga Group. The company began as a small investment firm and then became a real estate investment trust (REIT). In 1998 Starwood purchased ITT Corporation, a company seven times its size and at the time the world's largest lodging and gaming company. Starwood beat out the Hilton Hotels Corporation to get ITT, in what was one of the most dramatic takeover battles of the 1990s. Starwood is run by Barry Sternlicht, whose consummate dealsmanship parlayed the small trust into a global lodging company.

Shangri-La Hotels and Resorts

Hong Kong-based Shangri-La Hotels and Resorts is the largest Asian-based deluxe hotel group in the region and regarded as one of the world's finest hotel management companies. Shangri-La Hotels and Resorts is the trade name of Shangri-La Asia, which is listed on the Hong Kong Stock Exchange. This ownership change took place in 1997; before this the management company was a wholly owned subsidiary of the Kuok Group

Sheraton (by Starwood)

As the largest of the Starwood Hotels and Resorts Worldwide, Inc. brands. in more than 150 locations and commands a respectable position internationally.

The Taj Group of Hotels (India)

The Taj Group's operations cover over 60 hotels in India and abroad, and encompass a number of brands across various price segments. The Company has a dominant position in most areas it is present in. The Taj Group of Hotels is grouped into strategic business units to get consistency across the different units in the same brand and standardize the product and service across the brands, making them distinct and identifiable. These brands have been classified as Luxury, Business and Leisure.

ACTIVITY

a) Find out the locations/various prominent international hotel chain brands and their affiliates present in India.

b) Make a visit to a hotel of international hotel chain or it's affiliate property in your city or near by city and find out about it's corporate policy and mission.

QUESTIONS

1. How did the growth of international hotel chains took it's shape over the period of this century?

2. Exhibit the name of at least ten International brands of hotel chains and their affiliate properties.

12

MAJOR HOSPITALITY PLAYERS AND ASSOCIATIONS IN INDIA

— ASHISH DAHIYA[1] & PUSHKAR NEGI[2]

Hotels industry globally has witnessed a significant change and so has the Indian hospitality industry. The journey of hospitality industry in India may be inspirational for many amongst you and who knows one from you may become a New Hotelier in the 21st century. The beginning is always small, however, the dreams may be big. We do recommend to our dear students to spare some time to go through the book "Dare to Dream" a life of M.S Oberoi authored by Bachi J Karkaria and see how a boy from Bhaun (now in Pakistan) turned out to be 'Country's Only Exclusive Hotelier'.

Spare some time so as to learn how Conrad Hilton born in 1887 in the middle of New Mexican Dessert wandered taking a degree in mining and working as a bank cashier came with Hilton Hotels. How Jamsetji Tata born in 1839 at Navsari, grew up in Mumbai through the riches and then rags of his father's failing business and created a mark in history. It becomes important for us to know about the domestic players in India and we may expect few more amongst them in International sector in coming years. Thus in this unit we have explained about the various hospitality players in India. In our journey to meet Indian hospitality players we have also covered some associations in Indian Hospitality.

OBJECTIVES

After this unit you will be able to understand:

- ❖ The growth and development of hotel chains in India.
- ❖ Different hospitality units at national level in India.
- ❖ Various hospitality organizations in India.

---

1. Reader in Hotel Management at Centre for Mountain Tourism & Hospitality Studies, HNB Garhwal University, Srinagar, Garhwal, Uttarakhand.

2. Lecturer in Hotel Management at Centre for Mountain Tourism & Hospitality Studies, HNB Garhwal University, Srinagar, Garhwal, Uttarakhand.

Ambassador Group Hotels

Ambassador Group Hotels has sure come a long way, carving a niche for itself in Corporate Hospitality. Its deluxe accommodation furnished with various business specific needs has won the "thumbs-up" of many Business barons who have repeated their visits to the Hotel. Apart from a distinguished guest list of various Business travellers, the Hotel Group has had the continued honours of serving many leisure travellers who have more than appreciated the high standards of hospitality and service extend to them. The Ambassador Group also boasts of having one of the largest Flight Catering Unit in South East Asia; equipped with modern equipments, located at Mumbai and catering to several prestigious airlines. The dynamism of the Ambassador group is fairly evident in its spiralling growth and with its eyes set on the goal of being the best in business; it is proving to be a tough competitor for other Hotel Chains in India.

Ashok Group of Hotels

Owned by the India Tourism Development Corporation a public sector undertaking by Ministry of Tourism Government of India, the Ashok Group is India's one of the largest chain with various hotels in different major cities with the facilities beyond compare. The range varies from five-star deluxe to budget, depending upon tourist needs.

At all international airports ITDC runs duty free shops at arrivals and departure halls. ITDC also runs restaurants with specialized cuisine in Agra, Mascow and Wellinton.

Ashok group of Hotels are classified in three categories:-

- Elite group
- Classic hotels
- Comfort Hotels

Ashok group has very large networking and complete India experience with a combination of comfort and traditional Indian hospitality. The various hotels owned by ITDC are listed below:

The Ashok – Delhi

Samrat Hotel – Delhi

Lalitha Mahal Palace – Mysore

Hotel Bharatpur Ashok – Bharatpur

Hotel Jaipur Ashok – Jaipur

Hotel Kalinga Ashok – Bhubaneswar

Hotel Jammu Ashok – Jammu

Hotel Janpath – Delhi

Hotel Patliputra Ashok – Patna

Hotel Lakeview Ashok – Bhopal

Brahamputra Ashok - Guwahati

Donyi Polo Ashok - Pondicherry

Nilanchal Ashok - Puri

Ranchi Ashok – Ranchi

Kosi Tourist Complex

Bharat Hotels – The Grand Group

Bharat Hotels is a leading hotel company, presently offering fourteen luxurious hotels, with more than 3600 rooms in the five-star deluxe segment.

Bharat Hotels operate all hotels under 'THE GRAND' banner. These include InterContinental The Grand New Delhi, InterContinental The Grand Mumbai, InterContinental The Grand Goa Resort, InterContinental The Grand Palace Srinagar along with The Grand Ashok Bangalore, The Grand Laxmi Vilas Palace Udaipur and The Grand Temple View Khajuraho. Hotel projects under construction (to open in 2008-2009) include The Grand Great Eastern Kolkata, The Grand Resort Bekal, The Grand Ahmedabad, The Grand Chandigarh, The Grand Jaipur, The Grand Noida and The Grand Fort Dubai. The company also has plans for Hyderabad, Amritsar, Pune, Gulmarg, Chennai and other key locations.

Clarks Group of Hotels

An internationally renowned Hotel Group, **Clarks Group of Hotels** owned by U.P. Hotels Limited has made a name for itself in the Hospitality Industry by virtue of its blue ribbon service and warm hospitality. The USP of this Hotel Chain in India is undeniably the unique fusion of Indian tradition with the modern amenities pertaining to International Hospitality standards.

Clarks Group Hotels is the top pick of casual and business travellers alike. Various Clark Group Hotels patronized by elite clientele in India are:

- ❖ Hotel Clarks Shiraz, Agra
- ❖ Hotel Clarks Amer, Jaipur
- ❖ Clarks Hotel, Shimla
- ❖ Hotel Clarks, Varanasi
- ❖ Hotel Clarks Tower, Varanasi

ITC Welcomgroup

ITC Welcomgroup Hotels, has innumerable hotel units throughout India including Agra, Bangalore, Chennai, Hyderabad, Jaipur, Mumbai, Aurangabad, Baroda, Gwalior, New Delhi and Vishakapatnam. From 5-Star Sheraton hotels to heritage hotels, ITC - Welcomgroup Hotels, Palaces and Resorts, is today one of India's finest hotel chains. Each of the chain's hotels pays architectural tribute to ancient dynasties, which ruled India from time to time. The design concept and themes of these dynasties play an important part in their respective style and decor. With more and more hotels being added at strategic destinations, the group has joined hands with the Sheraton Corporation to strengthen its international marketing base. ITC-Welcomgroup's properties are classified under five distinct brands.

ITC Hotels - Luxury Collection are super deluxe and premium hotels located at strategic business and leisure locations.

ITC-Welcomgroup Sheraton Hotels offer warm, comforting services to the global traveller and a chance to connect.

WelcomHotels offer five-star hospitality for the discerning business and leisure traveller.

Fortune Hotel Fortune Park Hotels Ltd. is a subsidiary of ITC Ltd. Set up in 1995 to cater to the mid-priced market segment in business and leisure destinations. Today it is a professionally managed Hotel Management company, with twenty operating hotels and five hotels in various stages of completion.

Fortune Hotels operates across a wide spectrum and includes Select, Park, Inns, Resorts and Residences across the length and breadth of the country. Fortune Selects, Parks and Inns are business hotels in Metro and Non-metros, Fortune Resorts in popular holiday destinations and serviced apartments operate under the Fortune Residences brand.

WelcomHeritage includes a chain of palaces, forts, *havelis* and resorts that offer a unique experience. WelcomHeritage endeavours to preserve ancient royal homes and the historical Indian grandeur and opulence for the future Indian generations.

The Ecotel – Orchid Hotels

Kamats has been a name in Indian Hospitality. Kamat's is now a large hospitality Group with interests in Luxury Hotels, Budget Hotels Family Leisure and Sports Clubs, Travel Business, Catering and Educational Institutions, Departmental Stores and, of course, Restaurants.

Realising the importance of positioning of the property, as well as marketing company started a new brand unknown so far in the continent of Asia - a green hotel - environmentally sensitive - right from brick to paper and taking care of every little guest need at the same time. It was proved that 87% of international travellers do patronize green hotels. Kamat Hotels have tied up with an International Firm-HVS ECO SERVICES of HVS INTERNATIONAL, NEW YORK to undertake specific environmental programmes, designed to lower operating costs and increase revenues and evaluate the hotel's environmental performance in various areas. **THE ORCHID,** as it is aptly renamed, was awarded the prestigious 'ECOTEL' Certification' by HVS ECO SERVICES, USA, which is the hall mark of environmentally sensitive hotels.

H.R.H Group of Hotels

HRH Hotels Resorts and Palaces are one of the finest grand heritages and luxury hotels in Rajasthan. HRH Hotels Resorts and Palaces comprises nine hotels, resorts and authentic palace hotels in five locations across Rajasthan.

JAYPEE GROUP OF HOTELS

Jaypee Hotels, established in 1981, is a part of the Rs. 4000 crore conglomerate Jaypee Group, a diversified infrastructure industrial group with interests in civil engineering, hydropower, dam construction, cement, golf and real estate, IT, education and hotels.

The group has four five-star deluxe properties, strategically located to service the needs of discerning business and leisure travellers. In New Delhi, it has two hotels, the 119 room Jaypee Vasant Continental, located in Vasant Vihar and the Jaypee Siddharth, located in West Delhi

The largest and most famous hotel of the group is Jaypee Palace Hotel & Convention Centre at Agra. A hotel par excellence, Jaypee Palace Hotel & Convention Centre Agra blends the luxury of five-star deluxe comforts with the timeless world of Mughal opulence.

NEEMRANA HOTELS

Located 122 km from New Delhi, Neemrana derived its name from the brave local chieftain Nimola Meo, who when defeated by the Chauhans, pleaded that his name be given to his lost kingdom. Located in Neemrana are the heritage hotels of the Neemrana Group, offering a unique blend of royal experience and rich hospitality. The Eleven Neemrana hotels are The Hill Fort Kesroli, Neemrana Fort Palace, Bungalow on the Beach, Hotel De L'Orient, The Ramgarh Bungalows, The Verandah in the Forest, Villa Potipatti, Wallwood Garden, The Piramal Haveli, The Pataudi Place, and The Glasshouse of the Ganges.

NIRULA'S

Nirula's, a well-known name in the hospitality industry, had a small beginning. The company venture into the fast food business with the Pastry Shop, Snack Bar, Hot Shoppe and Ice Cream Parlour. The Potpourri restaurant with the first Salad Bar in India was also opened in this period. Later, they opened Family Style Restaurants at Vasant Vihar, Chanakya, Defence Colony, Noida and numerous other strategic locations in the NCR. Today, the Noida production facilities include the Bakery, Confectionery, Cheese Plant, Ice cream Plant, Food Processing Unit and Hot Kitchen. Nirula's widened its presence in North India with the opening of restaurants in Panipat, Dehradun, Chandigarh and Lucknow. In June 2006, Navis Capital Partners and Managing Director, Samir Kuckreja acquired the Nirula's Group of Companies.

Pride Hotels

The Pride Hotels, located in Pune, Nagpur and Ahmedabad epitomize luxury, extravagance, sophistication and impeccable service. Currently a new five-star hotel is under construction in Bangalore to cater to the heavy influx of corporate travellers. A part of Pride Group the hotels are benchmarks of excellence. Widely acclaimed by corporate and leisure travellers from India and abroad, The Pride Hotels epitomize legendary Indian hospitability.

Hospitality Associations

Associations play a vital role in any industry. They act as an interface between Industry and Academia, Industry and Government and not merely put forward current issues but also tend to provide or work upon solutions to the problems. Hospitality Industry is no exception. It is an application oriented industry. Thus a proper interface is required in order to deal with human resources, technology, legal and regulatory and other such issues. Being service oriented as such Hospitality industry is struggling and will have to struggle with high turnover, with high percentage of low skilled and skilled workers and drive society of trained personnel at various levels. Thus, it has become imperative for tourism and hospitality educational institutes to redesign refocus and rethink on the supply of trained manpower to this employees' intensive industry. Such associations can play a significant role in quality assurance, education and on human resources. Human Resource development is the key to development of Travel, Tourism and Hospitality Sector hospitality is not an exception. Various Hospitality associations in India are mentioned below:

Federation of Hotel and Restaurant Association of India (FHRAI)

Federation of Hotel and Restaurant Association of India is the trade association of entire hospitality industry in India. It was set up in 1955 and has its head office at New Delhi. It has a representation of 3135 members comprising of 2004 hotels, 990 restaurants, 137 associate and 4 regional associations (Jan 2007). The association includes suppliers to the hospitality industry, hospitality management institutes, consultants and travel agents.

The mission of the FHRAI is to represent, promote and develop the hospitality industry in India. It provides constant interface between industry, political leadership, policy formulation, academics and other stake-holders. The organization is committed to provide added values to its services and enhance the quality of benefits to the members. It promotes members business nationally as well as internationally. It finds out the latest national and international trends, news, best practices and statistics. It keeps the members updated on latest government circulars, notifications and legal issues. It helps the members in building capacity in the industry and develops Human Resource Potential for future expansion. The FHRAI has conducted about 50 training programmes in 16 cities for professional development of industry personnel. It has four regional associations, i.e. HRAEI (Hotel and Restaurant Association of Eastern India) having its head office at Kolkata. HRANI (Hotel and Restaurant association of Northern India) having its head office at Delhi, SIHRA (South India Hotels and Restaurant Association) having its head office at Chennai and HRAWI (Hotel and Restaurant Association of Western India) having its head office at Mumbai.

Hotel Association of India (HAI)

Hotel Association of India is an apex organization of the hospitality industry in India. It represents the entire cross-section of hotel industry ranging from small, medium, large and exclusive stand alone hotels and major hotel groups. It was established in year 1996. Hotel Association of India has an impressive membership of over 260 Hotels. The membership includes 1-star to 5-star deluxe category hotels, heritage hotels as well as public sector and government owned hotels. The HAI is committed to the attainment of following objectives:

- To create through a communication programme an awareness of the particular significance of the hotel industry in contributing to general economic development and employment.
- To secure for the industry its true status as a core infrastructure industry.
- To serve the members by establishing a data bank to provide timely information data, advisory and research services.
- To formulate strategies in areas of land, finance, taxation, training procedures and legislation to accelerate growth.
- To interface with central and state government and other authorities on issues concerning to hotel industry.
- To synergise with all segments of the hotel industry an apex bodies of the tourism sector in India and overseas and work for the creation of a common platform.

Association of Hospitality Trainers (AHT)

Association of Hospitality Trainers known as ***Trainers Forum*** is the largest online community of trainers in India and beyond. Established in year 2002, it has 2750 members with adding average of about 100 memberships every month. It started with a noble intention of bringing all trainers and educators together on one platform. The vision is to create a platform for all the trainers, educators and HR professionals from various industries and verticals, interact, share best practices, discuss & debate issues and concerns regarding Learning, Training and Development. Though the community is online it can be accessed in following cities via moderators at Mumbai, Chennai, Bangalore, New Delhi, Pune, Hyderabad, Ahmedabad, Bhubaneshwar, Indore and Cochin. About 900 messages are being posted in every month and free download facility is provided to all the members via website.

Indian Federation of Culinary Associations (IFCA)

Indian Federation of Culinary associations was established in year 2003 and has its office at Chennai. It is a member of World Association of Cook Societies. It has its Regional and State chapters. The membership is open for all chefs or people having an attitude for culinary. The recent activities of Federation includes:

- ❖ Cheering of under-privileged children on the occasion of International Chefs Day.
- ❖ Annual awards for excellence in culinary art.
- ❖ Development of culinary profession.
- ❖ Showcasing Indian culinary achievements.
- ❖ Encouraging talented and aspiring youngsters in the gastronomy field.
- ❖ Plans to publish a food magazine, a cook book and other such publications.
- ❖ Timely get together for charity for social cause.
- ❖ Spreading good word and positivism.
- ❖ Celebrating International Chefs Day.

By promoting International Chefs Day it endeavours to create cooking awareness for healthy, happy nation.

Indian Housekeepers Club

Indian Housekeepers Club is an association of housekeepers in India and came into existence in January 2006 at Alwar in Rajasthan. It is having 1200 members and has its registered office at Agra. The idea behind the association is to allow communication between hotel housekeepers on a national and international level – regardless of location of the participants. It aims at providing solutions to hotel housekeeping and related issues. Following are the activities in Indian Housekeepers Club:

- ❖ To bring maximum housekeepers/Asstt. Managers/Supervisors in the association to make them friendly with each other keeping the fact that there is hardly a time for social interaction in hotel industry this can bring a chance to bring family members to a get together of housekeepers.

- Inviting housekeeping companies to tell about new products and services.
- To enhance recruitment of housekeepers.
- To open an Institute on Housekeeping Management so as to teach poor students who had dreamed to work for hotel industry but failed to go for higher studies in this area due to heavy expenses.
- To facilitate distance education for those learners who are keen to enhance their qualifications while on job.
- To arrange seminars and workshops for housekeepers annually.

Hospitality Educators and Recruiters Association (HERA)

Hospitality Educators and Recruiters Association is an organization of Hospitality Educators, Human Resources and Training Professionals representing the finest hotels and hospitality institutions in India. The association came into existence in October 2006 and has its head office at Chennai. The main objectives of the association are:

- To upgrade the industrial technology and advancements with hospitality institutions.
- To organize the training need for the hospitality educators and students.
- To streamline the industrial release scheme (IRS) and recruitment process
- To create awards for best academic performer of the year, best institution of the year, best faculty of the year and grant scholarships to students.
- To conduct national and International seminar in hospitality education.

Indian Hospitality Congress (IHC)

Indian Hospitality Congress is an attempt to provide a common platform to hospitality educators, institutes, professionals and students. The IHC is a non-profit making organisation. It was formally set up in September, 2007 (World Tourism Day) at HNB Garhwal University Campus. It is having its head office at CMTHS-HNB Garhwal University and five regional offices at Ambala, Ahmedabad, Bhopal, Pondicherry and Ranchi. It has 1100 members with S.C Bagri (Professor & Director, Centre for Mountain Tourism & Hospitality Studies, HNB Garhwal University, Uttarakhand) as founder President, Manjula Chaudhary (Professor, Dept. of Hotel & Tourism Management Kurukshetra University) as Sr. Vice President, Mohinder Chand (Associate Professor, Dept. of Hotel & Tourism Management, Kurukshetra University) as Secretary and Ashish Dahiya (Reader, Centre for Mountain Tourism & Hospitality Studies HNB Garhwal University) as Jt. Secretary and Treasurer. The aims and objectives of the Congress are:

- ❖ Indian Hospitality Meet/ Seminar (annually).
- ❖ Indian Hospitality Newsletter.
- ❖ Promotion of Indian Literature in Hospitality.
- ❖ Inviting Authors to Develop Study Material on Hospitality in Indian Context.
- ❖ Promoting Research in Hospitality.
- ❖ Encouraging Hospitality Students – Annual Awards to be presented in Seminar at Annual Hospitality Meet.
- ❖ Industry-Institute Partnership.
- ❖ Offering Hospitality Youth Clubs.

ACTIVITIES

1 Visit the websites of all State Tourism Development Corporations of India and identify the growth of their accommodation properties.

2 Identify a hotel in your area and plan a visit to know its origin, growth and expansion.

QUESTIONS

1. Explain the growth and development of Bharat Hotels Ltd.
2. What are the various Hospitality Associations in India? Write notes about any two of them?

13

EMERGING TRENDS IN HOSPITALITY INDUSTRY - I (Defining Market, Basic Concept of Marketing, Marketing Mix, Market Segmentation, Hospitality Industry, etc.)

— J.S.TIWARI[1]

The travel and tourism sector creates more jobs per million rupees of investment than any other sector of the economy and is capable of providing employment to a wide spectrum of job seekers from the unskilled to the specialised, even in the remote parts of the country. The hospitality industry is a part of the travel and tourism industry. A proper marketing plan can increase the hospitality sale and keep the hospitality business a profitable venture. The current chapter is aimed to make the student aware of the meaning of market and marketing. To operate the hospitality business one must know the basic concept of marketing so that he can select the right set of market segment to promote the product and services. One should also keep an eye on the emerging markets for his product and services, so that he can trap the same to increase the volume of the business. The later part of the chapter deals with the role of support services and infrastructure in boosting the hospitality sales.

LEARNING OBJECTIVES

After reading this chapter you will be able to:

- ❖ Understand Marketing
- ❖ Understand emerging markets
- ❖ Understand role of support services and infrastructure in developing new market

Marketing is a comprehensive term and it includes all resources and a set of activities necessary to direct and facilitate the flow of goods and services from producer to consumers in the process of distribution. Businessman regards marketing as a management function to plan, promote and deliver products to the end users. Human efforts, finance and management constitute the primary resource of marketing.

---

1. Lecturer in Hotel Management at Babu Banarsidas Institute of Technology, Lucknow.

There are two major activities which are most significant in marketing:

1. Matching the product with the demand, i.e., consumer needs and desires or target market.

2. The transfer of the possession and ownership at every stage of flow of goods from primary producer to the end user.

DEFINING MARKETING

The American marketing association defines marketing as the process of planning and executing the conception, pricing, promotion and distribution of ideas, goods and services to create exchanges that satisfy individual and organizational objectives.

The British institute of marketing defines marketing as "the management process for identifying, anticipating and satisfying customers requirements profitably".

According to **Paul Mazur**, "marketing is the creation and delivery of stranded of living to society". This definition catches the real sprit of the marketing process. It has consumer orientation. It duly honours the marketing concept which indicates a shift from product to consumer-orientation, i.e., fulfilment of consumer needs and desires. It emphasis the major function of marketing, viz., satisfaction of customer and social demand for the material goods and services. It includes product planning and development.

According to **Philip Kotler**, "Marketing is the analysis, planning, implementation, and control of carefully formulated programmes designed to bring about voluntary exchange of values with target markets for the purpose of achieving organizational objectives. It relies heavily on designing the organization's offerings in terms of the target markets' needs and desires, and on using effective pricing, communication, and distributions to inform, motivate, and service the markets".

One can infer the following from the above mentioned definitions of the marketing:

- ❖ Marketing is a managerial process that involves the principles of management like analysis, planning, implementation and control.

- ❖ Marketing is identified as a process which identifies, expands and serves the material need of the peoples.

- ❖ Marketing attempts to bring voluntary exchanges of goods and service with values.

- ❖ Marketing is implementation of carefully formulated programmes.

BASIC CONCEPTS OF MARKETING

Before discussing any further on marketing we must understand the following basic key concepts which are the foundation stone of marketing. They are:

- Need
- Want
- Demand
- Product
- Value and Price
- Satisfaction.

Need

Need is among the basic concept of the marketing. It may be understood as a state of feeling of deprivation. It includes basic physical needs (food, warmth, clothing, safety etc.), social needs (belongingness, affection, fun, relaxation etc.), esteem needs (prestige, recognition, fame etc.). An unmet need is a driving force that stimulates the person to pursue it for satisfying him with appropriate kind of product or service.

Want

Want is the next important concept of marketing. Want may be understood as the way how one express or communicates his need. Like the basic need of hunger is may be expressed a want of bread and butter by a European; *bhojan thal* by an Indian; hamburger, French fries, and coke by an US citizen. Want may be described in terms of the objects which can satisfy the need. For Example:

- Need - I need food.
- Want – I want to go to restaurant for food.

Demand

Demand is the foundation stone and forms the basis of marketing. People are having unlimited wants but has limited resources. Demand is a want which is backed by the purchasing power.

Product

A product may be any thing that can be offered to satisfy a need or want. Peoples satisfy their needs and wants by using desired products. A consumer views products as bundles of benefits which will satisfy his basic as well as associated needs and wants e.g. when a person stays in a hotel he satisfies his basic need of shelter; along with this basic need, he also satisfies his needs of prestige, status and ego. Thus it is evident that a product should be able to satisfy the basic as well as hidden needs of the consumer.

Value and Price

A substance that can satisfy the needs of mankind is said to have value. When value of any item is expressed in terms of money is known as price. According to customers value is the difference between the benefits that he will gain from owning and/ or using a product and the cost of obtaining the product. The cost of obtaining a product can be both monetary as well as non-monetary.

Satisfaction

Satisfaction is another important aspect of marketing. Satisfaction is related with the actual performance of the product and service to the consumer's own perception of performance regarding that product. If the product meets the consumer's expectation it leads to satisfaction.

MARKETING MIX

The term marketing mix is used to indicate the integrating of several variables to satisfy specific consumer needs. The task of marketing manager is to inform these variables into marketing mix that meets the needs of each consumer group or market segment targeted by the organization. The most widely used model of the marketing mix known as "Four Ps". This model was introduced by E. J. McCarthy in his classic ***Basic Marketing***. This model can be represented by three concentric circles:

- ❖ The innermost circle contains the focal point of marketing effort - the consumer.
- ❖ The middle circle contains the marketing mix—Product, Price, Promotion and Place (known as Four Ps). These are the controllable variables.
- ❖ The outer circle represents the uncontrollable variables like economic environment, political and legal situations, and socio-cultural environment etc.

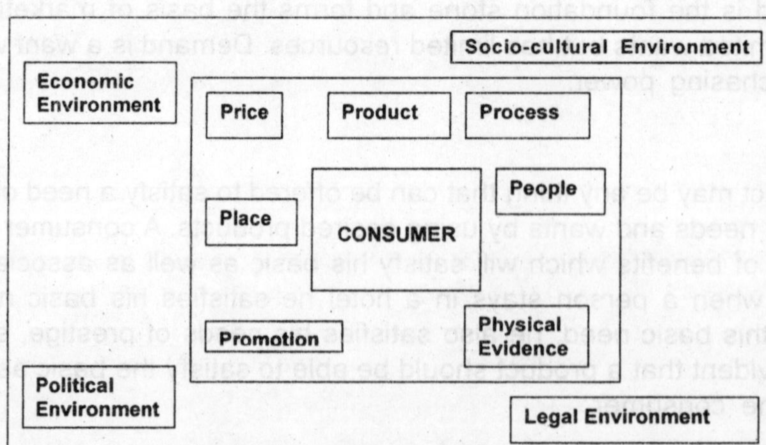

Fig. 12.1 The Marketing Mix

In the simplest manner, the basic marketing mix is the blending the four inputs or sub mixes which forms the core of the marketing system. They are:

- Product mix
- Place (Distribution Mix)
- Promotion Mix
- Price mix

Product Mix

The product or services mix is considered first because without product or service the industry has nothing to distribute, promote or price. Hospitality industry offers products like guest rooms, banquet space, food and beverages; and services like parking, housekeeping, express check-in and check-out services etc.

Place/Distribution Mix

Place refers to the accessibility of the products to end users. The distribution of consumer goods is achieved shipping the products to the consumer. In the case of hospitality products the consumer has to travel to the product. The distribution channels of hospitality products may be direct (having own sales force) or may be indirect (travel agent, tour operators, intersell agencies etc.)

Promotion Mix

Promotion mix includes all the ways how hotel communicates to its prospective guests. It consists of way like advertisement, sales promotion, personal selling, publicity, public relations, and exhibitions.

Price Mix

Pricing is very important among marketing mix. Hotels, especially large properties, often develop variable-rate policies to meet the needs of the different market segments. These policies are characterized by charging different prices to different buyers of the dame product, depending up on the competitive situations and the bargaining position of the buyer.

Apart from the above mentioned standard four Ps (Product, Price, Promotion and place), the service marketing relies upon following extra three Ps (People, Process and Physical evidence).

People

Any person coming in contact with the end-users can have an impact on overall satisfaction. Whether as a part of supporting services to a product or involved in a total service, peoples are particularly important because, in the consumer's eye they are inseparable from the total service. Hence they must be appropriately trained and well motivated to achieve organizations objectives.

Process

This is the process involved in providing a service and the behaviour of people, which can be crucial to guest satisfaction.

Physical evidence

Unlike a product, a service cannot be experienced before it is delivered, which makes it intangible. This may affect the customer's decision making regarding the favouring and choosing a service. To reduce the feeling of risk it is often vital to offer potential customers the chance to see what a service would be like. This is done by providing physical evidence like case studies, testimonials or demonstration.

MARKET SEGMENTATION

A marketing segment is a meaningful grouping of prospective buyers having similar wants. Segmentation is a consumer oriented marketing strategy. Market segmentation give formal recognition of the fact that wants and desires of the consumers are diverse and we can formulate a specific market offering to specific category or segment of the market so that the supply will have the best correlation with demand. Varied and complex buyer behaviour is the root cause of market segmentation. The hospitality market has two broad market segments:

- ❖ Group market segment
- ❖ Transient market segment

Group Market Segment

The group market includes that segment which provides large number of room sales. It includes corporate market, associations, and other segments like social groups, military, educational, religious and social institutions.

Transient Market Segments

The transient market includes that segment which provides comparatively low number of room sales than group market. It includes business and leisure travellers.

EMERGING MARKETS FOR HOSPITALITY INDUSTRY

The hospitality industry satisfies the need of shelter and requirement food and beverage of a traveller. In ancient times the magnitude and frequency of travelling was minimum due to speed and safety. That is a reason why there was less development of hotel industry. In the present age, the people are travelling more frequently as modes of transport are safer and faster than in the past. The mass tourism has given a boost to development of hospitality industry.

In early times the hotels were catering the needs of the local residents and the travellers. The demand variance of the hotel guest was almost non-existent as they were forced to stay in the available properties. Now-a-days the hotel guest is more demanding. The marketing strategies of the hotels are people-oriented. The hotel has started categorizing the target market based of the common wants of the prospective guests. The new emerging markets for the hospitality industry are:

* Meeting and Conferences
* Incentive Travel
* Trade Fairs and Exhibitions
* Extended stay market
* Honeymooners.

Meeting and Conferences

According to Oxford Dictionary a meeting is an assembly of people. For as long as there have been people there have been meetings. This fact is also been attested by archaeological investigations of old civilizations as there were ruins of some place of common gathering.

Meetings may be one of the major markets for the hotel industry. The meetings are generally organized by the corporate sectors, institutions, and other organizations for one or more of the following reasons:

* To evaluate the performance of the company, department of the company or the employees of the organization.
* To discuss the introduction of the new product/service by the company.
* To formulate new policies
* To introduce new methods of operation
* General body meeting.

The reason what so ever may be but it result in to requirement of the venue and other support services required to hold the meetings. Hotels having well-appointed meeting halls, board rooms can capture the market.

A conference centre is a specialized hospitality operation dedicated to facilitating and supporting conferences. A conference centre provides a venue for the conference, ministerial services required by attendee as well as organizer, telecommunication facility, public address system, audio-visual aids, flip charts, white boards, projectors, screens etc. In the case of residential conference and meeting the hotel or conference centre should have adequate number of the guest rooms to accommodate the attendee of the conference.

Incentive Travel

Incentive travel may be broadly defined as a lure of a travel trip to motivate employees at work. This is a popular mode of motivating the employees to outperform in 'their work and align their productivity to achieve organizations objectives. The organizations that offer incentive tours to their employees for one or more of the following reasons:

- Increasing sales volume or increased employee productivity
- Selling new accounts or selling slow moving items
- Introducing new products
- Pushing low season sales
- Overtaking competition
- Doing some thing profitable to the company
- Improving employee morale and goodwill
- Improving attendance
- Getting de-motivated employees to perform better.

The hotels can capture this market by approaching to the companies who are giving incentive travel to their employees. The chain hotels having properties at many locations can attract the prospective company by offering suitable package of incentive tour. The individual or small chain hotel may exercise the same by developing coalition among them.

Trade Fair and Exhibition

The trade shows and exhibitions are designated to bring together individuals associated with a common business or activity for the purpose of reviewing, demonstrating, marketing and selling materials and product related to their common interest. The basic function of a trade fair is to facilitate the exchange of information between the companies and the prospective buyers a trade show may be of following types on the basis of purpose:

- Industrial shows
- Trade shows
- Professional/scientific exhibitions.

The trade fairs and exhibition may or may not be open for common public. It caters to all those who have a specific demonstrative relationship to the event. The trade fairs attract a large number of attendee domestic as well as foreigner. The hotel may contact the officials arranging the trade show to become a co-sponsor or the official host of the show to gain more room sale. Trade shows lasts for several days thus have scope of increased room sales.

Extended Stay Market

In today's climate of downsizing, outsourcing, and mobility, businessmen are often away from their homes for extended periods of time and require more than a hotel room. The hospitality industry has responded to the growing demand for the extended-stay rooms. To capture this new segment a hotel property should feature its rooms with full kitchen, safes, larger closets and other amenities in the rooms.

Honeymooners

Most of the newlyweds plan a honeymoon; this may one of the emerging and profitable markets for the hospitality industry. Honeymooners are generally loyal guests; many return to their honeymoon property for anniversary visit or recommend it to their friends. Favourite honeymoon destinations in India include Goa, North Indian hill stations and sea beaches of Western *Ghats.* Another trend that can prove profitable to hospitality industry is the market of Destination wedding. Many couples are opting to travel to a specific location for both the wedding ceremony and honeymoon.

SUPPORT SERVICES

The services which are supportive in nature to boost the in flow of the tourists are known as support services. The below mentioned services are among the support services:

- ❖ Travel assistance
  - ✳ Passport Assistance
  - ✳ Visa assistance
  - ✳ E-Payment Services
  - ✳ Insurance Services
  - ✳ Airport Assistance
  - ✳ Tourist Information Services
  - ✳ Taxi/Cab rental.

Travel Assistance

Travel assistance which a hotel can provide through it travel desk is as under:

- ✳ Passport Assistance
- ✳ Visa assistance
- ✳ Taxi/ Cab rental

* Airport Assistance
* Tourist Information Services

Along with other services a hotel may have a branch of bank, insurance office in his offices area to assist tourists. The above mentioned services available at destination increases the tourism in the area. These services help tourists during their stay at the given destination.

INFRASTRUCTURE

Infrastructure elements comprise the system of services and utilities which are necessary to the operation of a tourism destination. The below mentioned are very significant in possible infrastructure:

- Transportation
- Communication
- Public Health Services

Transportation

Transportation is the movement of people and goods from one place to another. The term is derived from the Latin root ***trans*** (meaning across) and ***portare*** (meaning to carry). The field of transport has several aspects: loosely they can be divided into a triad of infrastructure, vehicles and operations. Infrastructure includes the transport networks like roads, railways, airways and terminals (railway stations, airport, seaport and bus/taxi stand). The vehicles include buses, car, bikes, airplane, helicopter, etc. The operations deals with the way the vehicles are operated on a network and the procedures set for the purpose including the legal environment and policies formulated by the local authorities.

Transport may be of following type:

- Air Transport
- Surface Transport
- Rail Transport
- Road Transport
- Waterways
  * Inland water ways
  * Sea transport.

Air transport

The air transport is the fastest method of transportation. The air transport includes airplane and air port and controlling towers. The cities connected with air transportation receive more and more tourists.

Rail transport

Rail transport is the transport of passengers and goods along the railways or railroads. A typical railway (rail road) tracks consists of two parallel steel or iron rails laid on the sleepers on specially treated surface. In rail transport, a train consists of rail vehicle that moves along the guides to transport freight or passengers from one place to another.

Road transport

The road transport includes the network of roadways laid especially for the movement of automobiles like buses, cars, bikes, trucks and vans. Road transport is the main mode of transport in hilly areas along with planes.

Waterways

This is the most ancient mode of the transport. The peoples were travelling in a vehicle called watercraft (boats and ships) using the rivers and seas. This mode of transport does not require any construction of the infrastructure like roads and railway. The use of the rivers and lakes for transportation is known as inland water ways and use of the oceans for the transportation is known as sea transport. Sea transport is achieved by using the vehicles known as ships.

Communication

Communication is one of the important infrastructures required for the overall development of any destination for tourists. The communication includes following modes:

- Post offices
- Telecommunication.

The place which has good communication facilities receives maximum tourists i.e. the clients for the hotel industry.

Public Health Services

Health care is the prevention, treatment and management of illness and the preservation of the mental and physical well being through the services offered by the medical, nursing, and allied health professionals. The destination should have adequate health service to attract more and more tourists.

ROLE OF SUPPORT SERVICES AND INFRASTRUCTURE

The support services and infrastructure mentioned above plays a vital role in marketing of the hospitality products and services. It plays following role in marketing:

- Attracts the target market
- Satisfies the guests needs
- Helps in achieving total guest satisfaction
- Boosts the hospitality sales.

Attracts the target market

The support service and infrastructure attracts the tourist to a destination. The support services assist them to travel to the place and infrastructures developments on the destination makes his journey and stay more pleasurable and memorable.

Satisfies the guests needs

The services and infrastructure satisfies the guest specific needs of travel, stay, experience, esteem needs as well as self-actualization needs.

Helps in achieving total guest satisfaction

These services help in achieving the total guest satisfaction as all the required information and needs are addressed by the available support services and infrastructure at the destination. A satisfied guest is an asset to the hospitality industry as he will turn into a loyal guest and will also perform the function of promoter of the hotel without any pay.

Boosts the hospitality sales

The places which are having the best infrastructure and support service are often visited by the more and more tourists. The inflow of tourist results into increasing the hospitality sales in both room sales as well as food and beverage sales.

ACTIVITY

1. Find out the various support services offered by a hotel to its existing as well as prospective guests in your location.
2. Find out the marketing plan of a hotel property located in your area.

QUESTIONS

1. Define marketing. Explain the four Ps of the marketing mix.
2. What do you understand by marketing mix? Explain in detail.
3. Explain the following terms:
   - need
   - want

- demand
- satisfaction.

4. What do you understand by support services and infrastructure?
5. What are the emerging markets for the hospitality industry? Explain each with suitable examples.
6. What role does support services and infrastructure play in increasing the sales of hospitality products?

14

EMERGING TRENDS IN HOSPITALITY INDUSTRY - II (Emerging Markets, Role of Support Services and Infrastructure)

— SURJEET KUMAR[1]

The tourism and hospitality industry is a thriving sector of world economy in present time and in India too this sector is growing very fast. Hospitality meets boarding, lodging and recreational needs of people in different areas. In India, it is one of the booming sector. Year 2006 has been the best year in term of foreign arrival, which reached a record 4.5 millions. Currently this sector is growing at the rate of 10-15 per cent. This is one of the vital sectors for Indian economy, since it contributes 5.9 per cent of the GDP and provides employment to 41.8 million people.

The Sanskrit saying, "Atithi Devo Bhava", or "The guest is truly a god" dictates the respect granted to guests in India. But with the passage of time there has been a significant change in the taste of guests and the service providers have become more conscious to their customers' needs. These new trends are widely visible in all aspects. This unit is an attempt to make you understand the various emerging trends in tourism and hospitality industry.

OBJECTIVES

After completion of this unit you will be able to understand:

- The present status of tourism and hospitality industry in the world.
- Role of support services and infrastructure, in hospitality Industry.

THE EMERGING MARKETS

Initially, tourism and hospitality industry developed in niche countries but saturation was felt by tourists who found new attractions of developing countries. Over the years, the travel to developing countries has increased the Pacific region has become an important destination. With globalization, these regions underwent economic changes and started becoming source markets. World is going through major

1. Lecturer in Hotel Management at Kurukshetra University, Kurukshetra, Haryana.

changes. These changes are omnipresent. The developed economies are showing the signs of slowing down whereas developing and under developing economies are growing at very fast phase. This trend is reflected in all the latest researches conducted by many international and national research organizations. Tourism and hospitality industry had also undergone through these changes. The traditional source market has shifted from west to east, countries i.e. China, India, Thailand, Malaysia are attracting huge amount of foreign direct investment (FDI).

These emerging economies have already created a great amount of interest in big hospitality investors and business houses. It is estimated that tourism and hospitality are the world's fastest growing industry and is going to be the second largest industry after agriculture by 2010. International Finance Corporation (IFC), part of the World Bank, states in its report that tourism and hospitality industry already provides direct or indirect employment to 231 million people (or one out of every 10 workers worldwide), which accounts for 11% of all international consumer expenditure, 11.3% of all capital investment and 6.7% of all government spending. This industry is also the world's largest tax contributors. As the latest trends show most of the emerging markets of tourism and hospitality exist in developing or underdeveloped countries. Let us have a cursory glance on thses emerging markets.

ASIA

Asia, the biggest continent, has now firmly established a central place in the world economy. Many analysts expect exponential growth in tourism and hospitality industry in Asia with major changes in travel patterns, both in types of travel and the profile of travellers. Travel in Asia is set to shoot to record levels, with overall spending on travel and tourism in the region forecasts to hit US$165 billion by 2014. Countries i.e. China, India, Japan, Korea, Taiwan, Sri Lanka, Maldives etc. are doing extremely well in tourism and hospitality.

China

China is expected to become the second largest destination globally by 2014. For this, China is improving its infrastructure with approximately 80 airports being constructed and about 30,000 kilometres of highways over the next 20 years. By that time China will have some 293 million people with household incomes of more than $4,000 annually. While China opens its doors to more foreign tourists, the Chinese themselves are fast becoming globe-trotters. They are not seen as big spenders, but are willing and able to travel, and will dominate the volume and value markets. The hospitality sector too in recent years has seen a sustained fast growth in the number of China's star rated hotels. By the end of 2002, there were a total of 8880 star-rated hotels in China. The total number of rooms was 879.2 thousand.

India

India's economic and social scene has undergone major changes with the opening of its economy in 1991, when the government redirected its controlled economy towards Liberalization, Privatization and Globalization (LPG). After that economy has grown faster and currently it's GDP is growing at 9.4% and rank 12th with 906,268 million US $ (World Bank GDP data). Services sector specially IT and IT-enabled services have totally changed the entire scene. Today development is visible in every segment of the economy. Year 2006 has been the best year till date, with foreign visitor arrivals reaching a record 4.5 millions. Foreign tourist arrivals have grown by 10-15 per cent in last one year but when it comes to domestic tourism, this figure is more impressive. India Pilgrimage tourism is growing at a rate of 20% annually. India has been ranked No. 5 among the top 10 world destinations by some of the most sophisticated and avid travellers (Conde Nast Travellers UK). Rajasthan, Goa, Kerela are some of the favourite tourist destinations.

The revenues of Hotel and Restaurant (H&R) industry in India during the financial year 2006-07 was INR 604.32 billion, a growth of 21.27% over the previous year, primarily driven by foreign tourist arrivals, which increased by 14.17%. Currently there are some 1,980 hotels approved and classified by the Ministry of Tourism, Government of India, with a total capacity of more than 1,40,000 hotel rooms. The hospitality industry is poised to grow at a faster rate and reach INR 826.76 billion by 2010. It is estimated that over the next two years 70,000-80,000 rooms will be added across different categories throughout the country.

Japan

Asia's most developed country Japan has seen a good growth in tourism and hospitality industry. There is a development of lots of luxury hotels. Due to years of peace and prosperity tourism and hospitality industry is witnessing a good growth. There is a new trend in Japan that is demand for theme parks, which is attracting huge FDI and become Japanese tourists first preference.

Thailand

Thai tourism and hospitality industry was adversely affected by devastating Tsunami but government and industry collective efforts have made Thailand to re-establish again on tourist map. In 2004 Thailand has recorded 11.68 million visitors; 13 million is 2005 and in 2006 which is considered to be the best year, records 15 million foreign tourists and 80 million domestic tourists to give it earning of US $ 22 billion.

The Thai Tourism Authority is organizing many educational and promotional tours to bring back tourist confidence shattered due to tsunami, recently more than 270 tour operators and travel journalists from important tourism generating countries in Northeast Asia and the Middle East had visited the Andaman coast provinces of Thailand to revive the tourism in six provinces affected by the Tsunami.

ASIA -PACIFIC AND AUSTRALIA

Over the years, this geographic region has grown considerably. According to a recently survey of 140 hotel executives conducted by New York University, the Asia

Pacific region is considered to be the next favourite destination. In this survey more than half of respondents (55%) predict the Asia/Pacific region will experience the greatest percentage increase in lodging investment over the next five years.

Australian hotel market also seems to be going from strength to strength. It is one of the most desired places to visit. As there is a major change in the behaviour of the western countries towards the Arab countries. The Southeast Asian capitals are enjoying an influx of big-spending tourists from Arab states, who feel they are unwelcome in Europe and the USA and London bombings. Malaysia, Thailand and Singapore are welcoming the cashed up Arabian visitors with open arms. Malaysia is drawing on its image as a modern and progressive Muslim country to target some 200,000 Arab tourists this year, a 40% increase in 2004 and far from the modest 21,731 arrivals recorded in 1999.

MIDDLE EAST

In Middle East, hospitality sector is witnessing huge investments. Governments of this region are encouraging private investors to develop major tourism and hospitality related projects. From past years Dubai shopping festival has become important event. Middle East hotels performances are equally impressive, they are growing at the rate 21%, in revenue per available room (revPAR).

Hotels in Qatar, Oman Saudi Arabia and Israel are doing extremely well. Cities i.e. Dubai, Abu Dhabi and Riyadh, Jerusalem and Tel Aviv continue to be a favourite tourist destinations.

RUSSIA

Russian economy has gone through major changes over the years. After its disintegration, for many years Russian have struggled to come over. But today the situation is changing very fast; the economy is showing signs of recovery. Under the leadership of President Putin the business confidence is back. Many companies predict that in coming years Russia specially Moscow city and nearby region will be the hot places to invest specially for tourism and hospitality companies. Jones Lang LaSalle Hotels sees Moscow as the emerging market to watch for hotel investment. Mark Wynne-Smith, European CEO, Jones Lang LaSalle Hotels says: "International investors have been viewing the hotel market in Russia with heightened interest and we predict that investment into hotels in Moscow could rival London, Paris and New York in the coming years."

WTTC/OEF forecast for Russia's Travel and Tourism is positive except there are few reservation. In 2006, Travel and Tourism Economy is expected to contribute 7.8 per cent of Russia's GDP – as against 11.8 per cent for Travel and Tourism in the European Union – and it should account for 4.5 million jobs, representing 6.6 per cent of total employment (11.8 per cent in the EU). Over the next ten years, Travel and Tourism in Russia is forecast to achieve annualized real growth of 6.4

per cent, in terms of GDP, compared with only 3.1 per cent in the EU, taking the share of Travel and Tourism GDP in Russia to 9.1 per cent in 2016.

This will solve Russia's problem of unemployment, allocation of funding in different sectors and give overall strength to Russian economy.

EUROPE

This continent can be studied is two parts: Western Europe and Eastern Europe.

Western Europe

This region is currently one of the hubs of tourism and hospitality industry. Maximum tourist destinations are located in this region. Spain, France, Italy and Switzerland are the countries, which keeps on fighting for the number one position. WTTC report suggest, within the span of few years, this region will have to face a stiff competition with Central and Eastern Europe. But this region will remain important for tourism and hospitality industry.

Eastern Europe

Eastern Europe seems to be one of the upcoming markets for tourism and hospitality currently lot of investment is coming to these countries. Currently, there are best opportunities for investors and developers. Travel and Tourism Demand in Central and Eastern Europe is expected to reach US$ 302,826.0 mn in 2007; by 2017 it will be US$ 700,536.0 mn. Countries i.e. Albania, Ukraine, Belarus, Poland, Slovakia, Hungary, Romania and Moldova will give a stiff competition to Western European countries.

AMERICAS

North America

Canada, USA and Mexico continued to enjoy the niche tourism destination for long time. But after the terror attack of September 11, 2001 the entire situation has changed, Stick rules imposed by US have adversely affected the tourism and hospitality industry. The US economy is showing the signs of slowing down which is a matter of concern. But recent survey shows that the hospitality and tourism industry is slowly recovering. Once again the hotel occupancy is rising.

Caribbean

Travel and Tourism Demand in Caribbean is expected to reach US$56,077.4 mn in 2007, growing to US$107,279.5 mn in 2017. According to World Travel and Tourism Council (WTTC) and its research partner, Oxford Economic Forecasting – the British Virgin Islands and Antigua and Barbuda – owe more than 75 per cent of their economies to Travel and Tourism. For another four countries Travel and Tourism generates between 50-75 per cent, and the respective shares are 25-50 per cent for a further ten countries, and 10 per cent for three others. Only four Caribbean economies –

Martinique, Curaçao, Puerto Rico and Haiti – owe less than 10 per cent of their economies to Travel & Tourism.

Latin America

In Latin America, the hospitality market is still recovering as the economies in the region continue to stabilize. Brazil is expected to recover fast as it is going to host 2010 Football World Cup.

AFRICA

According to statistics from the WTTC (World Travel and Tourism Council), the travel and tourism industry in North Africa represents 13.4 per cent of GDP and provides 12 per cent of employment. In Sub-Saharan Africa, the sector contributes 8 per cent of GDP and generates 10.5 million jobs, accounting for 6.6 per cent of total employment. Tourism revenue in Africa is expected to grow by 4.7 per cent per annum in real terms between 2007 and 2016.

Egypt and South Africa are considered to be the prime destinations in African continent. But Sub-Saharan region is becoming an important tourist destination. The international tourist arrival in the Sub-Saharan Africa has shown a growth of 11.1 per cent in the year 2006 compared to 2005. This growth was the second highest globally. In South Africa, South African government is spending huge sum of money on the airport modernization. The government is going to spend Rand 18 Million more on the construction part (terminal building) in the year 2007 compared to 2006.

In Northern Sahara region, the four countries Libya, Algeria, Morocco and Tunisia have a huge tourism potential but this is very much unrealized, but now the situation is changing very fast. Mauritius and Seychelles, small tiny islands nations located in Indian Ocean, are some of the emerging market, interesting to watch.

ROLE OF SUPPORT SERVICES AND INFRASTRUCTURE

Hospitality industry has a very wide spectrum. Today the hospitality industry is emerging as the largest employment provider. The whole industry encompasses a large number of sectors that network and integrate to satisfy the needs of clients. The people and functions of each sector are diverse yet complicated as a whole. Hospitality satisfies boarding, lodging and recreational needs of people in different areas. The nature and level of services delivered also differ with business plan of providers but all fall in the gambit of hospitality. The industry includes establishments that are owned by international companies, by domestic and by individuals. It ranges from the smallest kiosk that sells ice cream to the largest luxury hotel. Different types of tasks, methods and services are catered for by the industry in different establishments.

The hospitality industry has three domains: lodging, food and beverage, and travel/tourism. These domains are not independent; they have to depend on support services for their efficient working. For example, lodging operation, which consists of hotels, motels, resorts, camps, parks etc., which basic work is to take care of guest stay has to depend on various departments to give guest a lifetime experience. For this hotel has four major departments, which play a very vital role in hotel operations. These are front office, housekeeping, food and beverage production and food and beverage service.

But to run the show smoothly, these departments need the support of other departments which operate within the hotel like - security department, water supply department, personnel department, engineering and maintenance department, sales and marketing department, purchase department, accounts department, etc. These departments provide "back" up to the major departments in hotel or to the other key players in the hospitality sector and thus the services provided by them are known as Support services.

Engineering and Maintenance department deals in civil works, electrical works, mechanical works and computer works of the hotel. The role of this department is to provide utility services, which includes the day-to-day services of electricity, sanitation, hot water, steam, air-conditioning etc. Repair and maintenance work includes the preventive maintenance to reduce the break down of the heavy equipments and periodic repair and up keep of furniture and fixture of the hotel.

Security department's role is to make the place safe and secure for guests, visitors and employees. Security department is responsible for entire surveillance of the hotel, which include guest room, public area, boundaries, etc.

Human Resource department's role is to recruits the staff and train them so that they can give their best. Same way sales and marketing, accounts department all are support the major departments for smooth functioning so that ultimate goal of guest satisfaction can be achieved.

In case of food and beverage companies managing different operations and travel/tourism all are dependent on support service to made guest experience a memorable one. Over the year infrastructure has become an important ingredient for guest satisfaction. The country has made considerable progress in the past ten years in attracting private investment into the infrastructure sectors — in telecommunications, ports and roads and in other individual projects. The sector is estimated to grow at a 15 per cent over the next few years.

Clearly, it is a sector with colossal potential. According to the *Economic Survey 2005-2006*, India has the potential to absorb US$ 150 billion of foreign direct investment in the next five years in the infrastructure sector alone. When talking about infrastructure it includes **construction sector or Real Estate**, **Roads**, **Ports, Airports, Railways, Telecommunications and Power**. All these are necessary for tourism and hospitality sector to flourish.

Construction / Real Estate Sector

In India, construction is the second largest economic activity after agriculture. Investment in construction accounts for nearly 11 per cent of India's Gross Domestic Product (GDP) and nearly 50 per cent of its Gross Fixed Capital Formation (GFCF). Fund injection into the sector could go up to US$ 124.65 billion by FY2010. Construction accounts for nearly 65 per cent of the total investment in infrastructure and is expected to be the biggest beneficiary of the surge in infrastructure investment over the next five years.

Roads

The Indian road network, the largest in the world aggregating 3.32 million km, consists of 65,569 km of National Highways, 1,28,000 km of State Highways, 4,70,000 km of Major District Roads and about 26,50,000 km of other District and Rural Roads. National Highways account for only about 2 per cent of the total length of roads, but carry about 40 per cent of the total traffic across the length and breadth of the country. Considering the importance of the National Highways and the rapid increase in traffic, the Government has taken up the National Highways Development Project (NHDP), which consists of the following components:

- NHDP Phase-I: The Golden Quadrilateral (GQ; 5,846 km) connecting the four major cities of Delhi, Mumbai, Chennai and Kolkata.
- NHDP Phase-II: The North-South and East-West Corridors (NS-EW; 7,300 km) connecting Srinagar in the north to Kanyakumari in the south, including spur from Salem to Kochi, and Silchar in the east to Porbandar in the west
- Port connectivity and other projects — 1,157 km
- NHDP Phase III-A (4,015 km): 4-laning of over 4000 km in the year 2005 approved at an estimated cost of US$ 4.9 billion.

The Government has set ambitious plans for up gradation of the National Highways in a phased manner in the years to come. The details are as under:

- 4-laning of 10,000 km (NHDP Phase- III) including 4,000 km that has been already approved. An accelerated road development programme for the North Eastern region.
- 2-laning with paved shoulders of 20,000 km of National Highways under NHDP Phase-IV.
- 6-laning of GQ and some other selected stretches covering 6,500 km under NHDP Phase-V.
- Development of 1,000 km of express ways under NHDP Phase-VI.

- Development of ring roads, bypasses, grade separators, service roads, etc. under NHDP Phase-VII.

Ports

India, with an extensive coastline of 7,517 km (including the Andaman & Nicobar islands), has 12 major ports and 187 minor ports. The 12 major ports carry about three-fourths of the total traffic, with Viskhapatnam being the top traffic handler in each of the past five years. During 2004-05, Indian ports handled a total estimated traffic of over 500 million tonnes. Up to December 2005, cargo handled by major ports registered a 12.4 per cent growth, compared to 11.3 per cent observed in 2004-05. There has been an impressive growth of container traffic of 14.2 per cent per annum during the five years ending in 2004-05. Half of the world's traded goods are containerised and this proportion is expected to increase further.

Airports

Addressing the need for more efficient airports, the Indian Government has begun an aggressive drive to modernise existing airports. The international airports in Delhi and Mumbai are being upgraded with private sector participation. To ease matters further, the FDI cap in the sector has been moved to 49 per cent.

For the upgradation exercise, a joint venture will be formed in which the Airports Authority of India (AAI) and other public sector units will hold 26 per cent equity and the balance 74 per cent will be held by a strategic partner. The AAI has now identified 25 non-metro airports for development. These include Agatti, Aurangabad, Bhopal, Bhubaneswar, Coimbatore; Indore, Khajuraho, Nagpur, Patna, Port Blair, Rajkot, Trichy, Vadodra, Varanasi and Visakhapatnam.

Railways

The Indian Railways, which boasts of being the world's second largest rail network under a single management, has been one of the biggest contributors to the rise of industry and the change in the economic landscape of the country for over 150 years. Of the two main segments – freight and passenger of the Indian railways, the freight segment accounts for roughly two-thirds of its revenues.

Telecommunications

India's telecommunications story in many ways epitomises the new India. The image of young Indians with slick mobile phones has become a metaphor for economic growth in country. With rapid growth in the telecommunication sector, tele-density levels have surpassed all targets set by the Government. The total number of telephones (basic and mobile) rose from 22.8 million in 1999 to more than 125 million at the end of December 2005.

While 21.83 million telephones were added during 12 months of 2004-05, the first nine months of 2005-06 saw an addition of 27.47 million phones. Overall, tele-density has risen from a mere 2.32 million in 1999 to 11.32 million in December 2005.

The FDI scenario in the sector has also been on a roll. The Government allows 74 per cent of FDI in the sector and the total FDI approved up to September 2005 was US$ 9.3 billion. Some of the major investors are Hutchison, Singtel, AT&T and Distacom. Telecom major Vodaphone has extended now its entry into the sector with the acquisition of 10 per cent shares in Bharti Televentures for a consideration of 1.5 billion. The agenda for having world renowned Telecom and IT companies set up their R&D/manufacturing base in India, has been aggressively pursued to ensure timely delivery, high quality, cost effective supplies and very good after sale services.

Power

India's power market is the fifth largest in the world with an installed generation capacity of 123 GW, generation of more than 600 billion kWh, and a transmission and distribution network of more than 6.3 million circuit km.

With economic development in the country, per capita electricity consumption is bound to increase. The Government has taken significant policy initiatives to improve conditions for attracting private investment and FDI in the power sector. Broadly, 100 per cent foreign equity participation is allowed under the automatic approval route in all segments of the industry. For large generation projects, the Mega Power Policy extends incentives, such as capital import duty concessions, and the waiver of local levies to improve cost attractiveness, and a tax holiday for a period of 10 consecutive years out of 15 years from commencement.

This entire sector has an important role to play in guest satisfaction. In hospitality sector over few years India is attracting a huge investment. Lots of hotels, restaurants, retails etc. are coming up in every corner of country. There is only one reason that is growth in infrastructure sector. Some of the major hotel projects, which are going to come in India and were in news, are:

North India

- ❖ The Himalayan Ski Village Pvt. Ltd, the ski resort venture promoted by Alfred Ford, Chairman, of the Ford Motor Company Fund, has signed a memorandum of understanding with Government of Himachal Pradesh to develop a ski village.
- ❖ To revive tourism in Kashmir, Rs 40 crore had been sanctioned to rebuild the infrastructure in the state.
- ❖ Government has decided to release site for hotel to construct 40 five-star hotels in Delhi before the 2010 Commonwealth Games.

East India

- Sinclairs Hotels to invest Rs. 50 crore for expansion in the eastern India.

West India

- Tourism in Rajasthan is expected to get a major boost with the Union government giving its approval for assistance in developing eco-tourism in 10 districts of the state at the cost of 10 crores.
- Infocity, the IT park near Gandhinagar in Gujarat, and the Oberoi Group are jointly building a five-star business hotel at a cost of Rs.150 crore to cater to the needs of IT companies.
- Fomento Resorts Pvt. Ltd. Which owns the Cidade De Goa group of five-star hotels, has snapped up a 100 acre pick of land from the Maharashtra Tourism Development Corporation (MTDC) that is located on a hill site, 200 metres from the Aravali beach, in Sindhudurg district.

South India

- The Royal Orchid hotel group is planning to float a Rs. 100 crores expansion plans for Andhra Pradesh and Poona.
- Chennai based Empee Group is planning to build a 253 room five-star hotel in Chennai at an investment of Rs. 184 crore.
- Fortune Park Hotels Limited, the mid segment hotel brand of ITC Limited is planning to set up shop in Mumbai, Pune and Bangalore.
- The Andhra Pradesh Government is planning to give a major boost to tourism infrastructure in Hyderabad, which is a large convention centre overlooking the massive Golconda Fort. The Government is also planning to build a gigantic "View Tower", which will be the tallest structure in the city.
- The Kamat group of hotels has decided to set up a chain of bed and breakfast hotel facilities (nearly seven locations in Konkan), a five-star 'Orchid ecotel, four-star and three-star hotel facilities as well as a hotel management and research centre in the Konkan region.

It is well said that, india's international arrivals have touched the 3.5 million visitor-mark. If we can quickly set up the requisite infrastructure, the ten million figures will be barely a few years away. Domestic tourism is already witnessing a phenomenal growth of almost 15-20%. We expect this kind of growth for the next ten years or so.

ACTIVITY

a) Prepare a scrapbook and collect the latest hospitality news of emerging markets.

b) Enlist the role of support services for the smooth functioning of a hotel.

c) Identify the new hotel projects taking place in our country.

QUESTIONS

1. Discuss the emerging hospitality marks in the world.
2. What is the role of support services in smooth functioning of hotel?
3. How does infrastructure play a significant role in promotion of Hospitality Industry?

15

EMERGING TRENDS IN HOSPITALITY INDUSTRY - III (IT, Customer Reservation Management, Eco-Friendly Hospitality, Dining Experience Future Protections in HRM)

— *LATA S. PATIL*[1]

There are exciting times ahead for the Indian hospitality as the industry is on the verge of a boom. There have been booms and busts before and there will be more in the future, it is part of the business cycle. But more matured and organized industry welcoming latest trends with open arms. These are Information Technology, Eco-friendly Hospitality and Owning the Dining Experience.

OBJECTIVES

After reading this unit you will be able to understand (i) The role of information technology, CRM, eco-friendly hospitality and other emerging factors in the promotion of hospitality industry. (ii) the future projections of human resources in hospitality industry.

Information Technology

Internet changed the very concept of work and business in the hospitality industry. It became a catalyst for new business models, competitive strategies and organizational restructuring. The advent of technology redefines the business in the hospitality structure. Clearly there is a shift in the strategic thinking from products and service centricity to customer to customer centricity in the digital economy with client and the changing needs of the client increasingly at the centre of the strategy formulation paradigm.

The upswing in the hospitality industry's fortunes, value additions and cost cutting are the operating *mantras*. The interest involved as a medium with a potential to help the hospitality industry to excel in both these areas. Nobody can deny the attraction of a scenario in which the end customer can confirm a room of his choice, in a hotel of his choice at a fair price along with assurance that there will be surprises or shocks when he lands up at the hotel.

---

1. Vice Principal at Bharti Vidya Peeth's College of Hotel Management, Navi Mumbai.

As the hospitality industry started looking for ways to improve efficiencies, efforts and investments in the field of information technology intensified. One of the first deployments of it began at the front desk when receptionists began checking the name of the customer and then allotted a room to him. Big hotels also started putting in place accounting systems and back office software to improve processes. Further information technology was introduced in the hotel in three different ways. It is used to increase the efficiencies and lowering costs in internal operations of the hotels through Property Management Systems (PMS), Billing, Accounting, HR, Inventory Management etc. It is one big tool for marketing and distribution through GDS, CRS, Website, Online Reservations etc. Finally it is showing a impact on In-room technology and guest comforts. As hotel chains are tracking their assets across different regions through centralized systems. The Taj Group of Hotels, for instance, has implemented a WAN called Taj net, connecting the group's 55 properties in India, Nepal and Sri Lanka. Centralize system helps to monitor the performance of sales of all the properties and equally benefit to announce a special scheme for all its member hotels.

Says Pradeep Khetwal, Systems Manager, Le-Royal Meridien (Mumbai), "Most hospitality chains now realize that technology in the hospitality industry is critical to improve the operational efficiency of a hotel. The industry has moved from the traditional transaction-based processes such as check-in and reservations to features that are built and designed specifically for the customer. Services like providing wireless internet access to guests will only increase in the future."

CUSTOMER RESERVATION MANAGEMENT (CRM)

The CRM is also being adopted in a big way by almost all the big hotel chains in India. At present, every major hotel chain in India is investing in comprehensive systems that store complete profiles of their customers. The moment a guest checks in, he fills a form indicating his various preferences. If he is a regular client, the hotel immediately knows of his preferences and serves him accordingly. Says Prakash Shukla, Senior Vice President, Technology, and CIO, Taj Group of Hotels, "Every hotel has a major chunk of its revenue coming from its regular clientele. We too recognize this and have deployed Customer Information Systems (CIS) to service the customer in a better way." It helps the hotel to keep record of guest preferences, requests and their problem. Eventually this database is used to offer loyalty programmers to the customer.

According to Zahid Memon, Systems Manager, J W Marriott Hotel (Mumbai), "Most hotels know their customer preferences because relevant data can now be procured from the systems as and when needed. Earlier, data management systems contained only static information, which was used only to enhance efficiency of the hotel staff. But today, with the help of analytical tools, we can provide consistent service quality. The CRM and software tools for front line staff have enhanced successful one-to-one relationships."

In addition, most hotels have also embraced newer technologies. The Taj Group, for instance, extensively uses VOIP and video conferencing tools on its internal network to cut communication costs.

Wi Fi Service

It is the wireless mobile internet services commonly referred to as WiFi or wireless fidelity. It is one of the expected features for guests, especially business travellers. All the leading hotels in India provide WiFi access in many of their hotels in metros. Wireless technology today has matured and is all pervasive. It helps the staff to focus on guests' needs rather than specializing on which service depends.

Wi Max

The latest technology trend that will significantly change the outlook of the hospitality sector is Wi Max. It provides secure wireless network that can be deployed across metropolitalised areas by using cost effective standards based technologies. Wi Max and WiFi complement each other and often used together in a community wireless solution.

ECO-FRIENDLY HOSPITALITY

From multinational luxury chains to three rooms jungle lodges, hotels are cashing on the Eco-friend. They are recycling asking guest to reuse the towels and spending thousands of dollars to get Eco-certified while many hotel's are genuinely cleaning their act, a few are using Eco-label as a marketing. Ecotel concept covers Environmental Commitment and Community Involvement, Solid Waste Management, Energy Efficiency, Water Conservation and Preservation and last but not the least Employee Environment and Education.

Environmental Commitment

The hotels to environmental excellence say "Deluxe need not disturb Comfort need not compromise, and Entertainment need to be insensitive." Ecotel hotel participates in anti-plastic drive with help of school children, citizens and non-government organizations etc. Even they distribute Good Earth Keeping CD ROM to all the educational institutions and environmental organizational institutions and environmental organization. They have set up PUC check point to check the pollution inspection licence on their vehicle.

Solid Waste Management

The staff work together for the goal of Zero-garbage, most of the wood furnishings are recycled with cotton stocks. Rubber wood products are used through the hotel. Potted pots are replacing the cut flower.

Energy efficiency

Hotel energy efficiency effort is the ECO-Button. This function on the guest room to participate in the environmental programme. The hotel uses a thermal storage plant to decrease their needs for energy during peak period, leaving pressure on their utility company to use older and less pollution friendly equipment to generate power.

Water Conservation

Water conservation is nothing but hotel's own sewage transplantation. Water is treated thoroughly enough that the product can be used to irrigate the gardens on the grounds of the hotel.

Employee Environment Education

Ecotel hotels make effort to educate their industry employees about the Eco-friendly drive. Cash rewards are given to the employee who contributes most to the environmental programme.

OWNING THE DINING EXPERIENCE

One must own the dining experience. It means every one who comes into contact with guest, must take personal pride and responsibility to ensure guest has great dining experience whether the contact is direct or indirect. The bartender should think that mixing drink is made to the customer likings, the chef preparing the meal must be proud enough of the dish to serve personally, the dish washer cleaning the plates and silverware must feel good that they have contributed to a pleasant atmosphere, the food pick up waiter deliver the food must not leave before making sure the guest has everything they need to enjoy their meals, the manager on the floor must enforce the restaurant standard and visit the table to get the approval of the guest .At the end guest should have unforgettable experience. This ensure the **WOW FACTOR**

The restaurant business has developed in very varied one, with pubs, night clubs, restaurants, restobar, fast food chains to have different target but the major focus should be in overall dining experience.

Impact of National and International Events on the Hospitality Industry

Looking back over the past five decades, it is an interesting discovery to find that huge doses of hospitality sector infrastructure were driven by the decision to host international events be it conference, tradeshow, entertainment or sports-oriented activities.

Conferences, tradeshows are emerging on regular basis and they are directly promoting the hotel expansion. Sports facilities like the Nehru Stadium, Indira Gandhi villages, flyovers and upgrading of civic amenities – all on war footing – came in the run up to the Asian Games of 1982. During this period nine new hotels were constructed or expanded.

Fashion shows, Bollywood events/award ceremonies, National Film Festivals, Beauty pageants etc. are considered as national events in India. Country like India gaining its own popularity in the above-said events and at the same time attracting more and more number of national and international celebrities/personalities to participate whole-heartedly in all these events. This motivates the hospitality industry to expand or build up new hotels to accommodate all these guests. These all events are the positive impact on the hospitality industry.

FUTURE PROJECTIONS IN HUMAN RESOURCE MANAGEMENT: ISSUES AND TECHNOLOGIES

The Indian hotel industry is at the cross-roads. The industry suffering by market fluctuations, an oversupply of accommodation and outdated human resource management practices. Several recent research studies have underlined the significant costs of labour in overall industry costs, and the pressing need to reduce these costs and improve the profitability and competitiveness by effective and innovative human resource management strategies.

The challenge is to develop innovative human resource management practices which will enhance productivity and profitability without increasing staff levels. Significant contributions to industry viability will be achieved through comprehensive and integrated human resource management systems which ensure that the right staff are recruited, trained, monitored and appropriately rewarded in line with institutional and industry requirement. Change, globalization, increased competition for limited human resources along with technological advancements are just some of the vast challenges facing hospitality managers. The growing complexity of the customer and employee interaction driven by technology and the information age will shape human resource needs in the future. The customer, armed with more information, will expect frontline and other hotel staff to be at least as knowledgeable about the firm's offerings as they are themselves.

The above factors made human resource manager to revolve around the mission statements organizational goals and operational objectives. They have become the change agents as people skills were as important as financial skills to achieve success in the hospitality operations. Managers started acting as counsellors and coaches and began to manage their people instead of the job tasks.

Thus Human Resource Management is no longer referred as Personnel Department. The change is merely as nomenclature which represents a change in attitude, a change in conception and a change in status.

The following issues projecting the Human Resource Management

Service Standards

Most of the hotels converting the concept of "Service" into behavioural standards for Housekeeping, Front-office, and Food and Beverage occupations. They are focusing on general qualities such as the "friendliness", "refinement", "spontaneity" or "consistency" of staff. This standardization brings the quality service and the fulfilment of guest expectations.

Recruitment Opportunities and Options

The recruitment and selection practices should reflect actual expected occupational standards and overall management philosophies. Innovative sources and recruitment practices will ensure value added manpower who are already oriented to the demands and opportunities of career within the hotel industry. Employ the people with strong interpersonal and social skills to meet the high standard demand of the guest.

Industry Promotion and Institutional Development

The recruitment programmes should be innovative and focused and industry should adopt strategic and individual policies to appraise the perspective employees of the future opportunities offered by the industry. Community based programmes should be adopted to involve the local community or indigenous people especially in the resort areas or heritage hotel sites. This can be promoted by media, work experience programme and career advice.

To retain and to attract the quality, and productive staff, the development of employee careers should be activated. At this point human resource managers are beginning to recognize the productivity impact of increased flexibility. Including career planning and converting the penalties into incentives.

Job Rotation

Whatever may be the staffing at the initial stage recruitment, each and every employee should be multi skilled. Thus housekeeping staff may be recruited as base level, and eventually they rise through the various available supervisory levels in the departments. A more productive approach to employee motivation and commitment, involving every ones else's responsibility to serve the guest/customer. There should be an exp "our people are our most important asset." Focus should be given to adjust the present excessive hours of work. This programmed can be enhanced by job rotation, provision of multi skilling training programmes and team building opportunities.

Performance Management and Reward System

Performance management programmes should be developed to increase the career and adequate remuneration plans. Since hotel salaries are far lower than average even though they contribute significantly to overall operating costs. They should provide opportunities for modifications to penalty rates, vacations, increase in salaries, job stability training programme etc. Some hotels provide on premise health policies to show that they care for them and their families.

Training and Development

Orientation programmes, on the job training modules and intellectual supervision will no doubt fill the gap in human resource management for the hotel industry. Training is viewed as a fixed cost not the variable cost. Staff needs to be aware of current regulations, procedures and new technologies.

Employee Communication

To build enthusiasm, commitment and to increase potential of the employees, ongoing communication is integral part of human resource. Human resource activities, strategies, policies and procedures need to be conveyed. There should be staff-supervisor meetings, active use of guest feed back and grievance mechanism should be highlighted.

Turnover Wastage Analysis

Perception of the hotel occupations by the potential employees and their managers lead to low job satisfaction. This increases job turn over which should be analyzed and modification should be implemented.

Human Resource Planning

Comprehensive human resource planning helps to maintain strategic approaches to labour demand and supply projections to ensure the effective and cost – effective utilization of their employees to accountably contribute to the productivity of the hotels.

Human Resource and Information Technology

In HR there is need for computer proficiency, adaptation of sophisticated technology. Employers and employees will need to look for ways to utilize technology.

ACTIVITY

1. Make a scrap book and paste current news, events and activities of hospitality Industry.

QUESTION

1. Write a note on current emerging factors responsible for promoting hospitality Industry.
2. Discuss the future trends of growth of the hospitality industry by 2020.